# FEDERAL ROYAL COMMISSIONS IN CANADA, 1867-1967

## A Checklist

T0324007

# Federal
# Royal Commissions
# in Canada

## 1867-1966

## A CHECKLIST

*George Fletcher Henderson*

UNIVERSITY OF TORONTO PRESS

© University of Toronto Press 1967

Reprinted 2017

ISBN 978-1-4875-9161-8 (paper)

To Mother

# PREFACE

The subjects inquired into by Canadian federal royal commissions have ranged
over such a wide field that the reports and special studies prepared by the
400 commissions since Confederation have become an essential part of any research in Canadian studies.  In many cases the special studies which are always
prepared by the best experts available stand as the most important works ever
to appear on a given subject.  For example, the studies used by the Royal Commission on Dominion-Provincial Relations (1937-1940) are still used as required
reading in both graduate and undergraduate university courses almost thirty
years later.

In my work as Government Documents Librarian I witness the daily use of
royal commission material.  The importance attached to royal commission documents and the considerable difficulty in locating many of the earlier reports led
me to undertake the compilation of this checklist four years ago.

This work like all studies of this nature was completed only because of the
aid and co-operation of countless persons across Canada.  In the first place, I
wish to acknowledge the invaluable assistance given by the staff of the Privy
Council Office who enabled me to examine the Orders in Council establishing the
commissions.  Here Mr. J. L. Cross and Mr. Leo Lafrance were always most
helpful and co-operative.  Secondly, Mr. Erik J. Spicer, Parliamentary Librarian, and his staff were always ready to put their vast resources at my disposal.
Especially I wish to thank Miss Simone Chiasson, Chief of the Information and
Reference Division, who read the manuscript and offered many helpful suggestions for improving the work.  Miss Pamela Hardisty, Assistant Parliamentary
Librarian, was always most helpful in discussions regarding this checklist.

A work of this kind inevitably owes much to Dr. W. Kaye Lamb, National Librarian and Dominion Archivist, and his staff.  Dr. Lamb was always ready to
suggest possible hiding places of commission reports.  The National Library
staff allowed me to check the National Union Catalogue where I located several
missing reports.  As usual the people at the Public Archives of Canada were re-
markable in the facilities extended while this work was progressing.  For many
weeks they provided me with working space and generally made me at home while
I read Orders in Council and searched sets of private papers and record groups
for elusive reports.  Mr. R. S. Gordon, Chief of the Manuscript Division, was
always most helpful in suggesting possible avenues for locating additional reports.  Also he kindly permitted me to examine the manuscript of the Union List
of Manuscripts which revealed several sets of papers belonging to former commissioners.

I am deeply indebted to the many departmental librarians in Ottawa.  They
were particularly helpful in locating reports in their collections or suggesting
other likely repositories.  A great debt is also owed to the executive assistants
of many departments who were able to locate reports in their records.  They
were always prepared to make arrangements for me to examine the reports and
record the necessary bibliographical information.  Also I wish to record my
gratitude to the provincial archivists who undertook numerous searches of their

collections. Without their help many of the reports would have remained undis-
covered. Also I wish to thank Mr. James Maxwell, of Cornell University, Itha-
ca, New York, who discussed the project with me on several occasions and discovered several inaccuracies in the original draft of the work.

To the staff of Queen's University I owe many thanks. The completion of the
work would not have been possible without the several grants provided by the Arts
Research Committee. Also I wish to extend special thanks to several people who
frequently encouraged me to continue the work and provided time and supplies to
see the project on its way--Mr. Donald A. Redmond, Chief Librarian, Mr. H. P.
Gundy, his predecessor, and Mrs. H. A. Elliott, Head of the Acquisitions Department, Douglas Library. Without the understanding of these three people I
would never have been able to carry on the research during the last four years.
When I reached the stage of putting the Checklist into final form, Mr. W. F. E.
Morley, Curator of Special Collections, Douglas Library, was as usual ready
to spend many hours discussing the physical arrangement of the work. While
he was himself seeing a work through the Press, he was always ready to provide suggestions from his vast knowledge of bibliographical details. I must
also note the helpful suggestions provided by Mr. E. C. Beer, former Archivist.
The members of the Government Documents Department were always most co-
operative and painstaking in their work. In addition to typing correspondence
at short notice and xeroxing needed documents, they contributed in many ways
to final completion of the project. Especially, I wish to thank Bea Rombough
and Lynn Howard who frequently suggested many valuable ideas which have helped to improve the overall work. Also the Index would never have been completed without their help. Dr. John Meisel, Head of the Department of Political
Studies, also contributed valuable ideas during the preparation of the work. His
predecessor, Dr. J. E. Hodgetts, now Principal of Victoria College, University
of Toronto, discussed the work with me on many occasions during its early days.
His unequalled knowledge of royal commissions in Canada was extremely valuable as the work progressed.

A particular word of thanks goes to Nancy Rombough and Teddyanne Hunt for
their patience and understanding in the typing of this work from a very compli-
cated manuscript. Jackie Popma also kindly helped in the closing days.

To the staff of the University of Toronto Press, especially Miss M. Jean
Houston and Mr. J. E. Schreiber, many thanks are due for their unfailing cour-
tesy and understanding as they saw this difficult piece of work through the Press.

This work has been published with the help of a grant from the Social Science
Research Council of Canada using funds provided by the Canada Council. I am
indeed grateful to this organization for the generous grant provided for the project.

Above all, I wish to express my gratitude to my Mother whose encourage-
ment and aid in innumerable ways have helped to ensure the completion of this
work.

George F. Henderson

Wilton, Ontario.
September 7, 1967.

# CONTENTS

INTRODUCTION

The first obstacle that had to be faced in assembling the materials contained in this book was the problem of defining a royal commission. There are two sorts of definition: legal and historical, the former more precise, the latter vaguer, more general, and in the long run perhaps more useful. The pertinent legal definition of a royal commission is that provided by Part I of the Inquiries Act,[1] which establishes commissions of inquiry. But commissions appointed to investigate charges of political partisanship or to inquire into cases involving the revocation of naturalization or citizenship, while they fulfil this legal definition, cannot be included here. The former, amounting to several hundred since Confederation, tend to be numerous after every change of government in Ottawa[2] but have never tabled their reports; the latter since 1948 have been appointed under the Canadian Citizenship Act,[3] and are no longer considered to be true royal commissions.

The royal commission is a historical phenomenon as well as a legal one, however. It was one of the institutions Canada at its birth adopted from Britain, where it had experienced a resurgence of popularity in the nineteenth century after a long period of eclipse. A historical or working definition based on Canadian practice was provided by J. C. Courtney in a Ph. D. thesis on the subject:

> A royal commission of inquiry is an <u>ad hoc</u>, advisory organization of one or more commissioners, appointed by the Governor in Council to investigate, study and report upon a matter of immediate concern, that matter having been assigned to it by the Cabinet of the day; the term "royal" has been retained because of the executive nature of the appointment, the commissions being issued by the Crown under the Great Seal of Canada. Such power and authority as is granted to royal commissions for the conduct of their investigation is contained in the Inquiries Act.... The government is in no sense bound to enact legislatively any or all of the recommendations presented by a royal commission in its report(s); with the presentation of its final report a royal commission ceases to exist.[4]

From this definition it is apparent that sharp dividing lines may not exist in all instances. While I have generally included in this checklist commissions appointed under Part I of the Inquiries Act (with the exceptions noted above), I

---

[1] R. S. C., 1952, c. 154.
[2] For example, in the year following the 1930 general election, about 50 of these inquiries were initiated. Sixty-nine were established in the year following the 1935 election. (Keith B. Callard, Commissions of Inquiry in Canada, 1867-1949, Ottawa, 1950, p. 36.)

---

[3] R. S. C., 1952, c. 33.
[4] John C. Courtney, "Canadian Royal Commissions of Inquiry, 1946 to 1962: An Investigation of an Executive Instrument of Inquiry," Ph. D. thesis, Duke University, 1964, p. 14.

have necessarily been somewhat flexible.  Orders in council establishing commissions of inquiry have sometimes failed to state precisely the part of the Inquiries Act under which they were being appointed.  I have included those which
seem to have been concerned with matters of a public nature.  Undoubtedly there
will be disagreement with some of my inclusions; in any case certain departmental commissions of inquiry have inevitably strayed into this work.

Professor J. E. Hodgetts has classified royal commissions into four main
categories. [5]  In the first place, there is the group which has investigated sud-
den catastrophic incidents such as the Quebec City landslide of 1897, the fire
which destroyed the Parliament Buildings at Ottawa in 1916, the V-E Day riots
in Halifax in 1945, the fires at Rimouski and Cabano, Quebec, in 1950, and the
air crash near Montreal which claimed 118 lives in 1963.  Second  there are the
inquiries into social and cultural problems of national importance.  Into this cat-
egory fall commissions inquiring into broadcasting, Indian affairs, the development of the arts and sciences in Canada, the cost of living, and bilingualism and
biculturalism.  A third group of commissions has dealt with the Canadian economy in inquiries which have investigated matters ranging from banking and finance to the grain trade, from railways to the price spread of food.  Finally, on
several occasions the government has appointed commissions to investigate certain aspects of its own organization, as in the recent Glassco Commission, which
produced a report of two thousand pages.  The very first Canadian royal commission, in fact, was appointed to deal with the status and requirements of the
civil service.

Governments have appointed royal commissions for a variety of reasons: to
serve as a delaying measure in an embarrassing political situation, to gather
needed information in the face of new problems, to provide a firmer basis for a
decision on government policy, to sample public opinion on a potentially delicate
political matter before legislation is introduced, to educate public opinion, to
adjudicate disputes, and as a response to pressure groups.  On a few occasions
parliamentary committees have been converted into royal commissions upon
the prorogation of Parliament.

When an occasion arises which seems to justify the appointment of a royal
commission, the prime minister or the minister of the department concerned
submits to the governor in council a recommendation which lists the names of
the proposed commissioners and defines the scope of the proposed inquiry.
Once it has been approved, the memorandum reappears with few if any changes
as an order in council.  Then a commission under the Great Seal of Canada is
issued under section 3 of the Inquiries Act.

Usually one to three members serve on a royal commission.  One-member
commissions, historically the most common, have accounted for about 175 of
the commissions that have so far been appointed, compared with about 50 two-
member ones and 85 three-member ones.  Since the end of the Second World War
the major commissions have averaged five to six members, but both before and

---

[5]John Edwin Hodgetts, "The Role of Royal Commissions in Canadian Government," in Proceedings of the Third Annual Conference of the Institute of Public
Administration of Canada [1951], Toronto, 1952, pp. 354-55.

after the war larger commissions were sometimes appointed.

Over the years governments have shown a marked preference for judges and lawyers as commissioners, particularly in the case of single-member commissions. The public, it would seem, is more willing to accept a royal commission report as impartial if it has been written by a member of the legal community. Furthermore, as Professor Keith Callard has noted, Canada has "few men of integrity and reputation engaged in public life, who are not active participants in party strife."[6] Thus judges become particularly attractive nominees. At the same time they are in a better position than most other professional people to be temporarily released from their duties in order to devote time to gathering the materials for a report. Nowadays, however, with the advent of somewhat larger commissions, academic personnel are being appointed more and more often to multi-member bodies.

Of those on the staff of the commission who assist the commissioners in collecting information, the secretary occupies the most critical place. "His duties," writes Professor Hodgetts, "are many, ranging from the checking of baggage to the drafting of the report."[7] The secretary often an expert on the subject of the inquiry, particularly when the commissioners themselves are not experts,[8] is sometimes named in the order in council establishing the commission, but it is more usual to have the selection made by the department most directly concerned.

The terms of reference are set out in the order in council which establishes the commission. Critics of royal commissions have maintained that the government can influence the type of report it will ultimately receive. "The finest watch dog alive," they argue, "cannot bite a burglar if it has a muzzle on."[9] It is in any case true that the government has often taken a close interest in the terms of reference and on several occasions has extended or altered the terms after they were originally set forth.[10]

---

[6]Callard, Commissions of Inquiry, p. 19.

[7]John Edwin Hodgetts, "Royal Commissions of Inquiry in Canada: A Study in Investigative Technique," M. A. thesis, University of Toronto, 1940, pp. 137-38.

[8]Ibid., pp. 138-39.

[9]Toronto World, February 28, 1906. Quoted in Hodgetts, "Royal Commissions of Inquiry," p. 156.

[10]On May 15, 1963, two months before the establishment of the Royal Commission on Bilingualism and Biculturalism, Prime Minister Pearson consulted the ten provincial premiers about the proposed terms of reference. On several occasions, as in the case of the Royal Commission on the National Development in the Arts, Letters and Sciences (1949-1951), the government has extended the terms of reference by proposing additional subjects to be considered by the commission. (See Louis S. St. Laurent to Vincent Massey, April 25, 1950, quoted in the Report of the Royal Commission on National Development in the Arts, Letters and Sciences, Ottawa: King's Printer, 1951, p. xxi.)

Commissioners are granted wide powers under the Inquiries Act, including the power of summoning witnesses, of requiring them to give evidence on oath, and of ordering the presentation of any documents required by the inquiry. Witnesses testifying under oath before a royal commission are not subject to prosecution by a civil court on the basis of their testimony.[11]

The Inquiries Act does not specify the procedure which a royal commission is to follow; its silence on this point is in Professor Callard's opinion responsible for one of the principal assets of this type of inquiry: "Each investigation can be adapted to suit the requirements of the subject matter, of the commissioners and of the witnesses."[12] With the announcement of a royal commission, the members make plans for the initial meetings, and at these meetings they determine the organization of the commission and the procedure to be followed. A secretary is selected at this time, if one has not already been appointed. If public hearings are to be conducted across the country, the starting date must be decided and advertisements placed in newspapers in the provincial capitals and in other principal cities inviting written submissions by interested parties. If special studies are to be made, scholars and technical experts must be selected to prepare them. All these details must be predisposed before the commission can proceed with its proper business.

The information-gathering procedure of royal commissions is nowadays fairly standard. With major commissions, widespread public hearings are the general rule. Usually several hundred written submissions are received. People who have submitted briefs and witnesses who have been supboenaed may appear at the hearings. If necessary, commissioners may travel outside the country to gather additional information. The hearings, which may extend over a period of months, tend to be very formal, probably because the chairmen are often judges. Occasionally, as in the recent Royal Commission on Government Organization, project teams making use of specialist assistance have replaced public hearings; they have been augmented by advisory committees made up of prominent persons in various pertinent fields.

The time to prepare the final report may vary from a few weeks to many months, and the report itself may vary in size from a small pamphlet to several volumes. Between the conclusion of public hearings and the filing of the report, preliminary or interim reports may be issued, particularly when a long period is likely to ensue before the results can be assembled and published in final form. The interim reports may be little more than publicity releases, or they may themselves be significant documents synthesizing a part of the information gathered or offering an analysis of a part of the area of inquiry. In the latter case, like the final reports, they will become important research materials for future historians, economists, and political scientists.

The costs of royal commissions, like the length of their reports and the time taken in preparing them, have varied greatly, from a few hundred dollars to several million. In recent years the figures have tended to be high for major

---

[11] R. S. C., 1952, c. 307, s. 5.
[12] Callard, Commissions of Inquiry, p. 22.

commissions, and have covered not only the payment of commissioners and of legal counsel (the latter sometimes answering for 60 per cent of the total expenditure[13]) but fees to consultants (including the cost of preparing special studies), salaries of the secretariat, expense for travel, and the cost of printing the report.

Today major royal commissions have become temporary government departments. To a large extent this change from the earlier, simpler form, with a few commissioners, a secretary, and a stenographer who recorded evidence, has occurred because of the greater importance now attached to the gathering of data and to the preparation of "special studies." The first commission to prepare numerous studies (18 in its case) was the Royal Commission on Dominion-Provincial Relations (1937-1940). To date the largest number of special studies has been issued by the Royal Commission on Canada's Economic Prospects (1955-1957)--33 in all. This emphasis on special studies has tended to decrease the importance of formal public hearings--a "displacement of the lawyer and public hearing by the researcher and private inquiry," as Professor Hodgetts has termed it.[14]

Thus, even if no legislation directly results, the importance of the findings of royal commissions has if anything increased in recent years, and it has become more necessary than ever to provide a directory showing the names, contents, and locations of the diverse reports. The first attempt to do so appeared in 1939. Compiled by Arthur Harrison Cole of the Harvard University Library, A Finding-List of Royal Commission Reports in the British Dominions[15] provided a list of only 82 post-Confederation Canadian federal royal commissions. The chronological arrangement was rejected in favour of a broad subject classification with such headings as "Social Problems," "Governmental Administration," and "Agriculture and the Land." A year later, Miss Grace S. Lewis, the Librarian at the Dominion Bureau of Statistics, provided a listing of about 100 royal commission reports. Arranged chronologically, this list appeared in the Canada Year Book for 1940.[16] While the value of these two works to researchers during the last quarter century must not be underestimated, it is true that they made reference to only the most generally available reports. Any good research library in Canada should contain copies of most if not all of them. No attempt was made to provide a complete listing of Canadian royal commissions.

Two other lists of a more complete nature were produced, but both have remained in a generally unavailable format. The appendix of an M.A. thesis prepared by Professor Hodgetts in 1940 contained a valuable list of 276 commissions.[17] Then in 1950, as part of a special study for the Secretary to the Cabinet, Professor Callard tabulated 328 commissions of inquiry.[18] All of

[13]Hodgetts, "The Role of Royal Commissions," p. 360.

[14]John Edwin Hodgetts, "The Grand Inquest on the Canadian Public Service," Public Administration, XXII (September, 1963), p. 230.

[15]Cambridge, Massachusetts: Harvard University Press.

[16]Ottawa: King's Printer, pp. 1108-10.

[17]Hodgetts, "Royal Commissions of Inquiry."

[18]Callard, Commissions of Inquiry.

these works failed in one important respect. They did not seriously attempt to locate the reports of the more obscure royal commissions. Cole and Lewis simply ignored them. Hodgetts and Callard listed many of them but went no further.

I have used all these lists as a basis for this work. In addition, I have consulted the Registers to Orders in Council in the Privy Council Office, Ottawa, and checked all the returns for lists of royal commissions tabled in Parliament from time to time. After compiling a list based on all these sources, I attempted to weed out the departmental commissions of inquiry by checking the orders in council establishing all of the commissions involved. With the compilation of the list completed, the task of locating the reports commenced. About half of them were readily available, either in the <u>Sessional Paper</u> series [19] or as separate publications. The others which have been discovered turned up in various places from sets of private papers to the departmental files of the federal government.

In spite of this added effort only 300 out of 400 royal commission reports could be located. The discovery of each additional report was, therefore, regarded as a major victory. Several factors explain the failure to find the remaining 100 reports. In the first place, perhaps about 25 of them were destroyed in the fire which gutted the Parliament Buildings at Ottawa in February, 1916. This number of missing reports was actually tabled in Parliament. Since they had not been printed in the <u>Sessional Paper</u> series, they (along with all other pre-1916 unprinted sessional papers) do not now exist. Second, royal commissions have not always had the same prestige which they now enjoy. Thus, in some cases, a manuscript copy may be all that was ever presented by the commission.[20] Third, some commissions never submitted any reports.[21] Death of the commissioners or resignation of a person being investigated may have halted further inquiry.

There is consequently little doubt that copies of many of the elusive reports are hidden away in collections of private papers or in other unlikely repositories. If the publication of this checklist helps to bring some of them to light, its preparation will have been worthwhile. Should any reader know the whereabouts of a report that I have not located or of a commission here unlisted, the compiler would be most grateful if he would communicate with him through the Government Documents Department, Queen's University Library, Kingston, Ontario.

---

[19]Canada. Parliament, <u>Sessional Papers, 1867/68-1925</u>, Ottawa, 1868-1925.

[20]Many copies of reports located in federal departmental files were typewritten copies. See, for example, items 76, 104, 114, 116, and 149.

[21]See items 189 and 267.

FEDERAL ROYAL COMMISSIONS IN CANADA, 1867-1967

A Checklist

1   COMMISSION TO INQUIRE INTO THE PRESENT STATE AND PROBABLE
    REQUIREMENTS OF THE CIVIL SERVICE

Appointed on June 9, 1868 by Order in Council P. C. 528 on the recommendation of the Minister of Finance.  No indication of authorizing
statute given in Order in Council.
    Commissioners: Etienne Parent,[1] William Henry Griffin, Robert
Shore Milnes Bouchette, John Langton, William Smith, Thomas Reynolds
and Charles S. Ross.

### First Report

Main part of report undated.  Minority report of Bouchette dated
January 11, 1869.  Tabled in the House of Commons on April 26, 1869.
Sessional Paper no. 19 - 1869.  Printed as:
    First report of the Civil Service Commission.  Printed by order of
Parliament.  Ottawa, Printed by Hunter, Rose & Company, 1869.  59 p.
    Also issued as a separate.

### Second Report

Main part of report undated.  Minority report of Bouchette dated
March 30, 1869.  Tabled in the House of Commons on April 26, 1869.
Sessional Paper no. 19 - 1869.  Printed as:
    Second report of the Civil Service Commission.  Printed by order
of Parliament.  Ottawa, Printed by Hunter, Rose & Company, 1869.  45 p.
    Also issued as a separate.

### Third Report

Dated November 26, 1869.  Tabled in the House of Commons on May
7, 1870.  Sessional Paper no. 64-1870.  Printed as:
    Final report of the Civil Service Commissioners.  Printed by order
of Parliament.  Ottawa, Printed by I. B. Taylor, 29, 31 & 33 Rideau
Street, 1870.  24 p.
    Also issued as a separate.
    Notes: Commissioners met in Ottawa and in the other principal cities
of Canada.  Cost: $5,769.53.


2   ROYAL COMMISSION TO INQUIRE INTO THE CAUSE AND NATURE OF THE
    OBSTRUCTION OFFERED IN THE NORTH-WEST TERRITORIES TO THE
    PEACEABLE INGRESS OF THE HONOURABLE WILLIAM   MCDOUGALL

Appointed on December 17, 1869.[2]
Commissioner: Sir Donald Alexander Smith.

---

[1] Appointed on June 19, 1868 by Order in Council P. C. 633.
[2] The Commission under the Great Seal is dated December 17th.  Sessional Paper no. 12 - 1870, p. 49.

First Report

Dated April 12, 1870. Tabled in the House of Commons on April 28, 1870. Sessional Paper no. 12 - 1870. Printed as:

North-West Territories. Report of Donald A. Smith, Esq. In correspondence and papers connected with recent occurrences in the North-West Territories. Printed by order of Parliament. Ottawa, Printed by I. B. Taylor, 29, 31 & 33 Rideau Street, 1870. 13 p.

Also issued as a separate .

3   COMMISSION TO INQUIRE INTO THE STATE OF THE LAWS CONNECTED WITH THE ADMINISTRATION OF JUSTICE IN RUPERT'S LAND AND THE NORTH-WESTERN TERRITORIES

Appointed on September 13, 1870 by Order in Council P. C. 138 under An Act for the temporary Government of Rupert's Land and the North-Western Territory when united with Canada (32-33 Victoria, c. 3) on the recommendation of the Honourable Sir George Cartier acting in the absence of the Minister of Justice.

Commissioner: Francis Godshall Johnson.

Report

Not located.

Notes: Cost: $4,710.22.

4   ROYAL COMMISSION TO INQUIRE INTO THE BEST MEANS FOR THE IM-PROVEMENT OF THE WATER COMMUNICATIONS OF THE DOMINION AND THE DEVELOPMENT OF THE TRADE WITH THE NORTH-EASTERN PORTION OF NORTH AMERICA

Appointed on November 16, 1870 by Order in Council P. C. 17 under An Act respecting Inquiries concerning Public Matters (31 Victoria, c. 38) and on the recommendation of the Minister of Public Works.

Commissioners: Sir Hugh Allan, Chairman, Sir Casimir Stanislas Gzowski, Delino Dexter Calvin, George Laidlaw, Pierre Garneau, William James Stairs, [1] Alexander Jardine, Samuel Leonard Shannon. [2]

Secretary: Samuel Keefer.

Report

Dated February 24, 1871. Tabled in the House of Commons on March 27, 1871. Sessional Paper no. 54 - 1871. Printed as:

Canal Commission. Letter to the Honourable the Secretary of State from the Canal Commissioners, respecting the improvement of the inland

---

[1] Resigned from the Commission. He was replaced by Shannon.

[2] Appointed on December 6, 1870 by Order in Council P. C. 424.

navigation of the Dominion of Canada. Ottawa, 24th February, 1871.
190,  9 p.


5    COMMISSION TO INQUIRE INTO AND REPORT UPON THE ALLEGED OB-
     STRUCTIONS OF NAVIGABLE STREAMS AND RIVERS, IN THE PROV-
     INCES OF QUEBEC AND ONTARIO, BY DEALS, EDGINGS, SAW-DUST,
     AND OTHER REFUSE FROM SAWMILLS

          Established on October 27, 1871 by Order in Council P. C. 1459 on
     the recommendation of the Minister of Public Works.  No indication of
     authorizing statute given in Order in Council.  Members of the Commis-
     sion named on November 6, 1871 by Order in Council P. C. 1487.
          Commissioners: Hamilton Hartley Killaly, Chairman, John Mather,
     and R. W. Shepherd.

                                  Report
          Dated February, 1873.  Tabled in the House of Commons on March
     31, 1873.  Sessional Paper no. 29-1873.  Printed as:
          Report on the Commission appointed to enquire into the condition of
     navigable streams. Ottawa, Printed by I. B. Taylor, 29, 31 & 33 Rideau
     Street, 1873.  57 p.
          Also issued as a separate.
          Notes: Members of the Commission travelled extensively throughout
     Ontario and Quebec inspecting rivers and streams.


6    ROYAL COMMISSION TO INQUIRE INTO A CERTAIN RESOLUTION MOVED
     BY THE HONOURABLE MR. HUNTINGTON, IN PARLIAMENT, ON
     APRIL 2ND, 1873, RELATING TO THE CANADIAN PACIFIC RAILWAY

          Appointed on August 14, 1873 by Order in Council P. C. 1058 under
     An Act respecting Inquiries concerning Public Matters (31 Victoria,
     c. 38) and on the recommendation of the Minister of Justice.
          Commissioners: Charles Dewey Day, Chairman, Antoine Polette,
     and James Robert Gowan.
          Secretary: Salter Jehoshaphat Vankoughnet.

                                  Report
          Dated October 17, 1873.  Tabled in the House of Commons on
     October 23, 1873.  Text printed in the Journals of the House of Com-
     mons, Volume 7, 1873, Appendix 1.  Printed as:
          Report of the Royal Commission, appointed by Commission ad-
     dressed to them under the Great Seal of Canada, bearing date of the
     Fourteenth day of August, A. D. 1873.  227 p.
          Notes: Hearings held at Ottawa (September 1 - October 1, 1873).
     36 witnesses (including Sir John A. Macdonald) appeared before the Com-

mission.   Cost: $10,918.64.

7   ROYAL COMMISSION TO INQUIRE INTO THE CAUSE OF THE HIGH SPRING
    FLOODS WHICH OCCUR IN THE ST. LAWRENCE RIVER BETWEEN THE
    CITIES OF QUEBEC AND MONTREAL

      Established on September 8, 1873 by Order in Council P. C. 1152
on the recommendation of the Minister of Public Works.   No indication
of authorizing statute given in Order in Council.   Members of the Commission named on September 27, 1873 by Order in Council P. C. 1234.
      Commissioners: John Dickinson, Charles Logie Armstrong and
Jean Normand.

#### Report
      Dated December 8, 1873.   Tabled in the House of Commons on May
22, 1874.   Sessional Paper no. 76-1874.   Printed as:
      Report.... of the Commissioners named to enquire into the causes
of the high spring floods of the St. Lawrence, between Quebec and Montreal.   3 p.
      Notes: Commissioners examined the River during November, 1873
from  the steamer Richelieu.  Commission suspended on December 4,
1873.   Cost: $2,257.06.

8   ROYAL COMMISSION TO INQUIRE INTO AND REPORT UPON CLAIMS TO
    RIGHTS OF CUTTING HAY AND COMMON IN THE PROVINCE OF MANI-
    TOBA

      Appointed on December 22, 1873 by Order in Council P. C. 527 under
An Act respecting Inquiries concerning Public Matters (31 Victoria, c. 38)
and on the recommendation of the Minister of Justice.
      Commissioners: Joseph Dubuc  and John Farquhar Bain.

#### Report
      Not located.
      Notes: Cost: $817.60.

9   ROYAL COMMISSION TO INQUIRE INTO THE CONDITION AND MANAGE-
    MENT OF THE POST OFFICE AT MONTREAL

      Appointed on February 21, 1874 by Order in Council P. C. 112 on the
recommendation of the Postmaster General.   No indication of authorizing
statute given in Order in Council.
      Commissioners: John Mercier, John Dewe and William  Grannis
Parmelee.

Report

Not located .
Notes: Cost: $5,036.19.


10   COMMISSION TO INQUIRE INTO AND REPORT UPON CERTAIN MATTERS
     RELATIVE TO THE INTERCOLONIAL RAILWAY

     Appointed on May 11, 1874 by Order in Council P. C. 541 on the
     recommendation of the Minister of Public Works.  No indication of
     authorizing stature given in Order in Council.
     Commissioners: Never named.


11   COMMISSION TO INQUIRE INTO THE WORKING OF THE PROHIBITORY
     LIQUOR LAW IN THE UNITED STATES

     Appointed on July 28, 1874 by Order in Council P. C. 986 on the re-
     commendation of the Minister of Public Works.  No indication of author-
     izing statute given in Order in Council.
     Commissioners: Frederick Davis, Chairman, and Rev. J. W.
     Manning.

Report

     Undated.  Printed as:
     Report of Commissioners to enquire into the working of the prohibi-
     tory liquor law.  Ottawa, Printed by Maclean Roger & Co. , Wellington
     Street, 1875.  133 p.
     Notes: Visited 6 states, 13 cities, 10 towns and many rural districts.
     Cost: $2,110.60.
     Location: Library of Parliament, Ottawa.


12   ROYAL COMMISSION TO INQUIRE INTO CHARGES PREFERRED AGAINST
     EDWARD MEYER, CHIEF LANDING WAITER AT MONTREAL

     Appointed on January 23, 1875 by Order in Council P. C. 56 under
     An Act respecting Inquiries concerning Public Matters (31 Victoria, c. 38)
     and on the recommendation of the Minister of Customs.
     Commissioner: John W. Cudlip.

Report

     Not located.


13   COMMISSION TO ASCERTAIN PERSONS ENTITLED TO GRANTS OF LAND
     AND SCRIPT IN MANITOBA

Appointed on May 5, 1875 by Order in Council P. C. 449 on the recommendation of the Minister of the Interior. No indication of authorizing statute given in Order in Council.

Commissioners: John Maule Machar and Matthew Ryan.

Joint Secretaries: Amédée Emmanuel Forget and Henry Silas Goodhue.

### Report

Abstract of returns of Commissioners-- Half-Breed lands and scrip-claims investigated by Mr. Commissioner Machar and claims investigated by Mr. Commissioner Ryan. In Annual Report of the Department of the Interior for the year ended 30th June, 1875, Part III, p. 31. (Sessional Paper no. 9-1876). Complete text of report not located.

Notes: 9,293 claims were investigated and disposed of by the Commissioners. Cost: $8,963.21.

14   COMMISSION TO INVESTIGATE THE NATURE AND EXTENT OF THE COMMERCIAL ADVANTAGE TO BE DERIVED FROM THE CONSTRUCTION OF THE BAIE VERTE CANAL

Appointed on June 16, 1875 by Order in Council P. C. 556 on the recommendation of the Minister of Public Works. No indication of authorizing statute given in the Order in Council.

Commissioners: John Young, Chairman, Sir William Pearce Howland, Joseph Wilson Lawrence and Peter Jack.

Secretary: Frederick Braun.

### Report

Dated December 2, 1875. Tabled in the House of Commons on February 10, 1876. Sessional Paper no. 11-1876. Not printed in Sessional Papers Series. Printed as:

Report of the Commission appointed by the Government to investigate the nature and extent of the commercial advantages to be derived from the construction of the Baie Verte Canal; together with the evidence obtained. December, 1875. [Ottawa, 1875] vi, 20,138 p.

Location: New Brunswick Museum, St. John, N.B.

### Minority Report of J.W. Lawrence

Dated January, 1876. Printed as:

A minority report on the proposed Baie Verte Canal, by J.W. Lawrence, 1876. St. John, N.B., Daily Telegraph Steam Job Print, 1876. 45, 2 p.

Locations: New Brunswick Museum, St. John, N.B.; Public Archives of Canada, Ottawa; Queen's University Library, Kingston (Xerox copy).

Notes: Meetings held at Montreal and 15 towns and cities in the Maritimes. Cost: $8,099.50.

15 ROYAL COMMISSION TO INQUIRE INTO CONFLICTING CLAIMS TO LANDS OF OCCUPANTS IN MANITOBA

Appointed on January 7, 1876 by Order in Council P.C. 9 under the Act respecting conflicting claims of occupants in Manitoba (38 Victoria, c. 53).
Commissioner: Alexander Morris.

### Report
Not located.
Notes: Meetings of the Commission held in 5 counties. Cost: $818.08.

16 COMMISSION TO FIX AND DETERMINE THE NUMBER, EXTENT AND LOCALITY OF THE RESERVE OR RESERVES TO BE ALLOWED TO THE INDIANS OF BRITISH COLUMBIA

Appointed on May 6, 1876 and August 16, 1876 by Orders in Council P.C. 444 and 779 respectively on the recommendation of the Minister of the Interior. No indication of authorizing statute given in Order in Council.
Commissioners: Alexander Anderson, Archibald McKinley and Gilbert Malcolm Sproat.

### Report
Various drafts of reports (1876-1877) in Public Archives of Canada (Record Group 6, A-3, volume 2). 525 leaves.
Notes: Cost: $150,069.36.

17 ROYAL COMMISSION TO INQUIRE INTO THE MANAGEMENT OF THE CANADIAN NORTHERN RAILWAY COMPANY

Appointed on July 22, 1876 by Order in Council P.C. 720 under An Act respecting Inquiries concerning Public Matters (31 Victoria, c. 38) and on the recommendation of the Minister of Public Works.
Commissioners: Larratt William Smith, Chairman, John Peter Featherstone and Adam Hope.

### Report
Undated. Tabled in the House of Commons on February 15, 1877.

Sessional Paper no. 10-1877. Printed as:

Report of the Commission appointed "for investigating the books, accounts, and vouchers of the Northern Railway Company of Canada, and the disbursements and the expenditures of the said Company;" together with the evidence taken by the said Commission. Printed by order of Parliament. Ottawa, Printed by Maclean, Roger & Co., Wellington Street, 1877. 74 p.

Also issued as a separate.

18   COMMISSION TO INVESTIGATE CHARGES AGAINST MR. J. A. PROVEN-CHER, ACTING INDIAN SUPERINTENDENT OF THE MANITOBA SUPER-INTENDENCY

Appointed on November 3, 1877 by Order in Council P. C. 976 under An Act respecting Commissions, and Oaths of Allegiance and of Office (31 Victoria c. 36) and on the recommendation of the Minister of the Interior.

Commissioners: Ebenezer McCall and William Aird Ross.

Report

It appears unlikely that any report was issued. The commission was cancelled on November 12. 1877 by Order in Council P. C. 1004.

19   COMMISSION TO INVESTIGATE CHARGES AGAINST CAPTAIN JAMES COOPER, AGENT OF THE DEPARTMENT OF MARINE AND FISHERIES AT VICTORIA, BRITISH COLUMBIA

Appointed on November 3, 1877 by Order in Council P. C. 921 under An Act respecting Inquiries concerning Public Matters (31 Victoria, c. 38) and on the recommendation of the Minister of Marine and Fisheries.

Commissioner: John Hamilton Gray.

Report

Not located.

20   ROYAL COMMISSION TO INQUIRE INTO CONFLICTING CLAIMS TO LANDS OF OCCUPANTS IN MANITOBA

Appointed on May 23, 1878 by Order in Council P. C. 431 under An Act respecting conflicting claims to lands of occupants in Manitoba (38 Victoria, c. 53) and on the recommendation of the Minister of the Interior.

Commissioner: Edmund Burke Wood.

### Report

Tabled in the Senate on April 17, 1879. Sessional Paper no. 118-1879. Not printed in Sessional Paper Series. No copy located.
Notes: Cost: $4,971.43.


21  COMMISSION TO INVESTIGATE CHARGES AGAINST CERTAIN EMPLOY-
     EES OF THE WELLAND CANAL

Appointed on March 29, 1879 by Order in Council P. C. 440 on the recommendation of the Minister of Public Works.  No indication of authorizing statute given in Order in Council.
Commissioner: David Stark.

### Report

Not located.


22  COMMISSION TO INQUIRE INTO AND SETTLE THE DISPUTED TERRITORY
     FUND IN NEW BRUNSWICK

Appointed on May 19, 1879 by Order in Council P. C. 739 on the recommendation of the Minister of Finance.   No indication of authorizing statute given in Order in Council.
Commissioner: John Lorn McDougall.

### Report

Not located.


23  ROYAL COMMISSION TO INQUIRE INTO CHANGES AFFECTING THE AD-
     MINISTRATION OF JUSTICE IN THE NORTH-WEST TERRITORIES

Appointed on May 30, 1879 by Order in Council P. C. 749 on the recommendation of the Minister of the Interior.  No indication of authorizing statute given in Order in Council.
Commissioner: Edgar Dewdney.
Secretary: Elliott Torrance Galt.

### Report

Dated January 2, 1880.  In Annual Report of the Department of the Interior for the year ended 30th June, 1879 (Sessional Paper no. 4 - 1880) pp. 76-103.


24  ROYAL COMMISSION TO INQUIRE INTO MATTERS CONNECTED WITH
     THE CANADIAN PACIFIC RAILWAY

Established on May 22, 1880 by Order in Council P. C. 933 under
An Act respecting Inquiries concerning Public Matters (31 Victoria, c. 38)
and on the recommendation of the Minister of Railways and Canals.
Commissioners named on June 16, 1880 by Order in Council P. C. 1087.

Commissioners: George McKenzie Clark, Samuel Keefer and Edward
Miall.

### Report
Volumes 1 and 2 (Evidence) tabled in the House of Commons on
April 5, 1882. Volume 3 (Conclusions), dated April 8, 1882, tabled
in the House of Commons on April 11, 1882. Sessional Paper no. 48t-
1882. Not printed in Sessional Paper Series. Printed as:

Report of the Canadian Pacific Railway Royal Commission. Ottawa,
Printed by S. Stephenson & Co., Chatham, Ont., 1882. 3 v. (960, 949,
and 510 p.).

Notes: Hearings held at Ottawa (August 12, 1880- September 26,
1881). 105 witnesses (including Alexander Mackenzie and Sir Charles
Tupper) appeared before the Commission. Cost: $37,934.41.

### 25  ROYAL COMMISSION TO INQUIRE INTO THE ORGANIZATION OF THE CIVIL SERVICE COMMISSION

Appointed on June 16, 1880 by Order in Council P. C. 1093 on the
recommendation of the Sub-Committee of the Privy Council who were
charged with the duty of reporting upon the expediency of a renewed
enquiry into the organization of the civil service. No indication of authorizing statute given in Order in Council.

Commissioners: Donald McInnes, Edmond J. Barbeau, Alfred
Brunel, William White, John Tilton and William R. Mingaye.
Secretary: Martin Joseph Griffin.

### First Report
Dated March 5, 1881. Tabled in the House of Commons on March 8,
1881. Sessional Paper no. 113-1880/81. Printed as:

First report of the Civil Service Commission, with appendices. Pre-
sented to both Houses of Parliament by Command of His Excellency. 1881.
Ottawa, Printed by Maclean, Roger & Co., Wellington Street, 1881. 554p.
Also issued as a separate.

### Second Report
Dated July 28, 1881. Tabled in the House of Commons on February
15, 1882. Sessional Paper no. 32-1882. Printed as:

Second report of the Civil Service Commission, with appendix and
minority report. Ottawa, 28th July, 1881. Printed by order of Parliament. Ottawa, Printed by Maclean, Roger & Co., Wellington Street,
1882. 93 p.

Notes: Hearings held August 8 - December 20, 1880. Cost:
$11,003.45.

26  ROYAL COMMISSION TO INQUIRE RESPECTING CERTAIN CLAIMS TO
    LANDS IN MANITOBA

Appointed on February 25, 1881 by Order in Council P. C. 320
under An Act respecting Inquiries concerning Public Matters (31 Victoria,
c. 38).
Commissioners: Joseph Dubuc and James Andrews Miller.

Report
Tabled in the House of Commons on March 20, 1882. Sessional
Paper no. 30e-1882. Not printed. No copy located.

27  COMMISSION TO INQUIRE INTO AND REPORT ON THE SYSTEM OF LAWS
    REGULATING LABOUR IN THE STATE OF MASSACHUSETTS

Appointed on June 22, 1881 by Order in Council P. C. 959 on the
recommendation of the Minister of Finance. No indication of authorizing statute given in the Order in Council.
Commissioner: William Lukes.
Secretary: A. H. Blackeby.

Report
Undated. Tabled in the Senate on February 12, 1883. Sessional
Paper no. 16-1883. Printed as:
Report of A. H. Blackeby, the Commissioner appointed to enquire
into and report on the System of Laws regulating labor in the State of
Massachusetts. 22 p.

28  COMMISSION TO COLLECT, EXAMINE AND CLASSIFY THE STATUTES
    PASSED BY THE PARLIAMENT OF THE DOMINION OF CANADA,
    SINCE CONFEDERATION

Appointed on November 15, 1881 by Order in Council P. C. 1541 on
the recommendation of the Minister of Justice. No indication of authorizing statute given in Order in Council.
Commissioner: James Cockburn.
Secretary: Alexander Ferguson.

Report
Dated December 30, 1882. Tabled in the Senate on February 12,
1883. Sessional Paper no. 17-1883. Printed as:

Report of the Commissioners to collect, examine and classify the Statutes passed by the Parliament of the Dominion of Canada, since Confederation. 5 p.

Notes: Cost: $2,961.94.

29  COMMISSION TO INQUIRE INTO CHARGES PREFERRED AGAINST THE PULLMAN PALACE CAR COMPANY OF HAVING ON MANY OCCASIONS DURING A NUMBER OF YEARS PAST, BY THEIR EMPLOYEES AND AGENTS, INTRODUCED ILLICITLY INTO CANADA LARGE AND VALUABLE QUANTITIES OF GOODS LIABLE TO CUSTOMS DUTY WITHOUT REPORTING, ENTERING OR PAYING DUTY THEREON, AND OTHER VIOLATION OF CUSTOMS LAWS

Appointed on January 12, 1882 by Order in Council P. C. 35 under An Act respecting Inquiries concerning Public Matters (31 Victoria, c. 38) and on the recommendation of the Minister of Customs.

Commissioner: James Johnson.

Report

Not located.

30  ROYAL COMMISSION TO INQUIRE INTO CONFLICTING CLAIMS TO LANDS OF OCCUPANTS IN MANITOBA

Appointed on February 20, 1882 by Order in Council P. C. 298 under An Act respecting conflicting claims to lands of occupants in Manitoba (38 Victoria, c. 53) and An Act to amend "An Act respecting conflicting claims to lands of occupants in Manitoba" (41 Victoria, c. 14).

Commissioners: Aquila Walsh, William Pearce and Henry Hall Smith. [1]

Report

Not located.

31  ROYAL COMMISSION TO INQUIRE INTO CERTAIN CLAIMS CONNECTED WITH THE CONSTRUCTION OF THE INTERCOLONIAL RAILWAY

Established on July 28, 1882 by Order in Council P. C. 1634 on the recommendation of the Minister of Railways and Canals. Commissioners appointed on July 28, 1882 by Order in Council P. C. 1636.

---

[1] Smith who replaced Pearce was appointed on June 14, 1884 by Order in Council P. C. 1325.

Commissioners: George McKenzie Clark, Frederick Broughton, D'Arcy E. Boutton,[1] George Laidlaw,[2] and Sir Casimir Stanislaus Gzowski.[3]

Secretary: Louis Kossuth Jones.

Report

Dated March 20, 1884. Tabled in the House of Commons on April 1, 1884. Sessional Paper no. 53 - 1884, pp. 4-187. Printed as:

General Report of the Commissioners appointed to enquire into the claims arising out of the construction of the Intercolonial Railway. 183 p.

Notes: Cost: $22,025.49.


32 COMMISSION ON THE STATE OF THE MANUFACTURING INDUSTRIES OF ONTARIO AND QUEBEC

Appointed on May 5, 1884 by Order in Council P. C. 980 on the recommendation of the Minister of Finance. No indication of authorizing statute given in Order in Council.

Commissioner: A. H. Blackeby.

Report

Undated. Tabled in the House of Commons on February 11, 1885. Sessional Paper no. 37 - 1885, pp. 4-35. Printed as:

Report of A. H. Blackeby on the state of the manufacturing industries of Ontario and Quebec. 31 p.

Notes: The Commissioner visited factories in the major towns and cities of Ontario and Quebec.


33 ROYAL COMMISSION TO INQUIRE INTO CHINESE IMMIGRATION INTO BRITISH COLUMBIA

Appointed on July 4, 1884 by Order in Council P. C. 1458 under An Act respecting Inquiries concerning Public Matters (31 Victoria, c. 38) and on the recommendation of the Prime Minister.

Commissioners: Joseph Adolphe Chapleau and John Hamilton Gray.

Secretary: Nicholas Flood Davin.

Report

Dated February 21, 1885. Tabled in the House of Commons on

---

[1] Appointed on October 7, 1882 by Order in Council P. C. 1948.
[2] Unable to act.
[3] Appointed on September 14, 1882 by Order in Council P. C. 1831. However, he was unable to act.

February 25, 1885.  Sessional Paper no. 54a-1885.  Printed as:
Report of the Royal Commission on Chinese Immigration.  Report
and Evidence.  Ottawa, Printed by order of the Commission, 1885.
cxxxiv, cii, 487 p.
Also issued as a separate.
Notes: 31 witnesses examined viva voce.  39 witnesses examined
by sending out printed questionnaires.  The Commissioners also visited
San Francisco.  Cost: $ 9,755.05.

34  COMMISSION ON THE MANUFACTURING INDUSTRIES OF CERTAIN
    SECTIONS OF THE MARITIME PROVINCES

Appointed on September 14, 1884 by Order in Council P. C. 1794
on the recommendation of the Minister of Finance.  No indication of
authorizing statute given in Order in Council.
Commissioner: Edward W. Willis.

### Report

Undated.  Tabled in the House of Commons on February 11, 1885.
Sessional Paper no. 37-1885, pp. 35-197.  Printed as:
Report of Edward Willis, on the manufacturing industries of certain
sections of the Maritime Provinces.  Together with appendices containing notes and tabular statements of the working force and wages paid
in 1878 and 1884, and also the invested capital and annual output or pro-
duct.  162 p.
Notes: The Commission collected information in most of the major
towns and cities of the Maritime Provinces.

35  ROYAL COMMISSION TO INQUIRE INTO THE ENUMERATION OF HALF-
    BREEDS IN THE NORTH-WEST TERRITORIES

Appointed on March 30, 1885 by Order in Council P. C. 688 under
The Dominion Lands Act (46 Victoria, c. 17) and on the recommendation
of the Minister of the Interior.
Commissioners: William Purvis Rochfort Street, Chairman,
Roger Goulet, and Amédée Emmanuel Forget.

### Report

Not located.
Notes: Cost: $41,652.48.

36  COMMISSION TO INVESTIGATE AND REPORT UPON CERTAIN CLAIMS
    ARISING OUT OF THE RECENT OUTBREAK AND REBELLION IN THE
    NORTH WEST TERRITORIES

Appointed on October 15, 1885 by Order in Council P. C. 1917 under
An Act respecting Inquiries concerning Public Matters (31 Victoria, c. 38)
and on the recommendation of the Minister of Militia and Defence.

Commissioners: William Hayes Jackson, Edward Ashworth Whitehead, William Henry Forrest, George Grey, [1] and Adam John Laing
Peebles. [2]

Secretary: Edmund B. Holt.

### Reports

Reports Nos. 1 - 111 (September 8, 1885 - February 24, 1886).
In Report upon the suppression of the Rebellion in the North-West Territories, and matters in connection therewith, in 1885. (Sessional Paper
no. 6 - 1886), pp. 67 - 325.

Report Nos. 112 - 177 (March 2, 1886 - December 21, 1886). In
Final Report of the War Claims Commission. (Sessional Paper no. 9 -
1887, Appendix No. 15). 80 p.

Notes: Hearings held in Winnipeg, September 7, 1885 to February 25,
1886.

37  ROYAL COMMISSION TO INQUIRE INTO AND REPORT UPON CLAIMS FOR
COMPENSATION FOR LOSS OR DAMAGE ARISING OUT OF THE LATE
HALF-BREED AND INDIAN AND INDIAN INSURRECTION IN THE NORTH-
WEST TERRITORIES

Appointed on February 25, 1886 by Order in Council P. C. 5 under
An Act respecting Inquiries concerning Public Matters (31 Victoria, c. 38)
and on the recommendation of the Minister of the Interior.

Commissioners: Joseph Alphonse Ouimet, Chairman, Thomas McKay,
Henry Muma, and Lawrence Herchmer.

Secretary: George H. Young.

### Report

Dated July 4, 1887 . Printed as:
Rebellion N. W. T. Royal Commission on Rebellion Losses. Report to
the Honourable the Minister of the Interior. [ n. p. , n. d. ] 7, 19 p.

Locations: Manitoba Provincial Archives, Winnipeg; Queen's University Library, Kingston (Xerox copy).

Notes: Report not signed by Muma and Herchmer. Hearings held
in four towns and cities in the North -West Territories.

---

[1] Acted in the Absence of Whitehead.
[2] Appointed on November 17, 1885 by Order in Council P. C. 2155.

38  ROYAL COMMISSION TO INQUIRE INTO AND REPORT UPON THE ENUMER-
    ATION OF HALF-BREEDS IN THE NORTH-WEST TERRITORIES OUT-
    SIDE OF MANITOBA

    Appointed on March 1, 1886 by Order in Council P. C. 309 under the
    Dominion Lands Act (46 Victoria, c. 17) and on the recommendation of
    the Minister of the Interior.
        Commissioner: Roger Goulet.
        Secretary: Narcisse - omer Côté.

                                  Report
    Dated January 12, 1887. Report respecting claims by Half-Breeds.
    In Annual Report of the Department of the Interior for the year 1886.
    (Sessional Paper no. 7 - 1887), pp. 76-79.
        Notes: Held sittings at 16 places. The Commission received and
    investigated 1,414 claims.


39  ROYAL COMMISSION TO INQUIRE INTO CHARGES PREFERRED AGAINST
    JEREMIAH TRAVIS, STIPENDIARY MAGISTRATE, NORTH-WEST
    TERRITORIES

    Appointed on March 22, 1886 by Order in Council P. C. 505 under
    An Act respecting Inquiries concerning Public Matters (31 Victoria,
    c. 114) and on the recommendation of the Minister of Justice.
        Commissioner: Thomas Wardlaw Taylor.

                                  Report
        Tabled in the House of Commons on June 13, 1887. Sessional Paper
    no. 56a-1887. Not printed in Sessional Papers Series. No copy loca-
    ted.
        Notes: Cost: $1,278.00.


40  COMMISSION TO INQUIRE INTO THE CAUSE OF FLOODS AT MONTREAL

    Appointed on May 24, 1886 by Order in Council P. C. 1029 on the
    recommendation of the Minister of Public Works. No indication of
    authorizing statute given in Order in Council.
        Commissioners: Henry F. Perley, Thomas Coltrin Keefer, John
    Kennedy, Walter Shanly and Percival W. St. George.

                                 Reports
        Five interim reports (July 31, 1886 - August 12, 1887) included in
    the volume with the [final] report. Tabled in the Senate on April 25,
    1889. Sessional Paper no. 76-1889. Printed as:

Montreal Flood Commission. Reports of the Commission. Appointed by Order in Council of 28th May, 1886, to "Enquire into the causes of floods at Montreal and to suggest the necessary remedies to prevent their recurrence"; together with Order in Council appointed appointing the Commission, and Report of Chief Engineer of the Department of Public Works. 82 p.

Also issued as a separate with the following title:

Report of a commission of engineers appointed by the Government of Canada to inquire into the causes of the floods at Montreal and to suggest remedies for their removal.

Commissioners: Thos. C. Keefer, C. M. G. (Chairman), Henry F. Perley, John Kennedy, Percival W. St. George.

Published by Order of the City Council of Montreal, 1890. 76 p.

41  ROYAL COMMISSION TO INQUIRE INTO THE ADVISABILITY OF CONSTITUTING A COURT OF RAILWAY COMMISSIONERS

Appointed on July 6, 1886 by Order in Council P. C. 1355 on the recommendation of the Minister of Railways and Canals. No indication of authorizing statute given in Order in Council.

Commissioners: Sir Alexander Tilloch Galt, Chairman, Collingwood Schreiber, George Moberley, Egerton Ryerson Burpee and Thomas K. Kenny.[1]

Secretary: S. Lonergan.

Report

Dated January 14, 1888. Tabled in the House of Commons on February 29, 1888. Sessional Paper no. 8a-1888. Printed as:

Report of the Royal Commission on Railways, with Appendices. Ottawa, Printed by MacLean, Roger & Co., Wellington Street. 1888. 41 p.

Also issued as a separate.

Notes: Visited 9 cities in Canada. Two members (Burpee and Moberley) visited several American States. The Chairman visited Great Britain. Cost: $25, 746.65.

42  ROYAL COMMISSION TO INVESTIGATE AND REPORT UPON ALL QUESTIONS CONNECTED WITH THE PAST AND FUTURE LEASING OF WATERS FOR MANUFACTURING PURPOSES THROUGHOUT THE WHOLE LENGTH OF THE LACHINE CANAL

---

[1] Burpee and Kenny were appointed on August 14 1886 by Order in Council P. C. 1523.

Appointed on July 17, 1886 by Order in Council P. C. 1464 and on the recommendation of the Minister of Railways and Canals. No indication of authorizing statute given in Order in Council.

Commissioners: Etienne H. Parent, Chairman, Thomas Pringle and John Kennedy.

Secretary: Robert Chambers Douglas.

### Report

Dated May 31, 1887. Tabled in the House of Commons on March 2, 1888. Sessional Paper no. 30-1888. Not printed in Sessional Papers series. Printed as:

Report of Royal Commission on the leasing of water-power, Lachine Canal. Ottawa: Printed by Maclean, Roger & Co., Wellington Street 1887. 58 p.

Also issued as a separate.

Locations: Department of Transport Library, Ottawa. Queen's University Library, Kingston (Xerox copy).

Notes: 35 persons gave evidence before the Commission.

43  ROYAL COMMISSION TO INQUIRE INTO CHARGES PREFERRED AGAINST CHARLES THOMAS DUPONT, DISTRICT INSPECTOR OF INLAND REVENUE DIVISION OF BRITISH COLUMBIA

Appointed on October 26, 1886 by Order in Council P. C. 1942 under An Act to authorize making certain investigations under oath (43 Victoria, c. 12) and on the recommendation of the Minister of Inland Revenue.

Commissioner: John Kelly Barrett.

### Report

Not located.

44  COMMISSION TO INVESTIGATE ALLEGED IRREGULARITIES REGARDING A FUEL WOOD CONTRACT AT THE CITADEL, QUEBEC CITY

Appointed on November 24, 1886 by Order in Council P. C. 2100 on the recommendation of the Minister of Militia and Defence. Part of Inquiries Act not stated.

Commissioner: Jules Ernest LaRue.

### Report

Not located.

45  ROYAL COMMISSION TO INQUIRE INTO AND REPORT ON THE SUBJECT
    OF LABOUR,  ITS RELATION TO CAPITAL, THE HOURS OF LABOUR
    AND THE EARNINGS OF LABOURING MEN AND WOMEN

Appointed on December 7, 1886 by Order in Council P. C. 1938 on
the recommendation of the Prime Minister.  No indication of authorizing
statute given in Order in Council.

Commissioners: James Armstrong (Chairman, 1886-1888), [1]
Augustus Toplady Freed (Chairman, 1888-1889), [2] John Armstrong,
Samuel R. Heakes, Jules Helbronner, Michael Walsh, James Alfred
Clark, William A. Gibson, [3] Urias Carson, [3] Louis Côté, [3] Hugh A.
McLean, [3] John Kelly, [4] William Haggarty, [4] Guilliaume Boivon, [5] and
Patrick Kerwin. [3]

Secretary: A. H. Blackeby.

First Report

Dated February 23, 1889.  Sessional Paper Letter A - 1889, pp.
7 - 75.

Second Report

Undated.  Sessional Paper Letter A - 1889, pp. 7b-195.  Printed
as:

Report of the Royal Commission on the relations of labour and
capital in Canada.  Ottawa, Printed for the Queen's Printer and Controller of Stationery, A.  Senecal, Superintendent of Printing, 1889.
195 p.

Also issued as a separate.

Notes: Commissioners visited and took evidence in 36 towns and
cities in four Provinces.  About 1,800 witnesses appeared before the
Commission.  3,579 pages of printed evidence taken.


46  ROYAL COMMISSION TO INQUIRE INTO AND COMPLETE THE ENUMERA-
    TION OF HALF-BREEDS AND CLAIMS OF WHITE SETTLERS IN THE
    NORTH-WEST TERRITORIES

Appointed on May 9, 1887 by Order in Council P. C. 898 under
The Dominion Lands Act (R. S. C. , 1886, c. 54) and on the recommendation of the Minister of the Interior.

---

[1] Died on November 23, 1888.
[2] Appointed on January 9, 1889 by Order in Council P. C. 5.
[3] Appointed on November 22, 1887 by Order in Council P. C. 2321.
[4] Appointed on March 25, 1888 by Order in Council PC. 629.
[5] Appointed on March 17, 1888 by Order in Council P. C. 312.

Commissioners: Roger Goulet, Chairman , and Narcisse-Omer
Côté.
Secretary: James Anderson.

### Report

Dated January 10, 1888. North-West Half-Breed Commission In
Annual Report of the Department of the Interior for the year 1887, Part
V (Sessional Paper no. 14 - 1888) 6 p.
Notes: Hearings held at 30 centres. The Commissioners dealt with
565 applications.


47  COMMISSION APPOINTED TO CONSIDER THE ADVISABILITY OF EXTEND-
    ING THE TRENT VALLEY CANAL, AND TO WHAT EXTENT

Appointed on October 11, 1887 by Order in Council P. C. 2032 on
the recommendation of the Minister of Railways and Canals. No indication of authorizing statute given in Order in Council.
Commissioners: George McKenzie Clark,[1] Frank Turner, John
Kennedy and Charles A. Weller.[2]

### Report

Dated December  17, 1890. Tabled in the House of Commons on
March 24, 1892. Sessional Paper no. 47-1892. Printed as:
Report of the Commissioners appointed to consider the advisability
of extending the Trent Valley Canal, and to what extent. 2 p.
Notes: Commissioners travelled throughout the Trent Valley Canal
system by steamer. Commission held hearings at 11 towns and cities
as well as at several points on the line of the Erie Canal.


48  COMMISSION TO CONSIDER CERTAIN IMPROVEMENTS SUGGESTED
    FOR THE MONTREAL HARBOUR BY THE MONTREAL HARBOUR
    COMMISSIONERS

Appointed on April 10, 1890 by Order in Council P. C. 936 on the
recommendation of the Minister of Public Works. No indication of
authorizing statute given in Order in Council.
Commissioners: Casimir Stanislaus Gzowski and John Page.
Secretary: Joseph Rielle.

### Report

Not located.

---

[1] Resigned.
[2] Appointed on December 1, 1887 by Order in Council P. C. 2397.

49  COMMISSION TO CONSIDER THE ENLARGEMENT OF THE CORNWALL
    CANAL IN ACCORDANCE WITH THE GENERAL SCHEME NOW BEING
    CARRIED OUT TO AFFORD A NAVIGABLE DEPTH OF FOURTEEN
    FEET

    Commission established on February 17, 1891 by Order in Council
    P. C. 355 on the recommendation of the Minister of Railways and Canals.
    No indication of authorizing statute given in Order in Council.  Members
    named on April 24, 1891 by Order in Council P. C. 810.
    Commissioners: Walter Shanly, John Kennedy and Frank Turner.

                              Report
    Not located.


50  COMMISSION TO INQUIRE INTO AND REPORT ON THE FISHERIES AND
    FISHERIES REGULATIONS IN BRITISH COLUMBIA

    Appointed on August 25, 1891 by Order in Council P. C. 1985 on
    the recommendation of the Minister of Marine and Fisheries.  Addi-
    tional members named on December 23, 1891 by Order in Council
    P. C. 3021.
    Commissioners: Samuel Wilmot, Chairman, Charles T. Dupont, [1]
    Charles G. Major, [1] D. W. Higgins and William J. Armstrong.
    Secretary: Charles F. Winter.

                              Report
    Dated March 19, 1892.  Sessional Paper no. 10c-1893.  Printed as:
    British Columbia Fishery Commission Report, 1892.  Ottawa, Printed
    by S. E. Dawson, Printer to the Queen's Most Excellent Majesty, 1893.
    433 p. (Includes transcript of evidence).
    Also issued as a separate.
    Notes: Commission held hearings in 4 cities of British Columbia.
    112 witnesses were heard.


51  COMMISSION TO INQUIRE INTO CHARGES PREFERRED AGAINST
    COMMISSIONER LAWRENCE HERCHMER AND ASSISTANT COM-
    MISSIONER WILLIAM H. HERCHMER, OF THE NORTH-WEST
    MOUNTED POLICE

    Appointed on November 2, 1891 by Order in Council P. C. 2651 on
    the recommendation of the President of the Privy Council.  No indi-
    cation of authorizing statute given in order in Council.
    Commissioner: Edward Ludlow Wetmore.
    Secretary: Edward Joseph Duggar.

    _____

    [1] Unable to act.

Report
Tabled in the House of Commons on March 3, 1893. Sessional
Paper no. 47-1893. Not printed in Sessional Paper series. Copy
in Public Archives of Canada (R. C. M. P. Controller's Office Records,
File no. 720 of 1892). 200 p. (approx.)
Notes: Cost: $4,018.88.


52   ROYAL COMMISSION TO INQUIRE INTO THE PRESENT CONDITION OF
     THE CIVIL SERVICE AT OTTAWA

Appointed on November 14, 1891 by Order in Council P. C. 2716
under An Act respecting Inquiries concerning Public Matters (R. S. C.,
1886, c. 114) and on the recommendation of the Prime Minister.
Commissioners: George Hague, George Wheelock Burbidge,
Edmond J. Barbeau and John Mortimer Courtney.
Secretary: James Henry Flock.


Report
Dated April 21, 1892. Tabled in the House of Commons on May 20,
1892. Sessional Paper no. 16c-1892. Printed as:
Report of the Royal Commissioners appointed to enquire into
certain matters relating to the Civil Service of Canada. 1892. Printed
by order of Parliament. Ottawa, Printed by S. E. Dawson, Printer
to the Queen's Most Excellent Majesty, 1892. xcv, 733 p. (Includes
minutes of evidence).
Notes: Cost: $6,317.43.


53   ROYAL COMMISSION ON THE LIQUOR TRAFFIC IN CANADA

Appointed on March 8, 1892 by Order in Council P. C. 610 under
An Act respecting Inquiries concerning Public Matters (R. S. C., 1886,
c. 114) on the recommendation of the Prime Minister.
Commissioners: Sir Joseph Hickson, Chairman, Herbert Stone
McDonald, Edward F. Clarke, George Auguste Gigault, and Rev.
Joseph McLeod.
Secretary: Patrick Monaghan.


Reports
Interim Report dated June 4, 1894. No copy located.
Final Report dated March 29, 1895. [1] Tabled in the House of Com -
mons on April 24, 1895. Sessional Paper no. 21-1895. Printed as:

---

[1] The report of Rev. McLeod is dated April 5, 1895. It is printed in
the Final Report, pp. 509-691.

Report of the Royal Commission on the Liquor Traffic in Canada.
Printed by Order of Parliament. Ottawa, Printed by S. E. Dawson,
Printer to the Queen's Most Excellent Majesty, 1895. v, 1003 p.
Also issued as a separate.
Notes: Public hearings held July 25, 1892 - July 7, 1893.
Cost: $70,334.83.


54  ROYAL COMMISSION IN REFERENCE TO CERTAIN CHARGES MADE
    AGAINST THE HONOURABLE SIR A. P. CARON, K. C. M. G.

Appointed on June 16, 1892 by Order in Council P. C. 1705 under
An Act respecting Inquiries concerning Public Matters (R. S. C.,
1886, c. 114) and on the recommendation of the Prime Minister.
Commissioners: Adolphe Basile Routhier and Melbourne Mc-
Taggart Tait.

Report
Dated November 24, 1892. Tabled in the House of Commons on
February 6, 1893. Sessional Paper no. 27-1893. Printed as:
Report of the Royal Commission in reference to certain charges
made against Honourable Sir A. P. Caron, K. C. M. G. Session, 1893.
Printed by Order of Parliament. Ottawa, Printed by S. E. Dawson,
Printer to the Queen's Most Excellent Majesty, 1893. iv, 602 p. (In-
cludes transcript of evidence and exhibits).
Also issued as a separate.
Notes: Hearings held at Quebec City (September 8 - November 19,
1892). 17 witnesses were examined. Cost: $500.00.


55  COMMISSION TO INQUIRE INTO AND REPORT UPON THE DESCRIPTION
    OF NETS USED, THE SPAWNING PERIODS OF FISH, AND OTHER
    MATTERS CONNECTED WITH THE FISHERIES IN THE VARIOUS
    LAKES AND OTHER WATERS IN THE PROVINCE OF ONTARIO

Appointed on September 23, 1892 by Order in Council P. C. 2447
under An Act respecting Inquiries concerning Public Matters (R. S. C.,
1886, c. 114) and on the recommendation of the Minister of Marine
and Fisheries.
Commissioners: Samuel Wilmot, Chairman and Edward Harris.

Report
Dated March 1, 1893. Sessional Paper no. 10c - 1893. Printed
as:
Report of the Dominion Fishery Commission on the fisheries of
the Province of Ontario. 1893. Part I. Printed by Order of

Parliament. Ottawa, Printed by S. E. Dawson, Printer to the Queen's
Most Excellent Majesty, 1894. 34 p.

Notes: Hearings held in 21 towns and cities November 2 - November 10, 1893. 152 witnesses appeared before the Commission.

56   COMMISSION TO INQUIRE INTO AND REPORT UPON CLAIMS OF
     CERTAIN CONTRACTORS ARISING OUT OF THE CONSTRUCTION OF
     THE OXFORD AND NEW GLASGOW RAILWAY AND OF THE CAPE
     BRETON RAILWAY RESPECTIVELY

Appointed on December 29, 1892 by Order in Council P. C. 3250 under An Act respecting Inquiries concerning Public Matters (R. S. C., 1886, c. 114) and on the recommendation of the Minister of Railways and Canals.

Commissioner: George Wheelock Burbidge.

Report

Not located.

57   COMMISSION TO INVESTIGATE THE ADMINISTRATION AND AFFAIRS
     OF NEW WESTMINSTER PENITENTIARY

Appointed on May 21, 1894 by Order in Council P. C. 1527 on the recommendation of the Minister of Justice. No indication of authorizing statute given in Order in Council.

Commissioner: Montague William Tyrwhitt Drake.

Report

T he Report was read into the Senate Debates on July 8, 1895 by Senator Thomas B. McInnes. See Debates of the Senate, 1895, pp. 588 - 590.

Notes: Hearings opened at New Westminster on June 22, 1894.

58   COMMISSION TO INVESTIGATE CHARGES BY SHIPPERS THAT
     EXCESSIVE FREIGHT RATES ARE BEING CHARGED IN THE EXPORT
     OF CATTLE

Appointed on August 25, 1894 by Order in Council P. C. 2478 under An Act respecting Inquiries concerning Public Matters (R. S. C., 1886, c. 114) and on the recommendation of the Minister of Marine and Fisheries.

Commissioner: William Loftus Magee.

Report
Undated. Sessional Paper no. 11b-1895. Printed as:
Report of the Commissioner on cattle freight rates from the Port
of Montreal to ports in Europe. Ottawa, Printed by S. E. Dawson,
Printer to the Queen's Most Excellent Majesty, 1895. 16 p.
Also issued as a separate.

59   COMMISSION TO INQUIRE INTO AND REPORT ON COMPLAINTS AS TO
     DISCRIMINATION IN PASSENGER AND FREIGHT RATES IN MANITOBA
     AND THE NORTH-WEST TERRITORIES

Appointed on November 3, 1894 by Order in Council P. C. 2834
on the recommendation of the Minister of Railways and Canals. No
indication of authorizing statute given in Order in Council. Commission cancelled on November 26, 1894 by Order in Council P. C. 3462.
Commissioners: Peter Suther Archibald, Chairman, William
Pearce, and William H. Allison.
Secretary: H. H. Schaefer.

Report
Dated May 7, 1895. Tabled in the House of Commons on May 10,
1895. Sessional Paper no. 39 - 1895. Printed as:
Report of the Railway Rates Commission. 22 p.
Notes: On November 26, 1894 by Order in Council P. C. 3463
a Commission under the Railway Act (51 Victoria, c. 29) was appointed.
William H. Allison was added as Commissioner.

60   COMMISSION TO INQUIRE INTO THE PILOTAGE BUSINESS OF THE
     DISTRICT OF THE PORT OF ST. JOHN

Appointed on December 28, 1894 by Order in Council P. C. 3748
under An Act respecting Inquiries concerning Public Matters (R. S. C.,
1886, c 114) and on the recommendation of the Minister of Marine
and Fisheries.
Commissioner: W. H. Smith.

Report
Undated. Tabled in the House of Commons on January 24, 1896.
Sessional Paper no 11b - 1896. Printed as:
Report of an investigation into the Pilotage System at St. John,
N. B. by Captain W. H. Smith, R. N. R. , Chairman of the Board of
Examiners of Masters and Mates. Marine and Fisheries Department.
1895. Printed by order of Parliament. Ottawa, Printed by S. E.
Dawson, Printer to the Queen's Most Excellent Majesty, 1895. 360 p.
Also issued as a separate.

Notes: Hearings held at St. John, New Brunswick (February 7 - March 1, 1895). 52 witnesses appeared before the Commission.

61    COMMISSION TO INVESTIGATE ALLEGED VIOLATIONS OF "THE FISHERIES ACT" BY MESSRS. JAMES AND CHARLES NOBLE

Appointed on September 30, 1895 by Order in Council P. C. 2585 under An Act respecting Inquiries concerning Public Matters (R. S. C., 1886  c. 114) and on the recommendation of the Minister of Marine and Fisheries.
Commissioner: Frederick William Johnston.

Report
Dated March 1, 1897. Not printed. Copy in the Department of Fisheries files. 116 leaves (Includes transcript of evidence.)
Notes: Hearings held at Collingwood, Ontario, in February, 1896. 108 witnesses appeared before the Commission.

62    COMMISSION TO INVESTIGATE WHETHER, AND IF SO, TO WHAT EX-TENT, THE SWEATING SYSTEM IS PRACTISED IN THE VARIOUS INDUSTRIAL CENTRES OF THE DOMINION

Appointed on October 29, 1895 by Order in Council P. C. 3138 under An Act respecting Inquiries concerning Public Matters (R. S. C., 1886, c. 114) and on the recommendation of the Secretary of State.
Commissioner: Alexander Whyte Wright.

Reports[1]
Dated March 6, 1896. Tabled in the House of Commons on March 13, 1896. Sessional Paper no. 61-1896, pp. 1-19. Printed as:
Report upon the sweating system in Canada.
Notes: Seventy-nine days of inspection (October 29, 1895 - January 28, 1896). Commissioner also visited New York City and Jersey City, New Jersey.

63    COMMISSION TO INVESTIGATE REPORTS THAT THE DOMINION STEAMER "QUADRA" DID NOT REQUIRE THE EXTENSIVE REPAID CARRIED OUT AFTER RUNNING AGROUND ON FULFORD REEF, DISCOVERY ISLAND, BRITISH COLUMBIA

---

[1] A supplementary report which consists of evidence taken at Toronto, January 8-9 1896, is printed in Sessional Paper no. 61-1896, pp. 20-51.

Appointed on February 18, 1896 by Order in Council P. C. 586 under An Act respecting Inquiries concerning Public Matters (R. S. C. , 1886, c. 114) and on the recommendation of the Minister of Marine and Fisheries.
Commissioners: John Devereux and Richard Collister.

Report

Not located.

64   COMMISSION TO HOLD A CONFERENCE WITH THE GOVERNMENT OF
     MANITOBA, FOR THE PURPOSE OF ASCERTAINING WHETHER
     LEGISLATION CANNOT BE OBTAINED FROM THE LEGISLATURE
     OF MANITOBA DURING ITS PRESENT SESSION WHICH WILL DEAL
     IN A MANNER SATISFACTORY TO THE MINORITY IN MANITOBA
     WHICH ARE NOW BEFORE THE HOUSE OF COMMONS IN CONNECTION
     WITH THE REMEDIAL BILL (MANITOBA)

Appointed on March 21, 1896 by Order in Council P. C. 1105 on the recommendation of the Committee of the Privy Council. No indication of authorizing statute given in Order in Council. Amended on March 27 , 1896 by Order in Council P. C. 1199.
Commissioners: Donald Alexander Smith, Arthur Rupert Dickey and Alphonse Desjardins.

Report

Tabled in the House of Commons on April 11, 1896. Sessional Paper no. 39c-1896. Not printed in Sessional Papers Series. No copy located.

65   COMMISSION TO INQUIRE INTO THE RIGHT OF PROPERTY IN SALMON
     STAND BAY DU VIN CLAIMED BY DUDLEY PERLEY AND THOMAS
     WILLISTON

Appointed on April 22 , 1896 by Order in Council P. C. 1346 under An Act respecting Inquiries concerning Public Matters (R. S. C. , 1886, c. 114) and on the recommendation of the Minister of Marine and Fisheries.
Commissioner: David George Smith.

Report

Not located.

66    COMMISSION TO INQUIRE INTO AND REPORT  UPON CERTAIN CLAIMS
      OF MESSRS. BANCROFT, CONNOLLY AND COMPANY, REGARDING
      THE CONSTRUCTION OF THE KINGSTON GRAVING DOCK

         Appointed on May 7,  1896 by Order in Council P. C. 1765 on the
      recommendation of the Minister of Public Works.  No indication of
      authorizing statute given in Order in Council.
      Commissioner: George Wheelock Burbidge.

                              Report
             Not located.


67    COMMISSION TO INQUIRE INTO AND REPORT UPON CERTAIN CLAIMS
      OF JABEZ SNOWBALL, CONTRACTOR, REGARDING THE CONSTRUC-
      TION OF THE INDIANTOWN BRANCH OF THE INTERCOLONIAL
      RAILWAY

         Appointed on May 28, 1896 by Order in Council P. C. 1833 on the
      recommendation of the Minister of Railways and Canals.  No indica-
      tion of authorizing statute given in Order in Council.
      Commissioner : George Wheelock Burbidge.

                              Report
             Not located.


68    COMMISSION TO INQUIRE INTO AND REPORT UPON CLAIMS OF G. S.
      MAYERS REGARDING THE CONSTRUCTION OF A TRESTLE BRIDGE
      ON THE PICTOU BRANCH OF THE INTERCOLONIAL RAILWAY

         Appointed on June 11, 1896 by Order in Council P. C. 2020 on the
      recommendation of the Minister of Railways and Canals.  No indica-
      tion of authorizing statute given in the Order in Council.  Rescinded
      on October 14, 1896 by Order in Council P. C. 3490.
      Commissioner: George Wheelock Burbidge.

                              Report
             Apparently no report was issued.


69    COMMISSION TO INQUIRE INTO CHARGES REGARDING THE RESIGNA-
      TION OF WILLIAM SYKES, POSTMASTER, COBOURG, ONTARIO
      AND THE APPOINTMENT OF C. GUILLET,  POSTMASTER

         Appointed on October 24 , 1896 by Order in Council P. C. 3655

under An Act respecting Inquiries concerning Public Matters (R. S. C. ,
1886, c. 114) and on the recommendation of the Postmaster General.
Commissioner: Charles Seager.

Report

Not located.

70  COMMISSION TO INVESTIGATE THE REASONS FOR THE FAILURE OF
    THE ELECTION IN ALGOMA RIDING NOT TO BE HELD ON THE
    SAME DAY AS THE OTHER RIDINGS IN THE GENERAL ELECTION
    OF THAT YEAR

    Appointed on November 13, 1896 by Order in Council P. C. 3809
    under An Act respecting Inquiries concerning Public Matters (R. S. C. ,
    1886, c. 114) and on the recommendation of the President of the
    Privy Council.
    Commissioners: John Idington and John Crerar. [1]

Report

Not located.

71  COMMISSION TO INQUIRE INTO AND REPORT UPON CHARGES PRE-
    FERRED AGAINST EMILE DUBE OF FRAUDULENT CONDUCT IN
    SUPPLYING LUMBER TO THE INTERCOLONIAL RAILWAY

    Appointed on November 25, 1896 by Order in Council P. C. 3961
    under An Act respecting Inquiries concerning Public Matters (R. S. C. ,
    1886, c. 114) and An Act respecting the making of certain investiga-
    tions under oath (R. S. C. , 1886, c. 115) and on the recommendation of
    the Minister of Railways and Canals.
    Commissioner: Joseph Edouard Bédard.

Report

Not located.

72  COMMISSION TO INQUIRE INTO THE RESIGNATION OF C. E. EWING,
    COLLECTOR OF CUSTOMS, COBOURG, ONTARIO, AND THE PRO-
    MOTION OF D. MCALLISTER AND HAGERMAN AND THE ACTION
    OF G. GUILLET, M. P. , IN RELATION THERETO

---

[1] Replaced Idington. Crerar was appointed on November 16, 1896
by Order in Council P. C. 3843.

Appointed on November 25, 1896 by Order in Council P. C. 4009 under An Act respecting Inquiries concerning Public Matters (R. S. C., 1886, c. 114) and on the recommendation of the Minister of Trade and Commerce.

Commissioner: Charles Seager.

Report

Not located.

73  COMMISSION TO INVESTIGATE AN ACCIDENT ON THE PRINCE EDWARD ISLAND RAILWAY

Appointed on January 12, 1897 by Order in Council P. C. 76 on the recommendation of the Minister of Railways and Canals. No indication of authorizing statute given in Order in Council.

Commissioner: Herbert James Palmer.

Report

Not located.

74  COMMISSION TO INQUIRE INTO AND REPORT WITH RESPECT TO ALL
    MATERIAL FACTS RELATING TO ALLEGED SALE OF CERTAIN LOTS
    IN THE TOWN OF BANFF, NORTH-WEST TERRITORIES, PRIOR TO
    PASSING OF ROCKY MOUNTAINS PARK ACT, 50-51 VICTORIA,
    CHAPTER 32, TO ANY OTHER PERSONS WHO OR WHOSE ASSIGNEES
    OR OTHER LEGAL REPRESENTATIONS ARE NOW IN THE POSSES-
    SION OF SUCH LOTS

Appointed on February 2, 1897 by Order in Council P. C. 52 under An Act respecting Inquiries concerning Public Matters (R. S. C., 1886, c. 114) and on the recommendation of the Minister of the Interior.

Commissioner: Edwin Frederick Stephenson.

Report

Not located.

75  COMMISSION TO INVESTIGATE, INQUIRE INTO AND REPORT UPON
    CHARGES PREFERRED AGAINST CERTAIN OFFICERS AND GUARDS
    CONNECTED WITH THE STONY MOUNTAIN PENITENTIARY

Appointed on February 9, 1897 by Order in Council P. C. 242 under An Act respecting Inquiries concerning Public Matters (R. S. C., 1886, c. 114) and on the recommendation of the Minister of Justice.

Commissioner: Frederick Coate Wade.

Report

Letter of transmittal dated September 1, 1897.  Copy in Public
Archives of Canada (Partly typewritten and partly in manuscript).
(R. G. 33, no. 2). 221 leaves.
Notes: Cost: $408.75.


76   COMMISSION TO INVESTIGATE THE NATURE AND EXTENT OF LOSSES
     INCURRED BY INHABITANTS OF QUEBEC CITY IN CONSEQUENCE
     OF THE LANDSLIDE THAT OCCURRED IN SEPTEMBER, 1889

Appointed on March 2, 1897 by Order in Council P. C. 490 under
An Act respecting Inquiries concerning Public Matters (R. S. C. , 1886,
c. 114) and on the recommendation of the Minister of Justice.
     Commissioners: William Cook,  Fergus Murphy and John C. Howe.
     Secretary: J. D. Beattie.

Report

Dated April 12, 1897.  Not printed.  Carbon copy of typewritten
copy in Department of Justice files.  14 leaves.
     Notes: 77 witnesses were examined by the Commissioners.  81
claims were filed in writing with the Commission.  Hearings held at
Quebec City (March 22 - April 1, 1897).
     Cost: $1,838.50.


77   COMMISSION TO INVESTIGATE, INQUIRE INTO AND REPORT UPON
     THE STATE AND MANAGEMENT OF ST. VINCENT DE PAUL
     PENITENTIARY, MONTREAL

Appointed on March 25, 1897 by Order in Council P. C. 723 on
the recommendation of the Minister of Justice.  No indication of authorizing statute given in Order in Council.
     Commissioners: Edmund Allen Meredity, [1] James Noxon, Oliver
K. Fraser and David Arthur Lafortune. [1]

Report

Dated January 27, 1898.  Tabled in the House of Commons on
April 26, 1898.  Commissioners' Report on St. Vincent de Paul
Penitentiary.  In Report of the Minister of Justice as to Penitentiaries
of Canada for the year ended 30th June, 1898, Part II. (Sessional Paper
no. 18-1899), pp. 219-281.

---

[1] Unable to act because of other engagements.

Notes: Hearings held April 19 - December 7, 1897. Over 8,000 type-written pages of evidence recorded. 400 depositions from 160 witnesses were presented. Cost: $17,727.00.

78  COMMISSION TO INQUIRE INTO AND REPORT UPON CHARGES OF INTEMPERANCE AGAINST SHERIFF OWEN E. HUGHES OF THE JUDICIAL DISTRICT OF SASKATCHEWAN

Appointed on July 17, 1897 by Order in Council P.C. 2124 under An Act respecting Inquiries concerning Public Matters (R.S.C., 1886, c. 114) and on the recommendation of the Minister of Justice.
Commissioner: Thomas Horace McGuire.

Report

Dated August 28, 1897. Not printed. 2 leaves. Copy in Department of Justice Files.
Notes: The Commissioner reported to the Minister of Justice on August 28, 1897 that he commenced hearings on August 21, 1897 and that counsel for Sheriff Hughes requested an adjournment until August 24. On August 23 the Commissioner received a telegram from the Solicitor-General informing him that the Sheriff intended to resign in three months. No further inquiry was necessary.

79  COMMISSION TO INQUIRE INTO CERTAIN CHARGES PREFERRED AGAINST SHERIFF JAMES H. BENSON AND OTHERS OF REGINA, NORTH-WEST TERRITORIES

Appointed on July 21, 1897 by Order in Council P.C. 2252 under An Act respecting Inquiries concerning Public Matters (R.S.C., 1886, c. 114) and on the recommendation of the Minister of Justice.
Commissioner: Thomas Cooke Johnstone.

Report

Not located.

80  COMMISSION TO INVESTIGATE THE GRIEVANCES OF CERTAIN SETTLERS RESIDING WITHIN THE ESQUIMALT AND NANAÏMO RAILWAY COMPANY'S LAND BELT ON VANCOUVER ISLAND

Appointed on August 10, 1897 by Order in Council P.C. 2393 under An Act respecting Inquiries concerning Public Matters (R.S.C., 1886, c. 114) and on the recommendation of the Minister of the Interior.
Commissioner: Thomas Gainsford Rothwell.
Secretary: Beatrice Barber.

Report

Dated December 21, 1897. Tabled in the House of Commons on
April 27, 1898. Sessional Paper no. 70-1898. British Columbia
Claims Report of T. G. Rothwell, Commissioner, on claims of settlers
in Esquimalt and Nanaimo Railway Belt, British Columbia. In Annual
Report of the Department of the Interior for the year 1898, Part VII
(Sessional Paper no. 13-1899), pp. 459-469.

Notes: Hearings opened at Nanaimo on September 20, 1897.


81   COMMISSION TO INVESTIGATE AND REPORT UPON CERTAIN CHARGES
     OF CONSPIRACY TO DEFRAUD THE REVENUE, PREFERRED AGAINST
     JAMES DEVLIN, OF THE CITY OF KINGSTON, LATE ENGINEER OF
     THE KINGSTON PENITENTIARY

     Appointed on November 19, 1897 by Order in Council P. C. 3180
     under An Act respecting Inquiries concerning Public Matters (R. S. C.,
     1886, c. 114) and on the recommendation of the Minister of Justice.
     Commissioner: Charles Murphy.

                              Report

     Dated December 29, 1898. Tabled in the House of Commons on
     May 17, 1897. Sessional Paper No. 49-1897. Commissioner's Re-
     port on charges preferred against James Devlin, late Engineer of
     Kingston Penitentiary. In Report of the Minister of Justice as to
     Penitentiaries of Canada for the year ended 30th June, 1898, Part II.
     (Sessional Paper no. 18-1899), pp. 291-318.

     Notes: Hearings held January 20 - August 4, 1898 in seven towns
     and cities. Cost: $3,666.10.


82   COMMISSION TO INQUIRE INTO CHARGES OF UNJUST TREATMENT
     OF PERSONS ENGAGED IN THE CONSTRUCTION OF THE CROW'S
     NEST PASS RAILWAY

     Appointed on January 15, 1898 by Order in Council P. C. 55 under
     An Act respecting Inquiries concerning Public Matters (R. S. C., 1886,
     c. 114) and on the recommendation of the Minister of the Interior.

     Commissioners: Calixte Aime Dugas, Chairman, John Appleton
     and Francis Pedley.

                              Report

     Dated April 30, 1898. Tabled in the House of Commons on June 3,
     1898. Sessional Paper no. 90a-1898. Printed as:
     Report of the Commissioners in Crow's Nest Pass Complaints. 22 p.

     Notes: 282 witnesses examined.

83  COMMISSION TO INQUIRE INTO THE GRIEVANCES OF THE WORKMEN
    ON THE CROW'S NEST PASS RAILWAY, AND INTO THE CIRCUM-
    STANCES ATTENDING THE DEATHS OF TWO OF THE SAID EMPLOY-
    EES, CHARLES P. MACDONALD AND E. M. FRASER, AT OR NEAR
    PINCHER CREEK

        Appointed on July 1, 1898 by Order in Council P. C. 1742 under
    An Act respecting Inquiries concerning Public Matters (R. S. C. , 1886,
    c. 114) and on the recommendation of the Minister of Justice.
        Commissioner: Roger Conger Clute.

                              Report
        Dated January 17, 1899.  Tabled in the House of Commons on
    May 18, 1899.  Sessional Paper no. 70-1899.  Summary report
    printed as:
        Report of Mr. R. C. Clute on the Commission to inquire into the
    death of McDonald and Fraser on the Crow's Nest Pass Railway -
    Summary.  16 p.
        Complete report not located.
        Notes: Cost: $6,314.95.


84  COMMISSION ON THE LOBSTER INDUSTRY IN THE MARITIME
    PROVINCES

        Appointed on September 27, 1898 by Order in Council P. C. 2311
    on the recommendation of the Minister of Marine and Fisheries.  No
    indication of authorizing statute given in Order in Council.
        Commissioners: Edward Ernest Prince, Chairman, Moses H.
    Nickerson, William Whitman, Donald Campbell, Henry C. V. LeVatte,
    Archibald Currie, Stephen E. Gallant, Patrick J. Sweeney and Robert
    Lindsay.

                              Report
        Dated April 25, 1899.  Tabled in the House of Commons on June
    29, 1899.  Printed as :
        Report of the Canadian Lobster Commission, 1898.  (Supplement
    No. 1, to the Thirty-First Annual Report of the Department of Marine
    and Fisheries) 41 p.
        Notes: 65 sittings held in Quebec, New Brunswick, Nova Scotia
    and Prince Edward Island.  The Commissioners visited 49 centres.


85  COMMISSION TO INQUIRE INTO AND REPORT UPON CERTAIN CHARGES
    PREFERRED AGAINST MANY GOVERNMENT OFFICIALS IN THE
    YUKON TERRITORY

Appointed on October 7, 1898 by Order in Council P. C. 2371 under
An Act respecting Inquiries concerning Public Matters (R. S. C., 1886,
c. 114) and on the recommendation of the Minister of the Interior.
Commissioner: William Ogilvie.
Secretary: J. N. E. Brown.

### Report

Dated September 20, 1899. Tabled in the House of Commons on
June 7, 1900. Sessional Paper no. 33u-1900. Printed as:
Copy of Report of Mr. William Ogilvie, Commissioner of the
Yukon Territory, in connection with the administration of affairs in
that region. 33 p.

86  COMMISSION TO INVESTIGATE THE ADMINISTRATION OF THE LEPER
    LAZARETTO COLONY AT TRACADIE, NEW BRUNSWICK AND THE
    TREATMENT OF INMATES THEREOF

Appointed on October 26, 1898 by Order in Council P. C. 2499 on
the recommendation of the Minister of Agriculture. No indication of
authorizing statute given in the Order in Council.
Commissioners: Emmanuel Persillier Lachapelle and Arthur
Vallée.
Secretary: E. P. Benoit.

### Report

Dated November 14, 1898. Printed as:
Report of the Medical Commission appointed on October 26, 1898,
to investigate into the complaints made against the management of the
Tracadie Lazaretto. In Report of the Minister of Agriculture for the
Dominion of Canada for the year ended October 31, 1899, pp. 92-97.
(Sessional Paper no. 8-1900).
Notes: The Commissioners interviewed many of the lepers and
staff at the Lazaretto at Tracadie. They also visited Caraquet, New
Brunswick.

87  COMMISSION TO INVESTIGATE CHARGES OF ALLEGED DELAY IN
    THE CONSTRUCTION OF A PILE TRESTLE BRIDGE ON THE PICTOU
    BRANCH OF THE INTERCOLONIAL RAILWAY

Appointed on March 2, 1899 by Order in Council P. C. 126 on the
recommendation of the Minister of Railways and Canals. No indication
of authorizing statute given in Order in Council.
Commissioner: Frederick W. Holt.

Report

Not printed.  Complete report not located.  Summary of report
in Public Archives of Canada (R. G. 2, 3, vol. 142). 3 p.


88   COMMISSION TO INVESTIGATE THE CLAIMS WHICH MAY BE PRE-
     FERRED BY THE HALF-BREEDS IN THE NORTH-WEST TERRITORIES

Appointed on May 6, 1899 by Order in Council P. C. 918 on the
recommendation of the Superintendent General of Indian Affairs.  No
indication of authorizing statute given in Order in Council.
Commissioners:  James Walker and Joseph Arthur Côté.

Report

Dated September 30, 1899.  Printed as:
Report of Half-Breed Commissioners In Annual Report of the
Department of the Interior for the year 1899, Part VIII (Sessional
Paper no. 13-1900), pp. 3-7.
Notes:  Cost: $9,691.70.


89   COMMISSION TO INQUIRE INTO CLAIMS FOR PATENTS TO LANDS IN
     THE YUKON TERRITORY, AND ALSO TO INQUIRE INTO AND RE-
     PORT UPON ANY OTHER MATTERS IN ANY WAY CONNECTED WITH,
     OR WHICH IN ANY WAY CONCERN ANY LANDS IN THE YUKON
     TERRITORY

Appointed on August 2, 1899 by Orders in Council P. C. 1743,
P. C. 1744 and P. C. 1745 under An Act respecting Inquiries concerning
Public Matters (R. S. C. , 1886, c. 114) and on the recommendation of
the Minister of the Interior.
Commissioners:  Alexander McLeod and Raoul Rinfret.
Secretary:  W. F. Povak.

Report

Not located.
Notes:  Cost: $4,374.90.


90   ROYAL COMMISSION ON THE SHIPMENT AND TRANSPORTATION OF
     GRAIN

Appointed on October 7, 1899 by Order in Council P. C. 2181 under
An Act respecting Inquiries concerning Public Matters (R. S. C. , 1886,
c. 114) and on the recommendation of the Minister of the Interior.

Commissioners: Edmund John Senkler, Chairman, [1] Albert
Elswood Richards, Chairman (following Senkler's death), [2] William
Lothian, Charles C. Castle and W. F. Sirett.
Secretary: Charles Napier Bell.

Report
Dated March, 1900. Tabled in the House of Commons on April 4,
1900. Sessional Paper no. 81a-1900. Printed as:
.... Report.... of the Royal Commission on the shipment and
transportation of grain. 35 p.
Notes: Public Hearings held in 21 communities ( October - December, 1899). 227 persons appeared before the Commission.


91   COMMISSION RELATING TO UNREST AND DISCONTENT AMONG
     MINERS AND MINE-OWNERS IN THE PROVINCE OF BRITISH
     COLUMBIA

     Appointed on November 17, 1899 by Order in Council P. C.   2407
     under An Act respecting Inquiries concerning Public Matters (R. S. C.,
     1886, c. 114) and on the recommendation of the Minister of Justice.
     Commissioner: Roger Conger Clute.

First Report
Tabled in the House of Commons on May 23, 1900. Sessional
Paper no. 146-1900. Not printed in Sessional Papers series. No
copy located.

Second Report
Tabled in the House of Commons on June 6, 1900. Sessional
Paper no. 146a-1900. Not printed in Sessional Papers series. No
copy located.
Notes: Cost $6,711.51.


92   COMMISSION TO INVESTIGATE AND REPORT UPON CERTAIN HALF-
     BREED CLAIMS IN THE DISTRICT OF ATHABASKA AND ADJOINING
     COUNTRY COVERED BY THE SAID TREATY NO. 8

     Appointed on March 2, 1900 by Order in Council P. C. 460 on the
     recommendation of the Minister of the Interior and the Superintendent
     General of Indian Affairs.   No indication of authorizing statute given
     in Order in Council.

[1] Died on February 2, 1900.
[2] Appointed Chairman on February 13, 1900 by Order in Council
P. C. 342.

Commissioner: James Ansdell Macrae.

Report

Not located.


93   COMMISSION TO INQUIRE INTO AND REPORT UPON CLAIMS TO LANDS
     IN YUKON TERRITORY

Appointed on March 2, 1900 by Order in Council P. C. 509 under
An Act respecting Inquiries concerning Public Matters (R. S. C., 1886,
c. 114) and on the recommendation of the Minister of the Interior.
Commissioner: Raoul Rinfret.

Report

Not located.


94   COMMISSION TO INVESTIGATE ALLEGATIONS OF ELECTION FRAUDS
     PRIOR TO AND SUBSEQUENT TO THE GENERAL ELECTIONS OF
     1896

Appointed on June 4, 1900 by Order in Council P. C. 1446 under
An Act respecting Inquiries concerning Public Matters (R. S. C., 1886,
c. 114) and on the recommendation of the Minister of Justice.
   Commissioners: Sir John Alexander Boyd, William Glenholme
Falconbridge and Duncan Byron MacTavish.

Report

Dated June 15, 1901.   Copy attached to Order in Council P. C.
1368-a of June 25, 1901.   (In Public Archives of Canada, R. G. 2, 1,
Volume 876). 3 leaves.
   Notes: Cost: $2,298.41.


95   COMMISSION TO INVESTIGATE AND REPORT UPON ANY CLAIMS TO
     BOUNTY FOR SERVICES RENDERED AS SCOUTS OR OTHERWISE
     IN CONNECTION WITH THE SUPPRESSION OF THE NORTH-WEST
     REBELLION OF 1885, PREFERRED BEFORE THEM BY PERSONS
     RESIDENT IN THE DISTRICT OF SASKATCHEWAN, IN THE SAID
     NORTH-WEST TERRITORIES

Appointed on June 19, 1900 by Order in Council P. C. 1423 under
An Act respecting Inquiries concerning Public Matters (R. S. C., 1886,
c. 114) on the recommendation of the Minister of the Interior.
   Commissioners: Narcisse Omer Côte and Samuel McLeod.
   Secretary: Charles Fisher.

Report

Dated March 29, 1901.

Report of Commissioners Côte and McLeod In Annual Report of the Department of the Interior for the Year 1900-1901, Part VI. (Sessional Paper no. 25-1902), pp. 5-8.

Notes: Hearings held in 19 communities.

96    COMMISSION TO INQUIRE INTO AND REPORT UPON ANY CLAIMS TO BOUNTY FOR SERVICES RENDERED AS SCOUTS OR OTHERWISE IN CONNECTION WITH THE SUPPRESSION OF THE NORTH-WEST REBELLION OF 1885, PREFERRED BEFORE THEM BY PERSONS RESIDENT IN THE DISTRICTS OF ASSINIBOIA AND ALBERTA, IN THE SAID NORTH-WEST TERRITORIES

Appointed on June 19, 1900 by Order in Council P. C. 1423 under An Act respecting Inquiries concerning Public Matters (R. S. C. , 1886, c. 114) and on the recommendation of the Minister of the Interior.

Commissioners: James Andrew Joseph McKenna and James Walker.

Report

Dated March 11, 1901. Printed as:

Half-Breed Commissioners. Report of Commissioners McKenna and Walker. In Annual Report of the Department of the Interior for the Year 1900-1901, Part VI. (Sessional Paper no. 25-1902), pp. 3-5.

Notes: Hearings held at 25 communities (May 16 - December 6, 1900). 3,505 distinct written applications presenting the claims of 4,397 half-breeds were considered.

97    COMMISSION TO INVESTIGATE AND REPORT UPON ALL MATTERS CONNECTED WITH THE MANAGEMENT AND SALES OF LANDS COMPRISED WITHIN THE TOWN SITES OF REGINA, MOOSE JAW, QU'APPELLE AND VERDIN

Appointed on June 19, 1900 by Order in Council P. C. 1527 under An Act respecting Inquiries concerning Public Matters (R. S. C. , 1886, c. 114) and on the recommendation of the Minister of the Interior.

Commissioners: James Allan Smart and Edwin Frederick Stephenson.

Report

Not located.

98  COMMISSION TO INQUIRE INTO THE ABSTRACTION OF MONEY FROM
    A LETTER POSTED BY REV. J. M. WHITELAW

    Appointed on July 26, 1900 by Order in Council P. C. 1853 under
    An Act respecting Inquiries concerning Public Matters (R. S. C. , 1886,
    c. 114) and on the recommendation of the Postmaster General.
    Commissioner: William White.

                            Report
            Not located.


99  COMMISSION TO INQUIRE INTO AND REPORT UPON CERTAIN ALLEGED
    FRAUDULENT PRACTICES AND IRREGULARITIES IN CONNECTION
    WITH PUBLIC AUCTION SALES OF SCHOOL LANDS IN THE PROV-
    INCE OF MANITOBA

    Appointed on September 3, 1900 by Order in Council P. C. 2108
    under An Act respecting Inquiries concerning Public Matters (R. S. C. ,
    1886, c. 114) and on the recommendation of the Minister of the Interior.
    Commissioner: James Pierre Prendergast.

                            Report
            Tabled in the House of Commons on April 22, 1901.  Sessional
    Paper no. 76a-1901.  Not printed.  No copy located.


100 ROYAL COMMISSION TO INVESTIGATE CHINESE AND JAPANESE
    IMMIGRATION INTO BRITISH COLUMBIA

    Appointed on September 21, 1900 by Order in Council P. C. 2187
    under An Act respecting Inquiries concerning Public Matters (R. S. C. ,
    1886, c. 114) and on the recommendation of the Secretary of State.
        Commissioners: Roger Conger Clute, Chairman, Christopher
    Foley, [1] Ralph Smith, [2] and Daniel James Munn.
    Secretary: Francis J. Deane.

                            Report
            Part I (Chinese Immigration) dated February 18, 1902.
            Part II (Japanese Immigration) dated March 8, 1902.  Tabled
    in the House of Commons on April 14, 1902.  Sessional Paper no. 54-
    1902.  Printed as:

    _____

    [1] Appointed on January 8, 1901 by Order in Council P. C. 56
    [2] Resigned.

Report of the Royal Commission on Chinese and Japanese Immigration. Session 1902. Printed by Order of Parliament. Ottawa, Printed by S. E. Dawson, Printer to the King's Most Excellent Majesty, 1902. xiv, 430 p.

Also issued as a separate.

Notes: Hearings held in 12 towns and cities of British Columbia. 340 witnesses appeared before the Commission. Evidence ran to about 18,000 pages. Cost: $39,203.03.

101 ROYAL COMMISSION TO INVESTIGATE CHARGES MADE AGAINST GRAIN INSPECTORS AT MONTREAL

Appointed on January 2, 1901 by Order in Council P. C. 2809 under An Act respecting Inquiries concerning Public Matters (R. S. C., 1886, c. 114) and on the recommendation of the Minister of Inland Revenue.

Commissioners: David Horn, Chairman, William Grannis Parmelee and Thomas A. Crane.

Secretary: Charles Avila Wilson.

Report

Dated February, 1901. Tabled in the House of Commons on March 27, 1901. Sessional Paper no. 74-1901, pp. 2-5. Printed as:

Report of the commissioners appointed under date the second day of January, 1901, to investigate, inquire into and report upon certain complaints made with regard to the inspection of grain at the port of Montreal.

Notes: Cost: $2,538.45.

102 COMMISSION TO INVESTIGATE AND DEAL WITH CERTAIN HALF-BREED CLAIMS IN THE PROVINCE OF MANITOBA AND THE NORTH-WEST TERRITORIES

Appointed on March 16, 1901 by Order in Council P. C. 575 on the recommendation of the Minister of the Interior. No indication of authorizing statute given in the Order in Council.

Commissioner: James Andrew Joseph McKenna.

Report

Dated May 31, 1901. Printed as:

[Report from Mr. J. A. J. McKenna, Half-Breed Commissioner, in respect to the reserved claims in the North-West Territories].

In Canada Gazette, Volume XXXV (7), August 17, 1901, pp. 262-263.

103 COMMISSION TO INQUIRE INTO THE CIRCUMSTANCES ATTENDING
THE DEATH OF DIEUDONNE ST. MICHAEL IN THE SHIPYARD AT
SOREL

Appointed on April 19, 1901 by Order in Council P. C. 821 under
An Act respecting Inquiries concerning Public Matters (R. S. C., 1886,
c. 114) and on the recommendation of the Minister of Public Works.
Commissioners: Wilfrid Mercier and George Wheelock Burbridge. [1]

Report
Not located.

104 COMMISSION TO INVESTIGATE THE DETENTION OF THE STEAMSHIP
"YUKONER" AT DAWSON, BRITISH COLUMBIA IN THE SUMMER OF
1898

Appointed on May 29, 1901 by Order in Council P. C. 1011 under
An Act respecting Inquiries concerning Public Matters (R. S. C., 1886,
c. 114) and on the recommendation of the Minister of Customs.
Commissioner: Solon William McMichael.

Report
Not located.

105 COMMISSION TO INVESTIGATE AND REPORT UPON CERTAIN CLAIMS
FOR LOSS AND DAMAGE ALLEGED TO HAVE BEEN SUSTAINED BY
MESSRS. JAMES AND CHARLES NOBLE, BY REASONS OF SEIZURE
AND CONFISCATION OF FISHING TUGS AND NETS IN THE YEAR 1894

Appointed on August 16, 1901 by Order in Council P. C. 1660 on
the recommendation of the Minister of Marine and Fisheries. No
indication of authorizing statute given in Order in Council.
Commissioner: William Lount.

Report
Letter of transmittal dated April 6, 1902. Full text of Report not
located. Summary of Report contained in Department of Fisheries
files. (In Memorandum for the Honourable James Sutherland [ Minister
of Fisheries] Re Noble Investigation, April 16, 1902). 2 leaves.

---

[1] Appointed on August 6, 1901 by Order in Council P. C. 15 84.

106 COMMISSION TO INVESTIGATE THE QUESTION OF THE WEIGHING
    OF DAIRY PRODUCTS AT THE PORT OF MONTREAL, OR ELSE-
    WHERE IN THE DOMINION

     Appointed on December 7, 1901 by Order in Council P. C. 2175
under An Act respecting Inquiries concerning Public Matters (R. S. C.,
1886, c. 114) and on the recommendation of the Minister of Trade
and Commerce.
    Commissioner: William Grannis Parmelee.

Report
    Dated October 22, 1903. Tabled in the House of Commons on
August 5, 1904. Sessional Paper no. 143-1904. Not printed. No
copy located.
    Notes: Cost: $428.95.


107 COMMISSION ON THE SALMON FISHERY INDUSTRY IN BRITISH
    COLUMBIA
    Appointed on January 25, 1902 by Order in Council P. C. 91 on
the recommendation of the Minister of Marine and Fisheries. No
indication of authorizing statute given in Order in Council.
    Commissioners: Edward Ernest Prince, George Ritchie Maxwell, [1]
Aulay Morrison, [2] Ralph Smith and George Riley. [3]

Report
    Dated April 20, 1903. Tabled in the House of Commons on July
22, 1903. Sessional Paper no. 131-1903. Not printed. Typewritten
copy in the Department of Fisheries files. 7 leaves.
    Notes: 16 sittings held at four British Columbia towns and cities
(January 24-February 5, 1902). Over 70 witnesses appeared before
the Commission. Cost: $952.15. 189 typewritten pages of evidence
taken.


108 ROYAL COMMISSION ON THE TOBACCO TRADE

    Appointed on May 3, 1902 by Order in Council P. C. 732 under
An Act respecting Inquiries concerning Public Matters (R. S. C., 1886,
c. 114) and on the recommendation of the Minister of Justice.

---

[1] Resigned.
[2] Died before the Report was in its complete form. Ill health had
prevented him from taking an active part in the proceedings of the
Commission.
[3] Replaced Maxwell.

Commissioner: Duncan Byron MacTavish.

Report

Dated April 6, 1903.  Tabled in the House of Commons on April
16, 1903.  Sessional Paper no. 62-1903.  Printed as:

Report of the Royal Commission in re the tobacco trade of Canada.
Printed by Order of Parliament.  Ottawa, Printed by S. E. Dawson,
Printer to the King's Most Excellent Majesty, 1903.  10 p.

Also issued as a separate.

Notes: Investigation held in 8 towns and cities of Ontario and
Quebec.  119 witnesses appeared before the Commission.  Cost:
$2, 718. 72.

109 COMMISSION FOR THE REVISION AND CONSOLIDATION OF THE PUBLIC
STATUTES OF CANADA

Appointed on November 21, 1902 by Order in Council P. C. 1748
on the recommendation of the Minister of Justice.  No indication of·
authorizing statute given in Order in Council.

Commissioners: Sir Samuel Henry Strong, Chairman, Edmund
Leslie Newcombe, Augustus Power, Wentworth Eaton Roscoe, Edward
Robert Cameron, Henry Robertson, Thomas Metcalfe, Louis Philippe
Sirois, Charles Murphy and Francis Pedley.  Horace St. Louis and
Charles Murphy, Joint  Secretaries.

Report

Proclamation dated January 25, 1907.  Printed as:

The revised statutes of Canada, 1906.  Proclaimed and published
under the authority of the Act 3 Edward VII. , Chapter 61 (1903).
Ottawa, Printed by Samuel Edward Dawson, Law Printer to the King's
Most Excellent Majesty, from the roll of the said revised statutes
deposited in the office of the Clerk of the Parliaments, as authorized
by the said Act, 3 Edward VII. , Chapter 61, 1903, 1906.  4 v. (2, 949 p.
and index  various pagings).

Notes: Cost: $108, 079. 43.

110 COMMISSION TO INQUIRE INTO AND REPORT UPON THE WHOLE
QUESTION OF A DRY DOCK AT MONTREAL

Appointed on February 13, 1903 by Order in Council P. C. 213
under An Act respecting Inquiries concerning Public Matters (R. S. C. ,
1886, c. 114) and on the recommendation of the Ministers of Marine
and Fisheries and Public Works.

Commissioners: Percival Walker St. George,  Edward Henry
Keating, Maurice Perrault and W. J. Sproul (Assistant).

Report

Not located.


111 COMMISSION TO INQUIRE INTO AND REPORT UPON THE RECENT
    DEFALCATIONS IN THE DEPARTMENT OF MILITIA AND DEFENCE,
    AND INTO THE METHODS OF KEEPING THE ACCOUNTS IN THE
    SEVERAL DEPARTMENTS OF THE GOVERNMENT, PARTICULARLY
    IN RELATION TO THE ISSUING OF CHEQUES AND THE RECEIPT AND
    DISPOSAL OF PUBLIC MONEYS

    Appointed on March 6, 1903 by Order in Council P. C. 350 under
    An Act respecting Inquiries concerning Public Matters (R. S. C., 1886,
    c. 114) and on the recommendation of the Minister of Militia and De-
    fence.
        Commissioners: John Mortimer Courtney, George Burn and
    Ambrose Leonard Kent.

                              Report
        Undated. Tabled in the House of Commons on June 15, 1903.
    Sessional Paper no. 29b-1903. Printed as:
        Report of the Commission to inquire into the Martineau Defalcation,
    & c., & c. Printed by Order of Parliament. Ottawa, Printed by S. E.
    Dawson, Printer to the King's Most Excellent Majesty, 1903. 13 p.
        Also issued as a separate.
        Notes: The Commissioners examined the accounting practices of
    all the federal government Departments. Cost: $1,067.85.


112 ROYAL COMMISSION TO INVESTIGATE INDUSTRIAL DISPUTES IN THE
    PROVINCE OF BRITISH COLUMBIA

    Appointed on April 18, 1903 by Order in Council P. C. 613 under
    An Act respecting Inquiries concerning Public Matters (R. S. C., 1886,
    c. 114) and on the recommendation of the Minister of Labour.
        Commissioners: Gordon Hunter and Rev. Elliott S. Rowe.
        Secretary: William Lyon Mackenzie King.

                              Report
        Dated July 8, 1903. Tabled in the House of Commons on August
    24, 1903. Sessional Paper no. 36a-1904. Printed as:
        Report of the Royal Commission on Industrial Disputes in the
    Province of British Columbia. Issued by the Department of Labour,
    Canada. Printed by Order of Parliament. Ottawa, Printed by S. E.
    Dawson, Printer to the King's Most Excellent Majesty, 1903. 77 p.
        Also issued as a separate.

Notes: Hearings held in 7 towns and cities of British Columbia (May 4 - June 13, 1903). Cost: $9,951.21.


113 COMMISSION TO INVESTIGATE AND REPORT UPON CERTAIN CLAIMS FOR LABOUR, BOARDING HOUSE CLAIMS AND CLAIMS FOR MATERIAL AND SUPPLIES FURNISHED IN CONNECTION WITH THE SECTION OF THE ATLANTIC AND LAKE SUPERIOR RAILWAY BE- TWEEN CAPLIN AND PASPEBIAC

Appointed on May 6, 1903 by Order in Council P. C. 603 under An Act respecting Inquiries concerning Public Matters (R. S. C., 1886, c. 114) and on the recommendation of the Minister of Railways and Canals. Commissioner: George A. Mothersill.

Report

Not located.


114 ROYAL COMMISSION ON TRANSPORTATION OF CANADIAN PRODUCTS TO THE MARKETS OF THE WORLD THROUGH AND BY CANADIAN PORTS

Appointed on May 19, 1903 by Order in Council P. C. 583 under An Act respecting Inquiries concerning Public Matters (R. S. C., 1886, c. 114) and on the recommendation of the Minister of Public Works. New Commissioners named on August 26, 1903 by Order in Council P. C. 1475.

Commissioners: Sir William Van Horne, Chairman, John Bertram, [1] Robert Redford, Harold Kennedy, [2] Edward Carey Fry, [3] and James Henry Ashdown.

Secretaries: J. X. Perrault, [4] and Charles Napier Bell.

Reports

Five interim reports (January 21, 1904 - August 18, 1905) are printed in the Final Report, pp. 47-61.

Final Report dated December 11, 1905. Tabled in the House of Commons on April 17, 1906. Sessional Paper no. 19a-1906. Printed as:

Report of the Royal Commission on transportation. Appointed

---

[1] Unable to act. He died on November 28, 1904.
[2] Unable to act.
[3] Resigned early in 1905.
[4] Died on April 7, 1905.

May 19, 1903. Printed by Order of Parliament. Ottawa, Printed by
S. E. Dawson, Printer to the King's Most Excellent Majesty, 1906.
61 p.

(Also in Sessional Paper no. 19a-1906) "Printed for both distribution and sessional papers."

Notes: Sittings of the Commission held in 38 towns and cities.
Cost: $36, 333. 01.

115 COMMISSION TO INQUIRE INTO THE TREADGOLD AND OTHER CONCESSIONS IN THE YUKON TERRITORY

Appointed on May 27, 1903 by Order in Council P. C. 867 under
An Act respecting Inquiries concerning Public Matters (R.S.C., 1886,
c. 114) and on the recommendation of the Minister of Justice.

Commissioners: Byron Moffatt Britton, Benjamin Taylor A. Bell,[1]
and John Ernest Hardman. [2]

Secretaries: Hugh Howard Rowatt and G. A. Lacombe.

Report

Dated July 28, 1904. Tabled in the House of Commons on August
1, 1904. Sessional Paper no. 142-1904. Printed as:

[Report of the Commissioners to inquire into the Treadgold and
other Concessions in the Yukon Territory]. 49 p.

Notes: Public hearings held in 3 centres (August 17 - September
5, 1903). 154 witnesses were examined. 277 exhibits were filed with
the Commission.

116 COMMISSION TO INQUIRE INTO THE CONDUCT OF THE BUSINESS OF
THE OFFICE OF THE ASSISTANT RECEIVER GENERAL AT SAINT
JOHN, NEW BRUNSWICK

Appointed on November 5, 1903 by Order in Council P. C. 1832
under An Act respecting Inquiries concerning Public Matters (R.S.C.,
1886, c. 114) and on the recommendation of the Minister of Finance.

Commissioner: John Fraser.

Report

Dated November 30, 1903. Not printed. Typewritten copy in
the Department of Finance files. 5 leaves.

---

[1] Bell died at Ottawa on March 1, 1904.
[2] Removed on July 30, 1903 by Order in Council P. C. 1281.

117 COMMISSION TO INQUIRE INTO AND ASCERTAIN THE AMOUNT OF
SUBSIDY PAYABLE UNDER ACT 1 EDWARD VII., CHAPTER 7, IN
RESPECT OF CERTAIN WORK DONE UPON THE SUBSIDIZED SECTION
BETWEEN CAPLIN AND PASPEBIAC OF THE BAIE DES CHALEURS
DIVISION OF THE ATLANTIC AND LAKE SUPERIOR RAILWAY

Appointed on November 5, 1903 by Order in Council P. C. 1838
under An Act respecting Inquiries concerning Public Matters (R. S. C.,
1886, c. 114) and on the recommendation of the Minister of Railways
and Canals.
Commissioner: Henry A. F. McLeod.

Report

Not located.
Notes: Cost: $1,863.17.

118 COMMISSION TO INQUIRE INTO THE HERRING AND SARDINE INDUSTRY
OF THE BAY OF FUNDY, AS WELL AS INTO THE RAVAGES OF THE
DOG-FISH AND THE GENERAL CONDITION OF THE LOBSTER FISH-
ERY AT THE MAGDALEN ISLANDS, ST. MARY'S BAY AND THE BAY
OF FUNDY

Appointed on November 14, 1903 by Order in Council P. C. 1797
on the recommendation of the Minister of Marine and Fisheries. No
indication of authorizing statute given in Order in Council.
Commissioners: Joseph John Tucker, Chairman, Robert Norris
Venning, Albert James Smith Copp, E. C. Bowers, Robert Edwin
Armstrong and Rev. Joseph Samuel Turbide.

Report

Dated March 3, 1905. Not printed. Typewritten copy in the
Department of Fisheries files. 27 leaves.
Notes: Hearings held and visits made to fishing regions in the
Provinces of Nova Scotia and New Brunswick (November, 1903 - Sept-
ember, 1904). Cost: $3,575.64.

119 COMMISSION TO INQUIRE INTO AND REPORT UPON CERTAIN CLAIMS
FOR WAGES OF PERSONS EMPLOYED ON THE SUBSIDIZED LINE
OF RAILWAY FROM DUNCAN LAKE TOWARDS ARROW LAKE OR FOR
SUMS DUE FOR LABOUR OF PERSONS OR TEAMS SO EMPLOYED

Appointed on November 14, 1903 by Order in Council P. C. 1861
under An Act respecting inquiries concerning Public Matters (R. S. C.,
1886, c. 114) and on the recommendation of the Minister of Railways
and Canals.

Commissioner: Samuel Leonard Shannon.

Report
Dated January 7, 1904.  Copy not located.


120  COMMISSION TO MAKE AN INVESTIGATION INTO THE ORGANIZATION,
     METHODS AND SYSTEM ADOPTED AND IN USE IN MATTERS RE-
     LATING TO RAILWAYS IN THE UNITED STATES

Appointed on December 24, 1903 by Order in Council P. C. 2082
on the recommendation of the Minister of Railways and Canals.  No
indication of authorizing statute given in Order in Council.
Commissioners: Andrew George Blair and Arthur Hansard.

Report
Not located.


121  COMMISSION TO INVESTIGATE THE DIFFERENT ELECTRO-THERMIC
     PROCESSES FOR THE SMELTING OF IRON ORES AND THE MAKING
     OF STEEL IN OPERATION IN EUROPE

Appointed on January 23, 1904 by Order in Council P. C. 141 on
the recommendation of the Minister of the Interior.  No indication of
authorizing statute given in Order in Council.
Commissioners: Eugene Haanel, C. E. Brown and Erick Nystrom.
Secretary: Thomas Côté.

Report
Letter of Transmittal dated August 1, 1904.  Printed as:
Department of the Interior.  Hon. Clifford Sifton, Minister.
Report of the Commission appointed to investigate the different electro-
thermic processes for the smelting of iron ores and the making of
steel in operation in Europe. [Ottawa, 1904?] xiv, 223 p.
Notes: The Commissioners visited England, Sweden, France and
Italy during the late winter of 1904.


122  COMMISSION TO INVESTIGATE GRIEVANCES AND COMPLAINTS EX-
     ISTING IN REGARD TO SALMON AND LOBSTER FISHERIES IN GLOU-
     CESTER COUNTY, NEW BRUNSWICK

Appointed on April 11, 1904 by Order in Council P. C. 636 on the
recommendation of the Minister of Marine and Fisheries.  No indication
of authorizing statute given in Order in Council.

Commissioners: Edward Ernest Prince, and Peter Morais.
Secretary: P. J. Veniot.

### Report
Dated May 5, 1904. Tabled in the House of Commons on May 31,
1904. Sessional Paper no. 97-1904. Not printed in Sessional Papers
Series. Typewritten copy in the Department of Fisheries files. 12
leaves.
Notes: Hearings held at 4 centres in Nova Scotia (April 15 - April
20, 1904). About 60 witnesses appeared before the Commission.
Cost: $389. 92.


123 ROYAL COMMISSION TO INVESTIGATE ALLEGED EMPLOYMENT OF
ALIENS IN CONNECTION WITH THE SURVEYS OF THE PROPOSED
GRAND TRUNK PACIFIC RAILWAY

Appointed on May 23, 1904 by Order in Council P. C. 997 under
An Act respecting Inquiries concerning Public Matters (R. S. C. , 1886,
c. 114) and on the recommendation of the Minister of Labour.
Commissioner: John Winchester.

### Report
Dated January 26, 1905. Tabled in the House of Commons on
March 1, 1905. Sessional Paper no. 36a-1905. Printed as:
The Royal Commission in re the alleged employment of aliens in
connection with the surveys of the proposed Grand Trunk Pacific
Railway. Report of Commissioner. Printed by order of Parliament.
Ottawa, Printed for S. E. Dawson, Printer to the King's Most Excellent
Majesty, 1905. vii, 65 p. Also issued as a separate.
Notes: Hearings held at 7 cities (May 30 - August 30, 1904). 136
witnesses appeared before the Commission.


124 ROYAL COMMISSION TO INQUIRE INTO THE IMMIGRATION OF ITALIAN
LABOURERS TO MONTREAL AND THE ALLEGED FRAUDULENT
PRACTICES OF EMPLOYMENT AGENCIES

Appointed on June 20, 1904 by Order in Council P. C. 1230 under
An Act respecting Inquiries concerning Public Matters (R. S. C., 1886,
c. 114) and on the recommendation of the Minister of Labour.
Commissioner: John Winchester.

### Report
Dated March 24, 1905. Tabled in the House of Commons on May
19, 1905. Sessional Paper no. 36b-1905. Printed as:

The Royal Commission appointed to inquire into the immigration of Italian labourers to Montreal and the alleged fraudulent practices of employment agencies. Report of Commissioner and Evidence. Printed by Order of Parliament. Issued by the Department of Labour, Canada. Ottawa, Printed by S. E. Dawson, Printer to the King's Most Excellent Majesty, 1905. xli, 173 p. (Includes minutes of evidence).

Also issued as a separate.

Notes: Hearings held at Montreal (June 30 - July 26, 1904). 64 witnesses appeared before the Commission.

125 COMMISSION TO INQUIRE INTO AND EXAMINE CERTAIN RAILWAY CLAIMS ON THE SUBSIDIZED SECTION BETWEEN THE 70TH AND 100TH MILE OF THE BAIE DES CHALEURS DIVISION OF THE ATLANTIC AND LAKE SUPERIOR RAILWAY

Appointed on July 23, 1904 by Order in Council P. C. 1391 under An Act respecting Inquiries concerning Public Matters (R. S. C. , 1886, c. 114) and on the recommendation of the Minister of Railways and Canals.

Commissioners: Henry George Carroll and Francois Xavier Langelier. [1]

Report

Not located.

Notes: Cost $1,423.56.

126 COMMISSION TO INQUIRE INTO THE ADMINISTRATION OF THE VICTORIA AND ESQUIMALT PILOTAGE DISTRICT, BRITISH COLUMBIA

Appointed on September 28, 1904 by Order in Council P. C. 1830 under An Act respecting Inquiries concerning Public Matters (R. S. C. , 1886, c. 114) and on the recommendation of the Minister of Marine and Fisheries.

Commissioner: Richard Thomas Elliott.

Report

Not located.

Notes: Cost $247.14.

---

[1] Replaced Carroll. Langelier was appointed on August 3, 1904 by Order in Council P. C. 1510.

127 COMMISSION TO EXAMINE AND REPORT UPON ALL MATTERS CON-
    NECTED WITH THE OCCUPATION BY SQUATTERS OF THE GOVERN-
    MENT LIGHTHOUSE RESERVE AT PRESQU'ISLE, ONTARIO.

Appointed on December 23, 1904 by Order in Council P. C. 2295
under An Act respecting Inquiries concerning Public Matters (R. S. C.,
1886, c. 114) and on the recommendation of the Minister of Marine
and Fisheries.
Commissioner: William Patrick Anderson.

Report

Not located.

128 ROYAL COMMISSION TO INVESTIGATE ALLEGED EMPLOYMENT OF
    ALIENS BY THE PERE MARQUETTE RAILWAY COMPANY OF
    CANADA

Appointed on April 11, 1905 by Order in Council P. C. 636 under
An Act respecting Inquiries concerning Public Matters (R. S. C., 1886,
c. 114), and on the recommendation of the Minister of Labour.
Commissioner: John Winchester.

Report

Dated May 16, 1905. Tabled in the House of Commons on May 19,
1905. Sessional Paper no. 36c-1905. Printed as:
The Royal Commission in re the alleged employment of aliens by
the Père Marquette Railway Company in Canada. Report of Commissioner. Issued by the Department of Labour, Canada. Printed by order
of Parliament. Ottawa, Printed by S. E. Dawson, Printer to the King's
Most Excellent Majesty, 1905. 36 p.
Also issued as a separate.
Notes: Hearings held in 3 cities (April 24 - May 15, 1904). 38
witnesses appeared before the Commission.

129 COMMISSION TO INQUIRE INTO CERTAIN COMPLAINTS PREFERRED
    AGAINST R. C. MACDONALD OF WINNIPEG REGARDING RIGHTS
    OF CERTAIN HALF-BREEDS IN THE NORTH-WEST TERRITORIES

Appointed on June 21, 1905 by Order in Council P. C. 1148 under
An Act respecting Inquiries concerning Public Matters (R. S. C., 1886,
c. 114) and on the recommendation of the Minister of the Interior.
Commissioner: Robert Hill Myers.

Reports

Interim Report dated August 18, 1905. Not printed. 5 leaves.
Copy attached to Order in Council P. C. 2108 of January 6, 1906. (In
Public Archives of Canada, R. G. 2, 1, volume 995).

Final Report dated October 5, 1905. Not printed. 7 leaves.
Copy attached to Order in Council P. C. 2108 of January 6, 1906. (In
Public Archives of Canada, R. G. 2, 1, volume 995).

Notes: Hearings held at Killarney (July 25 - August 9, 1905). 48
persons gave evidence.

130 COMMISSION TO INQUIRE INTO FISHING IN GEORGIAN BAY

Appointed on July 22, 1905 by Order in Council P. C. 1446 on the
recommendation of the Minister of Marine and Fisheries. No indication of authorizing statute given in Order in Council.

Commissioners: Edward Ernest Prince, Chairman, James Noble
and John Birnie, Secretary.

Reports

Interim Report dated January 17, 1907. Text at pp. 34-41 of the
Final Report.

Final Report undated. Printed as:
Georgian Bay Fisheries Commission, 1905-1908. Report and
Recommendations (With Appendices) of the Dominion Fisheries
Commission appointed to enquire into the fisheries of Georgian Bay
and adjacent waters. Mr. John Birnie, K. C. , & c. , Collingwood,
Mr. James J. Noble, Little Current, Professor E. E. Prince, Ottawa,
Dominion Commissioner of Fisheries (Chairman) , Commissioners.
John Birnie, Secretary of the Commission. Ottawa, Government
Printing Bureau, 1908. iv, 55 p.

Notes: Commissioners held meetings at 51 fishing communities
in the Georgian Bay area. Cost: $18,807.10.

131 COMMISSION TO INVESTIGATE THE PRESENT STATE OF THE CANADIAN
FISHING INDUSTRIES ON THE PACIFIC COAST

Appointed on July 22, 1905 by Order in Council P. C. 1451 on the
recommendation of the Minister of Marine and Fisheries. No indication of authorizing statute given in Order in Council.

Commissioners: Edward Ernest Prince, Campbell Sweeney,
John Cunningham Brown, Richard Hall, John Pease Babcock and
Rev. G. W. Taylor.

Secretary: J. Charles McIntosh.

Reports

[First] Interim Report dated December 8, 1905. Printed as:
B. C. Fisheries Commission, 1905-06. Interim report of the
Commissioners. In Report of the Fisheries Commissioner for British
Columbia for the year 1906 (British Columbia Sessional Papers, 1907,
C16-C17). 2 p.

[Second] Interim Report dated October 2, 1906. Printed as:
Interim report of B. C. Fisheries Commission, In Report of the
Fisheries Commissioner for British Columbia for the year 1906 (British
Columbia Sessional Papers, 1907, C18-C22). 5 p.

Final Report [1] Not located.

Notes: Completed hearings in December, 1906. Cost: $20,488.06.

132 COMMISSION TO INQUIRE INTO THE TITLES OF PERSONS WHO TOOK
UP PARCELS OF LAND AT THE TOWNSITE OF FIELD, BRITISH
COLUMBIA

Appointed on July 29, 1905 by Order in Council P. C. 1498 under
An Act respecting Inquiries concerning Public Matters (R. S. C., 1886,
c. 114) and on the recommendation of the Minister of the Interior.
Commissioner: Thomas Gainsford Rothwell.

Report

Not located.
Notes: Cost: $1,159.40.

133 COMMISSION TO INVESTIGATE CHARGES AGAINST THE PILOTAGE
COMMISSIONER OF HOPEWELL CAPE, NEW BRUNSWICK

Appointed on February 3, 1906 by Order in Council P. C. 113
under An Act respecting Inquiries concerning Public Matters (R. S. C.,
1886, c. 114) on the recommendation of the Minister of Marine and
Fisheries.
Commissioner: James Friel.

Report

Not located.

134 ROYAL COMMISSION ON LIFE INSURANCE

---

[1] The final report was submitted in July, 1907. For summary see
Canadian Annual Review, 1908, pp. 522-523.

Appointed on February 28, 1906 by Order in Council P. C. 320 under An Act respecting Inquiries concerning Public Matters (R. S. C., 1886, c. 114) and on the recommendation of the Minister of Finance.

Commissioners: Duncan Byron MacTavish, Chairman, John Woodburn Langmuir and Ambrose Leonard Kent.

Secretary: Henry Taylor Ross.

### Report

Dated February 22, 1907. Tabled in the House of Commons on February 26, 1907. Sessional Paper no. 123a and no. 123b-1906/07. Printed as:

Report of the Royal Commission on life insurance. Printed by order of Parliament. Ottawa, Printed by S. E. Dawson, Printer to the King's Most Excellent Majesty, 1907. iv, 204 p.

Also issued as a separate.

Notes: Public hearings opened at Ottawa on March 7, 1906. 741 exhibits were placed before the Commission. Cost: $95,342.31.


135 ROYAL COMMISSION ON THE GRAIN TRADE OF CANADA

Appointed on July 19, 1906 by Order in Council P. C. 1475 on the recommendation of the Minister of Trade and Commerce. No indication of authorizing statute given in Order in Council.

Commissioners: John Millar, Chairman, George E. Goldie, and William L. McNair.

Secretary: E. Nield.

### Report

Dated October 11, 1907. Tabled in the House of Commons on January 8, 1908. Sessional Paper no. 59-1907/08. Printed as:

Report of the Royal Commission on the grain trade of Canada, 1906. Printed by order of Parliament. Ottawa, Printed by S. E. Dawson, Printer to the King's Most Excellent Majesty, 1908. 39 p.

Also issued as a separate.

Notes: Public hearings held in 30 towns and cities (August 29, 1906-late May, 1907). Commissioners also visited 11 British towns and cities. Cost: $30,774.31.


136 COMMISSION TO NEGOTIATE A TREATY WITH CERTAIN INDIANS IN THE PROVINCES OF ALBERTA AND SASKATCHEWAN, AND TO INVESTIGATE, HEAR AND DETERMINE THE CLAIMS OF HALF-BREEDS THEREIN

Appointed on July 20, 1906 by Order in Council P. C. 1459 on the recommendation of the Superintendent General of Indian Affairs.  No indication of authorizing statute given in Order in Council.

Commissioners: Andrew Joseph McKenna and Thomas A. Borthwick. 1

Reports

Report of First Commissioner for Treaty No. 10 (Signed by McKenna): Dated January 18, 1907.  Printed.  In Treaty No. 10 and Reports of Commissioners.  Ottawa, Queen's Printer, 1957, pp. 1-11.  (Reprinted from the edition of 1907).

Report of Second Commissioner for Treaty No. 10 (Signed by Borthwick): Dated October 14, 1907.  Printed.  In Treaty No. 10 and Reports of Commissioners.  Ottawa, Queen's Printer, 1957, pp. 12-14. (Reprinted from the edition of 1907).

Notes: Cost $7,210.84.

137  COMMISSION TO INVESTIGATE AND REPORT UPON THE CONDUCT OF DONALD MCPHAIDEN, ESQUIRE, AS SHIPPING MASTER FOR THE PORT OF VANCOUVER, BRITISH COLUMBIA

Appointed on August 16, 1906 by Order in Council P.C. 1587 under An Act respecting Inquiries concerning Public Matters (R.S.C., 1886, c. 114) and on the recommendation of the Minister of Marine and Fisheries.

Commissioner: Alexander Henderson.

Report

Not located.

Notes: Cost: $210.60.

138  COMMISSION TO INVESTIGATE AND REPORT UPON CERTAIN CLAIMS TO LANDS ON THE ST. PETER'S RESERVE, IN THE PROVINCE OF MANITOBA, AND OTHER MATTERS RESPECTING THE SAID RE-SERVE

Appointed on November 22, 1906 by Order in Council P.C. 2320 under An Act respecting Inquiries concerning Public Matters (R.S.C., 1886, c. 114) and on the recommendation of the Minister of the Interior.

Commissioner: Hector Mansfield Howell.

Report

Tabled in the House of Commons on January 27, 1910.  Sessional

--------

1 Appointed on April 6, 1907 by Order in Council P.C. 650.

Paper no. 78d-1910.  Not printed in <u>Sessional Paper</u> series.  No copy
located.


## 139 ROYAL COMMISSION REGARDING THE DISPUTE RESPECTING HOURS OF EMPLOYMENT BETWEEN THE BELL TELEPHONE COMPANY OF CANADA LIMITED AND OPERATORS AT TORONTO, ONTARIO

Appointed on February 2, 1907 by Order in Council P. C. 231
under the <u>Inquiries Act</u> (R. S. C. , 1906, c. 104) and on the recommendation of the Minister of Labour.
Commissioners:  William Lyon Mackenzie King, and John Winchester.

### Report
Dated August 27, 1907.  Tabled in the House of Commons on
February 24, 1908.  Sessional Paper no. 122-1907/08.  Printed as:
Report of the Royal Commission on a dispute respecting hours
of employment between the Bell Telephone Company of Canada, Ltd. ,
and operators at Toronto, Ontario.  Issued by the Department of
Labour, Canada.  Ottawa, Government Printing Bureau, 1907.  x, 102 p.
Also issued as a separate.
<u>Notes</u>:   $1,500.63.


## 140 COMMISSION TO INQUIRE INTO AND REPORT ON THE OPERATION OF THE EXISTING CIVIL SERVICE ACT AND RELATING LEGISLATION WITH VIEW TO PROPOSING SUCH CHANGES AS MAY BE DEEMED ADVISABLE

Appointed on May 8, 1907 by Order in Council P. C. 1108 under
Part I of the <u>Inquiries Act</u> (R. S. C. , 1906, c. 104) and on  the recom-
mendation of the Secretary of State.
<u>Commissioners</u>:  John Mortimer Courtney, Thomas Fyshe, J. G.
Garneau and Phillipe I. Bazin. [1]
<u>Secretary</u>:  Thomas S. Howe.

### Report
Dated March 17, 1908.  Tabled in the House of Commons on
March 26, 1908.  Sessional Paper no. 29a-1907/08.  Printed as:
Civil Service Commission, 1908.  Report of the Commissioners.
Printed by order of Parliament.  Ottawa, Printed by S. E. Dawson,
Printer to the King's Most Excellent Majesty, 1908.  275 p.
Also issued as a separate.

---

[1] Appointed on May 9, 1907 by Order in Council P. C. 1122.

Notes:  Cost: $18,431.30.

141 COMMISSION TO INVESTIGATE AND REPORT UPON CERTAIN CHARGES
      MADE BY JOSEPH S. PERRON, OF DAWSON, IN THE YUKON TER-
      RITORY, MINER, AGAINST OSWALD S. FINNIE, CHIEF CLERK IN
      THE OFFICE OF GOLD COMMISSIONER OF THE SAID YUKON TER-
      RITORY, OF WRONGFUL AND IRREGULAR ACTS ON THE PART OF
      THE SAID FINNIE

          Appointed on May 9, 1907 by Order in Council P. C. 1117 under
      Part I of the Inquiries Act (R. S. C., 1906, c. 104) and on the recom-
      mendation of the Minister of the Interior.
      Commissioner: James Craig.

                              Report
          Not located.

142 ROYAL COMMISSION ON THE QUEBEC BRIDGE INQUIRY

          Appointed on August 31, 1907 by Order in Council P. C. 1974
      under Part 2 of the Inquiries Act (R. S. C., 1906, c. 104) and on the
      recommendation of the Minister of Railways and Canals. [1]
          Commissioners: Henry Holgate, Chairman, John George Gale
      Kerry and John Galbraith.

                              Report
          Dated February 20, 1908. Tabled in the House of Commons on
      March 9, 1908. Sessional Paper no. 154-1907/08. Printed as:
          Royal Commission Quebec Bridge Inquiry. Report. Printed by
      order of Parliament. Ottawa, Printed by S. E. Dawson, Printer to
      the King's Most Excellent Majesty, 1908. 3 v. (206,585 p. and a volume
      of plans).
          Notes: Cost: $31,765.64.

143 ROYAL COMMISSION REGARDING LOSSES SUSTAINED BY THE JAP-
      ANESE POPULATION OF VANCOUVER, BRITISH COLUMBIA, ON
      THE OCCASION OF THE RIOTS IN THAT CITY IN SEPTEMBER,
      1907

---

[1] Strictly speaking this is a "Departmental Commission of Inquiry."
However, it is always known as a Royal Commission.

Appointed October 12, 1907 by Order in Council P. C. 2170 under Part I of the Inquiries Act (R. S. C. , 1906, c. 104) and on the recommendation of the Minister of Labour.

Commissioner: William Lyon Mackenzie King.

Secretary: Francis W. Giddens.

Report

Dated June 26, 1908. Tabled in the House of Commons on June 30, 1908. Sessional Paper no. 74g-1907/08. Printed as:

Report by W. L. Mackenzie King, C. M. G. , Deputy Minister of Labour, Commissioner, appointed to investigate into the losses sustained by the Japanese population of Vancouver, B. C. , on the occasion of the riots in that city in September, 1907. Printed by order of Parliament. Ottawa, Printed by S. E. Dawson, Printer to the King's Most Excellent Majesty, 1908. 22 p.

Also issued as a separate.

Notes: Sittings of the Commission held at Vancouver (October 22 - November 5, 1907). 80 witnesses were examined. Cost $632.00.

144 ROYAL COMMISSION TO INVESTIGATE METHODS BY WHICH ORIENTAL LABOURERS HAVE BEEN INDUCED TO COME TO CANADA

Appointed on November 5, 1907 by Order in Council P. C. 2435 under Part I of the Inquiries Act (R. S. C. , 1906, c. 104) and on the recommendation of the Secretary of State.

Commissioner: William Lyon Mackenzie King.

Report

Dated July 11, 1908. Tabled in the House of Commons on July 13, 1908. Sessional Paper no 741-1909. Printed as:

Report of the Royal Commission appointed to inquire into the methods by which Oriental labourers have been induced to come to Canada. W. L. Mackenzie King, C. M. G. , Commissioner. Ottawa, Government Printing Bureau, 1908. 81 p.

Also issued as a separate.

Notes: Hearings held at Victoria and Vancouver (November 11 - November 13, 1907). 101 witnesses were examined by the Commission. Cost: $2,216.68.

145 ROYAL COMMISSION TO INVESTIGATE LOSSES BY THE CHINESE POPULATION OF VANCOUVER, BRITISH COLUMBIA, ON THE OCCASION OF THE RIOTS IN THAT CITY IN SEPTEMBER, 1907

Appointed on March 7, 1908 by Order in Council P. C. 1814 under

the Inquiries Act (R. S. C. , 1906, c. 104) and on the recommendation
of the Secretary of State.   Part of Inquiries Act not stated in the Order
in Council.
Commissioner: William Lyon Mackenzie King.
Secretary: Francis W. Giddens.


Report
Dated June 26, 1908.   Tabled in the House of Commons on June 30,
1908.  Sessional Paper no. 74f-1907/08.  Printed as:
Report by W. L. Mackenzie King, C. M. G. , Deputy Minister of
Labour, Commissioner, appointed to investigate into the losses sus-
tained by the Chinese population of Vancouver, B. C. on the occasion
of the riots in that city in September, 1907.  Printed by order of
Parliament.  Ottawa, Printed by S. E. Dawson, Printer to the King's
Most Excellent Majesty, 1908.  18 p.
Also issued as a separate.
Notes: Sittings held at Vancouver (May 26 - June 5, 1908).  118
witnesses were examined.  Cost: $912. 90.


146 ROYAL COMMISSION TO INVESTIGATE INDUSTRIAL DISPUTES IN THE
    COTTON FACTORIES OF THE PROVINCE OF QUEBEC

Appointed on June 29, 1908 by Order in Council P. C. 1279 under
Part I of the Inquiries Act (R. S. C. , 1906, c. 104) and on the recom-
mendation of the Minister of Labour.
Commissioner: William Lyon Mackenzie King.
Secretary: Francis W. Giddens.


Report
Dated September 15, 1908.   Tabled in the House of Commons on
January 25, 1909.  Sessional Paper no. 39-1909.  Printed as:
Report of Royal Commission to inquire into industrial disputes in
the cotton factories of the Province of Quebec.  Commissioner: W. L.
Mackenzie King, C. M. G. , Deputy Minister of Labour.  Printed by
order of Parliament.  Ottawa, Printed by C. H. Parmelee, Printer
to the King's Most Excellent Majesty, 1909.  x, 32 p.
Also issued as a separate.
Notes: Hearings held in three Quebec centres.  45 exhibits placed
before the Commission.  56 witnesses examined by the Commission.
1, 200 typewritten pages of proceedings recorded.  Cost: $1, 404. 30.


147 COMMISSION TO INQUIRE WHETHER THE ST. ANDREWS COMPANY
    LIMITED, CHARLOTTE COUNTY, NEW BRUNSWICK, APPLICANT
    FOR FISHING LICENSES IS OPERATED IN THE INTERESTS OF
    UNITED STATES CITIZENS

Appointed on March 16, 1909 by Order in Council P. C. 535 under the Inquiries Act (R. S. C., 1906, c. 104) and on the recommendation of the Minister of Marine and Fisheries. Part of Inquiries Act not stated in the Order in Council.
Commissioner: John F. Calder.

Report

Dated May 14, 1909. Not printed. Copy in Department of Fisheries files. 8 leaves.
Notes: Hearings held at St. Andrews, New Brunswick (April 12 - May 4, 1909). 11 persons appeared before the Commission. 65 typewritten pages of evidence. Cost $249.95.

148 COMMISSION TO INQUIRE INTO AND REPORT UPON THE EXISTING REQUIREMENTS AND CONDITIONS OF THE FISHERIES IN THE PROVINCES OF MANITOBA, SASKATCHEWAN AND ALBERTA

Appointed on March 16, 1909 by Order in Council P. C. 534 on the recommendation of the Minister of Marine and Fisheries. No indication of authorizing statute given in Order in Council.
Commissioners: Ernest Edward Prince, Chairman, Daniel Fraser Reid, Thomas Llewellyn Metcalfe, [1] and Jabez Bowen Hugg. [2]

Reports

Interim Report dated December 2, 1909. Tabled in the House of Commons on January 20, 1910. Sessional Paper no. 90a-1910. Not printed in Sessional Papers series. No copy located.
Final Report dated February 28, 1911. Printed as: Manitoba Fisheries Commission, 1910-11. Report and recommendations. Ottawa, Government Printing Bureau, 1911. 43 p.
Notes: Cost: $6,702.34.

149 COMMISSION TO INVESTIGATE AND STUDY THE SWINE BREEDING INDUSTRY OF DENMARK, GREAT BRITAIN AND IRELAND

Appointed on June 11, 1909 by Order in Council P. C. 1353 on the recommendation of the Minister of Agriculture. No indication of authorizing statute given in Order in Council.
Commissioners: W. W. Ballantyne Chairman, William Jones, Gédéon Garceau, Joseph Rye and J. E. Sinclair.

---

[1] Replaced by Hugg.
[2] Appointed on September 3, 1909 by Order in Council P. C. 1833.

Secretary: J. B. Spencer.

### Report
Undated. Printed as:
Swine husbandry in the United Kingdom and Denmark; report of
the Canadian Commission, 1909. [Ottawa, 1910]. 60 p.
Location: Department of Agriculture Library, Ottawa.
Notes: Commissioners visited England, Ireland, Scotland, Denmark
and Holland.


150 COMMISSION ON THE LOBSTER INDUSTRY IN QUEBEC AND THE MARI-
    TIME PROVINCES

Appointed on June 21, 1909 by Order in Council P. C. 1470 on the
recommendation of the Minister of Marine and Fisheries. No indication of authorizing statute given in Order in Council.
Commissioner: William Wakeham.

### Report
Dated January 6, 1910. Tabled in the House of Commons on
February 3, 1910. Sessional Paper no. 22a-1910, following p. 1227
of Evidence. Printed as :
Report of Commander Wm. Wakeham, Special Commissioner and
Inspector of Fisheries for the Gulf of St. Lawrence, in the Lobster
Industry of the Maritime Provinces and the Province of Quebec. 9 p.
Notes: Hearings held in 58 centres (July 12 - September 22, 1909).
Cost: $2,292.54.


151 ROYAL COMMISSION ON INDUSTRIAL TRAINING AND TECHNICAL
    EDUCATION

Appointed on June 1, 1910 by Order in Council P. C. 1133 under
Part I of the Inquiries Act (R. S. C., 1906, c. 104) and on the recom-
mendation of the Minister of Labour.
Commissioners: James Wilson Robertson, James Simpson, John
Neville Armstrong, Gilbert Mackintosh Murray, Rev. George Bryce,
David Forsyth and M. Gaspard DeSerres.
Secretary: Thomas Bengough.

### Reports
Interim Report:[1] Dated March 28, 1911. Sessional Paper no.
191d-1913 pp. 58-65.
Final Report dated May 31, 1913. Tabled in the House of Commons
on June 5, 1913. Sessional Paper no. 191d-1913. Printed as:

[1] Termed "Interim Statement by the Commission."

Royal Commission on industrial training and technical education. Report of the Commissioners. Printed by Order of Parliament. Ottawa, Printed by C. H. Parmelee, Printer to the King's Most Excellent Majesty, 1913, 4 v. (2, 423 p. )

Also issued as a separate.

Notes: Held hearings (July 18, 1910 - February, 1911). Visited over 100 centres. 174 sessions held to receive testimony. 1470 persons gave evidence. About 180 memoranda and submissions presented to the Commission. Cost: $114, 859. 02.

152 COMMISSION TO INVESTIGATE INTO TITLES TO OWNERSHIP, BY THE UNITED KINGDOM OF GREAT BRITAIN AND IRELAND OF ALL LANDS IN THE ARCTIC SEAS, WHETHER ACQUIRED BY DISCOVERY, OCCUPATION OR OTHERWISE

Appointed on June 6, 1910 by Order in Council P. C. 1170 on the recommendation of the Prime Minister. No indication of authorizing statute given in Order in Council.

Commissioner: James Colebrooke Patterson.

Report

Not located.

153 COMMISSION TO INQUIRE INTO THE NUMBER OF BOATS TO BE EMPLOYED BY SALMON CANNERIES IN THE PROVINCE OF BRITISH COLUMBIA

Appointed on June 8, 1910 by Order in Council P. C. 1234 on the recommendation of the Minister of Marine and Fisheries. No indication of authorizing statute given in the Order in Council. (Termed "Special Commission of Inquiry" in the Order in Council)

Commissioners: John T. Williams and John Pease Babcock.

Report

Dated July 14, 1910. Not printed. Typewritten copy in the Department of Fisheries files. 70 leaves.

Notes: The Commissioners visited all the canneries in British Columbia during late June and early July, 1910. Cost: $490. 60.

154 COMMISSION TO INVESTIGATE AND REPORT UPON THE CONDITIONS AND REQUIREMENTS OF THE FISHERIES OF THE PROVINCES OF ALBERTA AND SASKATCHEWAN

Appointed on July 6, 1910 by Order in Council P. C. 1432 on the recommendation of the Minister of Marine and Fisheries.  No indication of authorizing statute given in Order in Council.

Commissioners:  Edward Ernest Prince, Chairman, Thomas Horace McGuire and Euston Sisley.

Reports

Interim Report:  Tabled in the House of Commons on July 28, 1911. Sessional Paper no. 211-1911.  Not printed in Sessional Paper Series. Copy not located.

Final Report:  Prefatory note dated January, 1912.  Printed as:

Dominion Alberta and Saskatchewan Fisheries Commission, 1910-1911:  Report and Recommendations with Appendices.  Ottawa, Government Printing Bureau, 1912. vii, 71 p.

Notes:  Commission sat September 7 - October 31, 1910 and July 17 - November 7, 1911.  Sittings held in 42 centres.  230 witnesses appeared before the Commission.  Cost: $15,405.61.

155 COMMISSION TO INVESTIGATE ALLEGED CHINESE FRAUDS AND OPIUM SMUGGLING ON THE PACIFIC COAST

Appointed on November 12, 1910 by Order in Council P. C. 2281 under the Inquiries Act (R. S. C., 1906, c. 104) and on the recommendation of the Minister of Trade and Commerce.  Part of Inquiries Act not stated in the Order in Council.

Commissioner:  Dennis Murphy.

Report

Dated May 1, 1911.  Tabled in the House of Commons on July 21, 1911.  Sessional Paper no. 207-1911.  Not printed in Sessional Papers series.

Report of Mr. Justice Murphy, Royal Commissioner appointed to investigate alleged Chinese frauds and opium smuggling on the Pacific Coast. 1910-11.  Ottawa, Government Printing Bureau, 1913.  54 p.

Location:  Library of Parliament, Ottawa.

Notes:  Sittings held at 3 British Columbia towns and cities during the Winter, 1910-1911.  Cost: $5,000.

156 COMMISSION TO INVESTIGATE THE CONDITIONS OF SHEEP BREEDING AND THE MARKETING OF THEIR PRODUCTS IN THE UNITED KINGDOM, CANADA AND THE UNITED STATES

Appointed on November 19, 1910 by Order in Council P. C. 1/2317 on the recommendation of the Minister of Agriculture.  No indication of authorizing statute given in the Order in Council.

Commissioners: W. A. Dryden and W. T. Ritch.

Report

Letter of transmittal dated November 1, 1911. Printed as:

The sheep industry in Canada, Great Britain and the United States; report of the Commissioners. [Ottawa, 1911] xi, 187 p.

Notes: The Commissioners travelled widely throughout Canada as well as in Great Britain and the United States.

157 COMMISSION TO INVESTIGATE ALL PROPOSED POWER DEVELOPMENT WORKS ON THE PORTION OF THE ST. LAWRENCE RIVER BETWEEN THE HEAD OF LAKE ST. FRANCIS AND THE CITY OF MONTREAL

Appointed on August 29, 1911 by Order in Council P. C. 1971 on the recommendation of the Minister of Public Works. No indication of authorizing statute given in Order in Council.

Commissioners: C. M. McLeod, Chairman, William Inkerman Gear and Arthur Surveyer.

Report

Not located.

158 COMMISSION TO INQUIRE INTO THE PUBLIC SERVICE

Appointed on December 21, 1911 by Order in Council P. C. 2928 under Part I of the Inquiries Act (R. S. C., 1906, c. 104) and on the recommendation of the Prime Minister.

Commissioners: Alfred Bishop Morine, Chairman, [1] Guillaume Narcisse Ducharme and Richard Stuart Lake.

Report

Dated November 9, 1912. Tabled in the House of Commons on December 9, 1912. Sessional Paper no. 57-1913. Printed as:

Public Service Commission, 1912. Report of the Commissioners. Printed by Order of Parliament. Ottawa, Printed by C. H. Parmelee, Printer to the King's Most Excellent Majesty, 1913. 387 p.

Also issued as a separate.

Notes: Cost: $50,942.28.

159 COMMISSION TO INQUIRE INTO AND INVESTIGATE AND REPORT UPON

---

[1] Resigned on May 30, 1912.

ALL MATTERS IN RESPECT TO THE CONSTRUCTION OF THE NA-
TIONAL TRANSCONTINENTAL RAILWAY BETWEEN MONCTON, IN
THE PROVINCE OF NEW BRUNSWICK, AND THE CITY OF WINNIPEG,
IN THE PROVINCE OF MANITOBA

Appointed on January 29, 1912 by Order in Council P. C. 169 under
the Inquiries Act (R. S. C., 1906, c. 104) and on the recommendation
of the Minister of Railways and Canals. Part of Inquiries Act not
stated in the Order in Council.
    Commissioners: George Lynch-Staunton, Chairman and Frederick
Passmore Gutelius.

Report

Dated February 11, 1914. Tabled in the House of Commons on
February 12, 1914. Sessional Paper no. 123-1914. Printed as:
Report of the National Transcontinental Railway Investigating
Commission. Printed by Order of Parliament. Ottawa, Printed by
the King's Printer to His Most Excellent Majesty, 1914. 659 p. (In-
cludes transcript of evidence). [1]
    Notes: Cost: $66,237.47


160 ROYAL COMMISSION OF INQUIRY IN THE MATTER OF THE FARMERS'
    BANK OF CANADA

Appointed on February 12, 1912 by Order in Council P. C. 325
under Part I of the Inquiries Act (R. S. C., 1906, c. 104) and on the
recommendation of the Minister of Finance.
    Commissioner: Sir William Ralph Meredith.

Report

Dated February 21, 1913. Tabled in the House of Commons on
February 26, 1913. Sessional Paper no. 153a-1913. [2] Printed as:
[Report of the Honourable Sir William Ralph Meredith, Kt., Com-
missioner appointed to make investigation into all matters connected
with the Farmers' Bank of Canada]. 12 p.
    Notes: Held hearings (March 4, 1912 - January 7, 1913).
Cost: $14,828.37.


161 COMMISSION TO INVESTIGATE AND REPORT UPON THE WORKING OF
    THE LAW BRANCH OF THE HOUSE OF COMMONS OF CANADA

---

[1] A volume of exhibits (including numerous maps) is also included in
Sessional Paper no. 123-1914.
[2] The Proceedings are also reproduced in this Sessional paper. They
run to 1198 pages.

Appointed on April 10, 1912 by Order in Council P. C. 870 under the Inquiries Act (R. S. C. , 1906, c. 104) and on the recommendation of the Acting Prime Minister. Part of Inquiries Act not stated in the Order in Council.

Commissioners: William Drummond Hogg and Adam Shortt.

#### Report

Dated May 7, 1912. Copy with the Privy Council Dormants (No. 870 of April 10, 1912). In the Public Archives of Canada. (R. G. 2, 3, vol. 177) 9 leaves.

Notes: Occupied 12 days in taking evidence from those who were connected with the Office of the Law Branch of the House of Commons. Cost: $1,488.

162 COMMISSION TO INVESTIGATE AND REPORT UPON, WITH RESPECT TO CLAIMS PUT FORWARD BY AND ON BEHALF OF THE INDIANS OF BRITISH COLUMBIA, AS TO LANDS, RIGHTS AND ALL QUESTIONS AT ISSUE BETWEEN THE DOMINION AND PROVINCIAL GOVERNMENTS AND THE INDIANS IN RESPECT THERETO, AND TO REPRESENT THE GOVERNMENT OF CANADA THEREIN

Appointed on May 24, 1912 by Order in Council P. C. 20/1398 on the recommendation of the Treasury Board. No indication of authorizing statute given in Order in Council.

Commissioner: James Andrew Joseph McKenna.

#### Report

Interim Report dated October 26, 1912. Copy attached to Order in Council P. C. 3277 of November 27, 1912 (In Public Archives of Canada, R G. 2, 1, Volume 1234). 3 leaves. No further report located.

Notes: Cost: $3,454.92.

163 COMMISSION TO INVESTIGATE INTO AND REPORT UPON THE CONDITIONS AND REQUIREMENTS OF THE SHELL FISHERIES OF THE MARITIME PROVINCES

Appointed on July 4, 1912 by Order in Council P. C. 1901 on the recommendation of the Minister of Marine and Fisheries. No indication of authorizing statute given in Order in Council.

Commissioners: Edward Ernest Prince, Chairman, Richard O'Leary, John McLean and S. Y. Wilson.

#### Report

Dated May 24, 1913, Printed as:

Dominion Shell-fish fishery Commission, 1912-1913: Report and Recommendations. Ottawa, Government Printing Bureau, 1913. 90 p.

Notes: 50 public sittings held throughout Nova Scotia, Prince Edward Island, and New Brunswick (September 3 - November 20, 1912). 284 witnesses appeared before the Commission. Cost: $9,333.67.

164 ROYAL COMMISSION TO INQUIRE INTO ALLEGED COMPLAINTS RE-
LATING TO THE WEIGHING OF BUTTER AND CHEESE IN MONTREAL

Appointed on July 19, 1912 by Order in Council P. C. 1955 under Part I of the Inquiries Act (R. S. C., 1906, c. 104) and on the recommendation of the Minister of Agriculture.

Commissioners: Robert Alexander Pringle, Chairman, Arthur Jacob Hodgson and Samuel J. Macdonnell.

Report

Undated. Tabled in the House of Commons on May 30, 1913. Sessional Paper no. 153b-1913. Printed as:

Report of Royal Commission to enquire into alleged complaints relating to weighing of butter and cheese in Montreal. Printed by Order of Parliament. Ottawa, Printed by C. H. Parmelee, Printer to the King's Most Excellent Majesty, 1913. 17 p.

Also issued as a separate.

Notes: Held hearings in 5 towns and cities (July 29, 1912 - January 4, 1913). Evidence of about 50 persons taken at the hearings. Cost: $3,532.38.

165 COMMISSION TO INVESTIGATE HERRING WEIR LICENSES BY FREDERICK BUTLER, MUSQUASH, CHARLOTTE COUNTY, NEW BRUNSWICK

Appointed on September 20, 1912 by Order in Council P. C. 2576 under Part I of the Inquiries Act (R. S. C., 1906, c. 104) and on the recommendation of the Minister of Marine and Fisheries.

Commissioner: John F. Calder.

Report

Dated October 28, 1912. Tabled in the House of Commons on June 6, 1913. Sessional Paper no. 230-1913. Not printed in Sessional Paper Series. Typewritten copy in the Department of Fisheries files. 4 leaves.

Notes: Hearings held at Deans Hall, New Brunswick on October 8, 1912. Three witnesses appeared before the Commission. 7 typewritten pages of evidence taken.

166 COMMISSION TO INQUIRE INTO CERTAIN MATTERS AFFECTING THE
OPERATION OF THE CIVIL SERVICE ACTS, THE ORGANIZATION
OF THE PUBLIC SERVICE AND THE METHODS OF ADMINISTRATION
UNDER WHICH THE PUBLIC SERVICE OF CANADA IS CARRIED ON

Appointed on October 7, 1912 by Order in Council P. C. 2751 under
the Inquiries Act (R. S. C., 1906, c. 104) and on the recommendation
of the Prime Minister.
Commissioner: Sir George H. Murray.

Report

Dated November 30, 1912. Tabled in the House of Commons on
December 18, 1912. Sessional Paper no. 57a-1913. Printed as:
Report on the organization of the public service of Canada, by
Sir George Murray. Printed by Order of Parliament. Ottawa, Printed
by C. H. Parmlee, Printer to the King's Most Excellent Majesty, 1912.
27 p.
Also issued as a separate.


167 ROYAL COMMISSION TO INQUIRE INTO THE STATE OF THE RECORDS
OF THE PUBLIC DEPARTMENTS OF THE DOMINION OF CANADA

Appointed on November 9, 1912 by Order in Council P. C. 3054
under the Inquiries Act (R. S. C., 1906  c. 104) and on the recommenda-
tion of the Secretary of State. Part of Inquiries Act not stated in the
Order in Council. Termed "Royal Commission" in the Order in Council.
Commissioners: Sir Joseph Pope, Ernest Frederick Jarvis and
Arthur George Doughty.

Report

Dated March 3, 1914. Printed as:[1]
Report of the Royal Commission appointed to inquire into the state
of the records of the public departments of the Dominion of Canada (in
1912). Ottawa, F. A. Acland, Printer to the King's Most Excellent
Majesty, 1924 [ ?] 16 p.
Notes: The Commissioners visited all the Departments of the
federal government at Ottawa (December 11, 1912 - November 28, 1913).
Almost 200 meetings and inspections were held. Cost: $166.00.


168 COMMISSION TO CONSIDER AND REPORT UPON THE CLAIMS OF THE

[1] The thirty-three Appendices were not printed. The manuscript copy
is located in the Manuscript Division, Public Archives of Canada,
Ottawa.

PROVINCE OF BRITISH COLUMBIA FOR BETTER TERMS

Appointed on February 1, 1913 by Order in Council P. C. 260.
under Part I of the Inquiries Act and on the recommendation of the
Prime Minister. Members named on March 26, 1913 by Order in
Council P. C. 645. [1]
Commissioners: Zebulon Aytoun Lash and Ernest Victor Bodwell.
Secretary: Frederick Cook.

Report
Not located.
Notes: Cost: $10, 115. 00.


169 COMMISSION TO INVESTIGATE AND REPORT UPON THE WATER LEVELS
OF THE ST. LAWRENCE RIVER AT AND BELOW MONTREAL

Appointed on March 21, 1913 by Order in Council P. C. 614 on
the recommendation of the Minister of Marine and Fisheries. No
indication of authorizing statute given in Order in Council.
Commissioners: Eugene E. Haskell, William James Stewart and
Victor F. W. Forneret.

Report
Dated March 1, 1915. Tabled in the House of Commons on March
16, 1915. Sessional Paper no. 166-1915. Not printed in Sessional
Papers Series. Printed as:
Investigation of water levels, River St. Lawrence between Montreal
and Lake St. Peter. Ottawa, Government Printing Bureau, 1915. 15p.
(and 7 maps).
Locations: Department of Transport Library, Ottawa; Queen's
University Library, Kingston (Xerox copy - without maps).


170 COMMISSION RESPECTING INDIAN LANDS AND INDIAN AFFAIRS
GENERALLY IN THE PROVINCE OF BRITISH COLUMBIA

Appointed on March 31, 1913 by Order in Council P. C. 644 under
Part I of the Inquiries Act (R. S. C. , 1906, c. 104) and on the recommendation of the Prime Minister.

---

[1] Gave authority for the appointment of a third Commissioner by the
agreement of the other two Commissioners, or failing such agreement, by the Secretary of State for the Colonies. However, it appears
that he was never appointed.

Commissioners: Nathaniel W. White, [1] James Andrew Joseph
McKenna, James Pearson Shaw, Day Hort Macdowell, Edward Ludlow
Wetmore, [1] and Samurez Carmichael.
Secretary: C. H. Gibbons.

### Report

Ninety-eight Interim Reports (May 21, 1913 - April 27, 1916).
Contained in pp. 23-137 of General Report.
Five Progress Reports (November 26, 1913 - December 20, 1915).
Contained in pp. 141-175 of General Report.
General Report: Undated. Tabled in the House of Commons on
March 11, 1920. Sessional Paper no. 66-1920. Not printed in Sessional
Papers Series. Printed as:
Report of the Royal Commission on Indian Affairs for the Province
of British Columbia. Printed by Order. Victoria, British Columbia.
In four volumes. Printed by the Acme Press, Limited, 1916. 4 v.
(956 p. and folded tables).
Notes: 5,655 folio pages of typewritten evidence taken. 253
exhibits presented to the Commission.

171 COMMISSION TO INVESTIGATE INTO AND REPORT UPON CLAIMS OF
CERTAIN CANADIAN PELAGIC SEALERS ALLEGED TO HAVE BEEN
DAMIFIED BY REASON OF THE PELAGIC SEALING TREATY OF THE
SEVENTH JULY, 1911, BETWEEN GREAT BRITAIN AND THE UNITED
STATES, RUSSIA, AND JAPAN, AND BY THE PARIS AWARD REGU-
LATIONS OF 1893

Appointed on June 10, 1913 by Order in Council P. C. 1054 under
the Inquiries Act (R. S. C., 1906, c. 104) and on the recommendation
of the Minister of Marine and Fisheries. Part of Inquiries Act not
stated in the Order in Council.
Commissioner: Louis Arthur Audette.

### Report

Undated. Tabled in the House of Commons on February 9, 1916.
Sessional Paper no. 79-1916. Printed as:
Pelagic Sealing Commission. Commissioner's Report. 62 p.
Notes: Hearings held in 4 cities. 1,605 claims submitted to the
Commission. Cost: $35,546.93.

172 COMMISSION TO INVESTIGATE AND REPORT UPON ALL MATTERS

---

[1] Resigned.

CONNECTED WITH THE SALE, LEASE, GRANT, EXCHANGE OR
DISPOSITION BY ANY MEANS WHATSOEVER, SINCE THE FIRST
DAY OF JULY, 1896 OF (A) DOMINION LANDS; (B) TIMBER AND
MINERAL LANDS AND MINING RIGHTS AND PRIVILEGES, INCLUDING
COAL, PETROLEUM AND GAS LANDS AND RIGHTS; (C) WATER
POWERS AND RIGHTS UNDER THE AUTHORITY OF OR PURPORTING
TO BE UNDER THE AUTHORITY OF THE DOMINION LANDS ACT,
THE IRRIGATION ACT, OR OTHER STATUTES OF THE PARLIAMENT
OF CANADA

Appointed on June 27, 1913 by Order in Council P. C. 1589 under
Part I of the Inquiries Act (R. S. C. , 1906, c. 104) and on the recom-
mendation of the Acting Minister of the Interior.
Commissioner: Thomas Roberts Ferguson.

Report
Tabled in the House of Commons on April 13, 1915.  Sessional
Paper no. 281-1915.  Not printed.  No copy located.


173 COMMISSION TO INVESTIGATE RELATIONS BETWEEN EMPLOYERS
    AND EMPLOYEES IN INDUSTRIES IN PORT ARTHUR AND FORT
    WILLIAM

Appointed on June 27, 1913 by Order in Council P. C. 1593 under
Part I of the Inquiries Act (R. S. C. , 1906, c. 104) and on the recom-
mendation of the Minister of Labour.
Commissioner: Samuel Price.

Report
Not located.
Notes: Cost $132. 60.


174 ROYAL COMMISSION TO INVESTIGATE COAL-MINING DISPUTES ON
    VANCOUVER ISLAND

Appointed on June 27, 1913 by Order in Council P. C. 1594 under
Part I of the Inquiries Act (R. S. C. , 1906, c. 104) and on the recom-
mendation of the Minister of Labour.
Commissioner: Samuel Price.

Report
Dated August 14, 1913.  Printed as:
Report of Royal Commissioner on coal mining disputes on Vancouver Island.  By Samuel Price.  Issued by authority of the Minister
of Labour.  Ottawa, Government Printing Bureau, 1913.  43 p.

Notes: Cost: $1,320.85.


175 COMMISSION TO INVESTIGATE CERTAIN CHARGES OF MALFEASANCE
IN OFFICE BROUGHT AGAINST J. E. MILLER, INSPECTOR OF IN-
LAND REVENUE FROM THE PROVINCE OF BRITISH COLUMBIA AND
E. B. PARKINSON, COLLECTOR OF INTERNAL REVENUE AT VAN-
COUVER, AND INTO ALL MATTERS PERTAINING TO INTERNAL
REVENUE IN THE SAID PROVINCE

Appointed on July 26, 1913 by Order in Council P. C. 1910 under
the Inquiries Act (R. S. C., 1906, c. 104) and on the recommendation
of the Minister of Inland Revenue. Part of Inquiries Act not stated in
the Order in Council.
Commissioners: Henry Lawlor and John Kelly Barrett.

Report
Not located.


176 ROYAL COMMISSION TO INVESTIGATE THE STATE AND MANAGEMENT
OF THE KINGSTON PENITENTIARY

Appointed on August 25, 1913 by Order in Council P. C. 2205 under
Part II of the Inquiries Act (R. S. C., 1906, c. 104) and on the recom-
mendation of the Minister of Justice. [1]
Commissioners: George Milnes Macdonnell, Chairman, Frederick
Etherington and Joseph Patrick Downey.

Report
Undated. Tabled in the House of Commons on April 22, 1914.
Sessional Paper no. 252-1914. Printed as:
Report of the Royal Commission on Penitentiaries. Printed by
order of Parliament. Ottawa, Printed by J. de L. Taché, Printer to
the King's Most Excellent Majesty, 1914. 44 p.
Also issued as a separate.
Notes: Sittings held at Kingston (September 13, 1913 - March 27,
1914). The Commissioners visited many of the leading penal institu-
tions of the United States. Cost: $8,715.79.


177 COMMISSION TO INQUIRE INTO AND REPORT UPON CERTAIN ALLE-
GATIONS MADE BY JEANNETTE M. CAIN THAT HER HUSBAND,

---

[1] While this Commission was established under Part II of the Inquiries
Act, it is known as a "Royal Commission."

THE REVEREND JOHN CAIN, WHO HAD CONTRACTED FOR THE
PURCHASE OF AN ANNUITY UNDER THE PROVISIONS OF THE
GOVERNMENT ANNUITIES ACT, 1908, WAS AT THE TIME HE
ENTERED INTO THE CONTRACT, INCAPABLE OF UNDERSTANDING
BUSINESS, AND DID NOT UNDERSTAND THE CONTRACT REFERRED
TO

Appointed on December 4, 1913 by Order in Council P. C. 3063 on
the recommendation of the Postmaster General. No indication of
authorizing statute given in Order in Council.
Commissioner: Elzéar Lucien Fiset.

Report
Not located.

178 COMMISSION TO INVESTIGATE THE INCREASE IN THE COST OF LIVING
IN CANADA AND INTO THE CAUSES WHICH HAVE OCCASIONED OR
CONTRIBUTED TO SUCH RESULT

Appointed on December 20, 1913 by Order in Council P. C. 3195 on
the recommendation of the Prime Minister. No indication of authori-
zing statute given in Order in Council.
Commissioners: John McDougald, Charles Canniff James, Robert
Hamilton Coats and Joseph Ulric Vincent.
Secretary: T. J. Linton.

Report
Dated August 1, 1914. Tabled in the House of Commons on Febru-
ary 16, 1916. Sessional Paper no. 84–1916. Not printed in Sessional
Papers Series. Printed as:
Board of Inquiry into cost of living. Report of the Board. Ottawa,
Printed by J. de L. Taché, Printer to the King's Most Excellent
Majesty, 1915. 2 v. (2063 p. ).

179 COMMISSION TO INQUIRE INTO AND REPORT UPON THE PROPOSED
CONSTRUCTION OF A DEEP INLAND WATERWAY PROVIDING FOR
THE ACCOMODATION OF THE LARGE LAKE CARRIERS FROM THE
GEORGIAN BAY TO THE PORT OF MONTREAL

Appointed on March 18, 1914 by Order in Council P. C. 551 on
the recommendation of the Minister of Public Works. No indication
of authorizing statute given in Order in Council.
Commissioners: William Sanford Evans, Chairman, Edouard
Gohier and Frank Stephen Meighen.

Reports

First Interim Report tabled in the House of Commons on April 14,
1916. Sessional Paper no. 16b-1916. Printed as:

First Interim Report. Interim Report. Statistical Examination
of certain general conditions of transportation bearing on the economic
problem of the proposed Georgian Bay Canal. By W. Sandford Evans,
Chairman, Georgian Bay Canal Commission. 1916. Printed by Order
of Parliament. Ottawa, Printed by J. de L. Taché, Printer to the
King's Most Excellent Majesty, 1916. 150 p.

Also issued as a separate.

Second Interim Report: Tabled in the House of Commons on May
13, 1918. Sessional Paper no. 141-1918. Printed as:

Interim Report No. 1 [i.e., No. 2]. Georgian Bay Canal Commis-
sion. Wheat prices and a comparative study of United States and
Canadian markets. By W. Sanford Evans. Printed by authority of
Parliament. Ottawa, J. de Labroquerie Taché, Printer to the King's
Most Excellent Majesty, 1918. 48 p.

Also issued as a separate.

Third Interim Report: Tabled in the House of Commons on May
13, 1918. Sessional Paper no. 142-1918. Printed as:

Interim Report No. 3. Georgian Bay Canal Commission. Trans-
atlantic passenger and freight traffic and steamship subsidies. By W.
Sanford Evans. Printed by order of Parliament. Ottawa, J. de
Labroquerie Taché, Printer to the King's Most Excellent Majesty,
1918. 53 p.

Also issued as a separate.

No further reports located.

Notes: Cost: $56,285.18.


180 COMMISSION TO INQUIRE INTO AND REPORT ON THE WORKS EMBRACED
IN THE CONSTRUCTION OF A LINE OF RAILWAY FROM A POINT AT
OR NEAR MILLVILLE, IN THE PROVINCE OF NEW BRUNSWICK, TO
A POINT ON THE ST. JOHN RIVER, NEAR THE POKICK BRIDGE, IN
THE SAID PROVINCE, BY THE SOUTHAMPTON RAILWAY COMPANY,
INCLUDING THE ACTUAL, NECESSARY AND REASONABLE COST OF
SUCH CONSTRUCTION IN ORDER TO COMPLETE THE SAID RAILWAY
IN ACCORDANCE WITH THE REQUIREMENTS OF A SUBSIDY CON-
TRACT BEARING DATE THE FOURTEENTH DAY OF MAY, 1912, BE-
TWEEN HIS MAJESTY REPRESENTED BY THE MINISTER OF RAIL-
WAYS AND CANALS AND THE SAID SOUTHAMPTON RAILWAY COM-
PANY

Appointed on March 30, 1914 by Order in Council P.C. 871 under
Part I of the Inquiries Act (R.S.C., 1906, c. 104) and on the recommendation of the Minister of Railways and Canals.

Commissioner: Robert Abercrombie Pringle.

Report

Tabled in the House of Commons on February 8, 1915. Sessional Paper no. 41-1915. Not printed. No copy located.
Notes: Cost: $8,464.70.

181 COMMISSION TO INVESTIGATE CONDITION OF INDIAN AFFAIRS IN BRITISH COLUMBIA

Appointed on April 3, 1914 by Order in Council P.C. 923 under Part I of the Inquiries Act (R.S.C., 1906, c. 104) and on the recommendation of the Prime Minister.
Commissioner: Samurez Carmichael.

Report

Not located.

182 COMMISSION TO INQUIRE INTO THE CIRCUMSTANCES ATTACHED TO THE ACQUISITION BY THE PAS TOWNSITE COMPANY OF A PIECE OF LAND FOR THE PURPOSES OF A WIRELESS STATION OF THE HUDSON BAY RAILWAY

Appointed on May 13, 1914 by Order in Council P.C. 1281 under Part I of the Inquiries Act (R.S.C., 1906, c. 104) and on the recommendation of the Minister of Railways and Canals and the Minister of the Interior.
Commissioners: R. H. Fraser and Harry G. Cuttle.

Report

Not located.

183 COMMISSION TO INVESTIGATE HINDU CLAIMS FOLLOWING REFUSAL OF IMMIGRATION OFFICIALS TO ALLOW OVER 300 HINDUS ABOARD THE S. S. KOMAGATA MARU TO LAND AT VANCOUVER

Appointed on September 26, 1914 by Order in Council P.C. 2432 under Part I of the Inquiries Act (R.S.C., 1906, c. 104) and on the recommendation of the Minister of the Interior.
Commissioner: H. C. Clogston.

Report

Not located.

184 COMMISSION TO INVESTIGATE THE FALLING OFF OF SARDINE
FISHERIES IN L'ETANY RIVER ALLEGED TO BE CAUSED BY
POLLUTION OF WATER FROM A SARDINE CANNERY

Appointed on October 6, 1914 by Order in Council P. C. 2508
under the Inquiries Act (R. S. C., 1906, c. 104) and on the recommendation of the Minister of Naval Service.  Part of Inquiries Act not stated
in the Order in Council.
Commissioner: William Ambrose Found.

Report
Dated October 24, 1914.  Not printed.  Typewritten copy in the
Department of Fisheries files.  6 leaves.
Notes: Hearings held at St. George, New Brunswick (October 20-
21, 1914).  3 witnesses appeared before the Commission.  16 pages of
evidence taken.

185 COMMISSION TO INVESTIGATE CHARGES OF CORRUPTION AND FRAUD
IN RELATION TO CONTRACTS FOR CONSTRUCTION OF DRILL SHEDS
IN THE PROVINCE OF ONTARIO

Appointed on January 9, 1915 by Order in Council P. C. 55 under
Part I of the Inquiries Act (R. S. C., 1906, c. 104) and on the recom-
mendation of the Prime Minister.
Commissioner: Robert Abercrombie Pringle.

Report
Tabled in the House of Commons on April 15, 1915.  Sessional
Paper no. 294-1915.  Not printed in Sessional Paper Series.  No copy
located.

186 COMMISSION TO INVESTIGATE A SCHEME OF SCIENTIFIC FISHING
FOR SEA HERRING IN THE ATLANTIC WATERS OF THE DOMINION

Appointed on February 2, 1915 by Order in Council P. C. 249 on
the recommendation of the Minister of Naval Service.  No indication
of authorizing statute given in Order in Council.
Commissioner: Johan Hjort.

Report
Not located.

187 COMMISSION TO INQUIRE INTO, INVESTIGATE AND REPORT UPON
THE PURCHASE BY AND ON BEHALF OF THE GOVERNMENT OF

CANADA, THROUGH WHATEVER AGENCY THE PURCHASE MAY
HAVE BEEN EFFECTED, OF ARMS AND MUNITIONS, IMPLEMENTS,
MATERIALS, HORSES, SUPPLIES AND OTHER THINGS FOR THE
PURPOSES OF THE PRESENT WAR AND AS TO THE EXPENDITURES
AND PAYMENTS MADE OR AGREED TO BE MADE THEREFOR

Appointed on June 2, 1915 by Order in Council P. C. 1287 under
Part I of the Inquiries Act (R. S. C. , 1906, c. 104) and on the recom-
mendation of the Minister of Justice.
Commissioner: Sir Charles Peers Davidson.

Reports
Report concerning military cloth (Auburn Woollen Mills Company):
Undated.  Tabled in the House of Commons on January 30, 1917.
Sessional Paper no. 60-1917.  Not printed in Sessional Papers Series.
Printed as:

Royal Commission.  Report of the Commissioner concerning
military cloth (Auburn Woollen Mills Co. ) Commissioner: The
Honourable Sir Charles Davidson, Knight.  Ottawa, Printed by J. de
L. Taché, Printer to the King's Most Excellent Majesty, 1917.  35 p.
Report concerning purchase of submarines:
Undated.  Tabled in the House of Commons on January 30, 1917.
Sessional Paper no. 60-1917.  Not printed in Sessional Papers Series.
Printed as:

Royal Commission.  Report of the Commissioner concerning
purchase of submarines.  Commissioner: The Honourable Sir Charles
Davidson, Knight.  Ottawa, Printed by J. de L. Taché,  Printer to
the King's Most Excellent Majesty, 1917.  25 p.
Report on purchase of surgical field dressings and other surgical
supplies:
Undated.  Tabled in the House of Commons on January 30, 1917.
Sessional Paper no. 60-1917.  Not printed in Sessional Papers Series.
Printed as:

Royal Commission.  Report of the Commissioner on purchase of
surgical field dressings and other surgical supplies.  Commissioner:
The Honourable Sir Charles Davidson, Knight.  Ottawa, Printed by J.
de L. Taché, Printer to the King's Most Excellent Majesty, 1917.  28 p.
Report concerning the sale of small arms and munitions:
Undated.  Tabled in the House of Commons on January 30, 1917.
Sessional Paper no. 60-1917.  Not printed in Sessional Papers Series.
Printed as:

Royal Commission.  Report of the Commissioner concerning sale of small arms and munitions. Commissioner: The Honourable Sir Charles Davidson, Knight. Ottawa, Printer to the King's Most Excellent Majesty, 1917. 56 p.

Notes: Cost: $30,592.45.


188 COMMISSION TO EXAMINE AND REPORT UPON CERTAIN MATTERS RELATING TO THE HARBOUR OF MONTREAL

Appointed on June 12, 1915 by Order in Council P. C. 1378 on the recommendation of the Minister of Marine and Fisheries. No indication of authorizing statute given in Order in Council.

Commissioners: Eugene Haskell, William James Stewart, Frederick William Cowie and Victor W. Forneret. [1]

Report

Not located.


189 COMMISSION TO INVESTIGATE METHODS OF STIMULATING AGRICULTURAL PRODUCTION

Appointed on October 19, 1915 by Order in Council P. C. 2436 under Part I of the Inquiries Act (R. S. C. , 1906, c. 104) and on the recommendation of the Prime Minister.

Commissioners: James Alexander Lougheed, Sir Joseph Wesley Flavelle, St. Jean-Baptiste Rolland, William Benjamin Ross, Edward N. Hopkins, John Gunion Rutherford, William Smith, James Cameron Watters and William Farrell.

Secretary: William John Black.

Report

Undated. Copy attached to Order in Council P. C. 2401 of September 30, 1918. (In Public Archives of Canada, R. G. 2, 1, Volume 1516). 225 leaves.

Notes: Cost: $23,250.57.


190 COMMISSION TO INQUIRE INTO THE PURCHASE OF COAL FOR THE DREDGING PLANT OF THE DEPARTMENT OF PUBLIC WORKS IN BRITISH COLUMBIA

Appointed on November 20, 1915 by Order in Council P. C. 2714

---

[1] Replaced by Cowie.

under Part I of the Inquiries Act (R. S. C. , 1906, c. 104) and on the
recommendation of the Minister of Public Works.
Commissioner: Hamnett Pinhey Hill.

Report
Not located.

191 COMMISSION TO INVESTIGATE THE SUPPLY AND SUFFICIENCY OF
RAW MATERIALS IN CANADA REQUIRED FOR THE PRODUCTION
OF MUNITIONS OF WAR AND AS TO THE BEST METHOD OF CON-
SERVING THE SAME

Appointed on November 27, 1915 by Order in Council P. C. 2755
under Part I of the Inquiries Act (R. S. C. , 1906, c. 104) and on the
recommendation of the Prime Minister. Additional Members added
on November 30, 1915 by Order in Council P. C. 2806.
Commissioners: Thomas Cantley, Chairman, Robert Hobson,
William Cameron Edwards, Ebenezer Carnegie, George W. Watts
and George Cleghorn Mackenzie, Secretary.

First Report
Letter of transmittal dated February 28, 1918. Tabled in the
House of Commons on May 20, 1918. Sessional Paper no. 153-1918.
Printed as: Munition Resources Commission. Canada. First Report
of the work of the Commission, November, 1915, to February, 1918
inclusive. Ottawa, The Mortimer Company Limited, 1918. viii, 47 p.

Final Report
Undated. Tabled in the House of Commons on May 31, 1920.
Sessional Paper no. 184-1920. Printed as: Munition Resources
Commission. Canada. Final Report of the Work of the Commission,
November, 1915, to March, 1919 inclusive. Toronto, Industrial and
Technical Press Limited, 1920. xiii, 260 p.

192 ROYAL COMMISSION TO INVESTIGATE THE ORIGIN AND ALL MATTERS
CONNECTED WITH THE PARLIAMENT BUILDINGS FIRE AT OTTAWA,
FEBRUARY 3, 1916

Appointed on February 7, 1916 by Order in Council P. C. 246 under
Part I of the Inquiries Act (R. S. C. , 1906, c. 104) and on the recom-
mendation of the Prime Minister.
Commissioners: Robert Abercrombie Pringle and Duncan Byron
MacTavish.

Report

Dated May 15, 1916. Tabled in the House of Commons on May 16, 1916. Sessional Paper no. 72a-1916. Printed as:

Royal Commission re Parliament Buildings Fire at Ottawa, February 3, 1916. Report of Commissioners and Evidence. Printed by Order of Parliament. Ottawa, Printed by J. de L. Taché, Printer to the King's Most Excellent Majesty, 1916. 159 p. (Includes minutes of evidence).

Also issued as a separate.

Notes: Met at Ottawa (February 10 - May 5, 1916). 80 witnesses appeared before the Commission. Cost: $124.40.


193 COMMISSION TO CONSIDER THE WHOLE MATTER OF THE HANDLING AND MARKETING OF GRAIN

Appointed on March 22, 1916 by Order in Council P. C. 657 under Part I of the Inquiries Act and on the recommendation of the Minister of Trade and Commerce.

Commissioners: Robert Magill, W. D. Staples and J. P. Jones.

Report

No report had been issued by this Commission as late as June 14, 1922.


194 COMMISSION TO INQUIRE INTO AND INVESTIGATE INTO AND REPORT UPON CERTAIN CONTRACTS MADE BY THE COMMITTEE KNOWN AS THE SHELL COMMITTEE, AND UPON SUCH OTHER MATTERS RELATING TO THE ACTS OR PROCEEDINGS OF THE SAID SHELL COMMITTEE AS MAY BE REFERRED TO THE SAID COMMITTEE BY ORDER IN COUNCIL FROM TIME TO TIME

Appointed on April 3, 1916 by Order in Council P. C. 775 under Part I of the Inquiries Act (R. S. C., 1906, c. 104) and on the recommendation of the Prime Minister.

Commissioners: Sir William Ralph Meredith, Chairman, and Sir Lyman Poore Duff.

Secretary: J. A. Ritchie.

Report

Dated July 20, 1916. Printed as:

Royal Commission on shell contracts. Commissioners: The Honourable Sir William Meredith, Knight, Chief Justice of Ontario; The Honourable Sir Lyman Poore Duff, Justice of the Supreme Court. Secretary, J. A. Ritchie, Esquire, Barrister-at-law. Report. Ottawa, Printed by J. de L. Taché, Printer to the King's Most Excellent

Majesty, 1916.  29 p.
   Location:  Library of Parliament, Ottawa.
   Notes:  Hearings held April 19, 1916 - June 9, 1916 at Ottawa.
Cost: $54,872.41.


195 COMMISSION TO INVESTIGATE INTO AND REPORT UPON UNREST IN
   CERTAIN INDUSTRIES OF TORONTO AND HAMILTON

   Appointed on April 11, 1916 by Order in Council P. C. 832 under
Part I of the Inquiries Act (R. S. C., 1906, c. 104) and on the recommendation of the Minister of Labour.
   Commissioners:  Colin George Snider, Chairman, William Inglis
and John A. McClelland.

Report
Dated May 6, 1916.  Printed as:
"Munitions Industry Inquiry.  Report of Commissioners Appointed
by the Minister of Labour to Inquire into Certain Concerns in Toronto
and Hamilton" in Labour Gazette, XVI, June 1916, pp. 1295-1297.
   Notes:  Sittings held at Toronto and Hamilton (April-May, 1916).
Cost: $984.30.


196 COMMISSION TO INQUIRE IN THE UNITED KINGDOM, FRANCE, BEL-
   GIUM AND ITALY, INTO THE POSSIBILITIES FOR THE SUPPLY OF
   CANADIAN PRODUCTS, NATURAL AND MANUFACTURED, WHICH
   MAY BE NEEDED FOR THE WORK OF RECONSTRUCTION IN THE
   SAID COUNTRIES DURING AND AFTER THE WAR, AND ALSO AS
   TO THE SOURCES OF SUPPLY IN THOSE COUNTRIES FOR COM-
   MODITIES NEEDED IN CANADA AND WHICH FORMERLY WERE
   OBTAINED FROM GERMANY AND AUSTRIA, AND TO REPORT UPON
   THE SAME

   Appointed on May 9, 1916 by Order in Council P. C. 1010 on the
recommendation of the Minister of Trade and Commerce.  No indication of authorizing statute given in Order in Council.
   Commissioners:  James W. Woods, Chairman, Hector Edmond
Dupré, W. Frank Hatheway, Theo. H. Wardleworth, Frank Pauzé
and George William Allan.
   Secretary:  Roy Campbell.

Report
Letter of transmittal dated November 18, 1916.  Tabled in the
House of Commons on July 5, 1917.  Sessional Paper no. 221 -1917.
Not printed in the Sessional Papers Series.  Printed as:

Report of Special Trade Commission to Great Britain, France and
Italy. May - September, 1916. Published by Authority of Right Hon-
ourable Sir George E. Foster, K. C. M. G. , M. P. , Minister of Trade
and Commerce. [Ottawa, 1916?] 158 p.
 Notes: The Commissioners visited England, France, and Italy
(May - August, 1917). Cost: $14,615.01.


197 COMMISSION TO INVESTIGATE AND REPORT UPON THE FACTS AND
    CIRCUMSTANCES OF OR CONNECTED WITH THE SALE OR DISPOSAL,
    BY THE GOVERNMENT OF CANADA, OF SMALL ARMS MUNITIONS
    SINCE THE 4TH AUGUST, 1914, REFERRED TO IN CERTAIN RETURNS
    MADE TO THE HOUSE OF COMMONS ON THE FIRST AND SECOND
    DAYS OF MAY, 1916

        Appointed on May 9, 1916 by Order in Council P. C. 1093 under
    Part I of the Inquiries Act (R. S. C. , 1906, c. 104) and on the recom-
    mendation of the Minister of Justice.
        Commissioner: Sir Charles Peers Davidson.

                            Report
        Not located.


198 ROYAL COMMISSION TO INQUIRE INTO RAILWAYS AND TRANSPORTA-
    TION IN CANADA

        Appointed on June 14, 1916 by Order in Council P. C. 1680 under
    Part I of the Inquiries Act (R. S. C. , 1906, c. 104) and on the recom-
    mendation of the Prime Minister.
        Commissioners: Alfred Holland Smith, Chairman, Sir Henry
    Lumley Drayton, Sir George Paish, [1] and William Mitchell Acworth. [2]

                            Report
        Dated April 25, 1917. Tabled in the House of Commons on May 2,
    1917. Sessional Paper no. 20g-1917. Printed as:
        Report of the Royal Commission to inquire into railways and trans-
    portation in Canada. Printed by Order of Parliament. Ottawa, Printed
    by J. de L. Taché, Printer to the King's Most Excellent Majesty, 1917.
    cv, 86 p.
        Also issued as a separate.
        Notes: Cost: $335,549.

───────────

[1] Resigned from the Commission on October 21, 1916 because of ill-
health.
[2] Appointed on October 21, 1916 by Order in Council P. C. 2567.

199 COMMISSION TO INQUIRE INTO AND REPORT UPON THE CAUSE OF
   UNREST IN THE ASBESTOS MINING INDUSTRY IN THE DISTRICT
   OF THETFORD MINES, IN THE PROVINCE OF QUEBEC, INCLUDING
   THE RELATIONS BETWEEN EMPLOYERS AND EMPLOYEES IN THE
   SAID INDUSTRY

   Appointed on August 3, 1916 by Order in Council P. C. 1860 under
   Part I of the Inquiries Act (R. S. C., 1906, c. 104) and on the recom-
   mendation of the Minister of Labour.
   Commissioner: Charles Albert Emile Blanchet.

                               Report
   Tabled in the House of Commons on April 19, 1917. Sessional
   Paper no. 103-1917. Not printed in Sessional Papers Series. No
   copy located.
   Notes: Cost: $551. 15.

200 COMMISSION TO INQUIRE INTO AND REPORT UPON THE UNREST IN
   THE MINING INDUSTRY AT COBALT, IN THE PROVINCE OF ON-
   TARIO, AND THE NATURE AND CAUSES THEREOF

   Appointed on August 28, 1916 by Order in Council P. C. 1976 under
   Part I of the Inquiries Act (R. S. C., 1906, c. 104) and on the recom-
   mendation of the Minister of Labour.
   Commissioners: Emerson Coatsworth, E. T. Corkill and Joseph
   Gibbons.

                               Report
   Dated September 12, 1916. Printed as:
   "Report of Royal Commission appointed to investigate unrest in
   the mining industry in the Cobalt District. " in Labour Gazette, XVI,
   October, 1916, pp. 1634-1638.
   Notes: Cost: $1,003. 35.

201 ROYAL COMMISSION TO INQUIRE INTO AND REPORT UPON THE CON-
   DITIONS IN REGARD TO THE DELIVERY OF CARGOES OF COAL TO
   COASTING VESSELS IN THE MARITIME PROVINCES

   Appointed on September 20, 1916 by Order in Council P. C. 2242
   under Part I of the Inquiries Act (R. S. C., 1906, c. 104) and on the
   recommendation of the Minister of Trade and Commerce.
   Commissioners: Wilfred Eddy Tupper, Archibald Tibbits and
   J. Fred McDonald.

Report
Dated December 6, 1916. Tabled in the House of Commons on
May 7, 1917. Sessional Paper no. 142-1917. Not printed in Sessional
Papers Series. Copy in Sessional Paper Office, Parliament Buildings,
Ottawa. 19 leaves.
Notes: Held meetings in Halifax, Sydney and Charlottetown (October
6 - October 12, 1916). The Commissioners also visited several other
ports during the same period.

202 COMMISSION TO INVESTIGATE THE SEIZURE OF THREE BOATS BY
THE CAPTAIN OF THE FISHERIES PATROL BOAT HUTSON WHEN
ILLEGALLY LOBSTER FISHING OFF RICHIBUCTO, NEW BRUNS-
WICK

Appointed on October 28, 1916 by Order in Council P.C. 2650
under Part I of the Inquiries Act (R.S.C., 1906, c. 104) and on the
recommendation of the Minister of Naval Service.
Commissioner: George Teed.

Report
Dated December 27, 1916. Not printed. Typewritten copy in the
Department of Fisheries files. 12 leaves.
Notes: Hearing held at Richibucto on December 4, 1916. 10
persons gave evidence. 93 typewritten pages of evidence taken.

203 COMMISSION TO INQUIRE INTO THE PRICES OF FOOD, CLOTHING AND
FUEL IN THE COAL MINING DISTRICTS OF FERNIE, LETHBRIDGE
AND CALGARY

Appointed on December 1, 1916 by Order in Council P.C. 2969
under Part I of the Inquiries Act (R.S.C., 1906, c. 104) and on the
recommendation of the Minister of Labour.
Commissioner: Frederick Ernest Harrison.

Report
Not located.

204 COMMISSION TO INQUIRE INTO AND REPORT UPON THE MANUFAC-
TURE, SALE, PRICE AND SUPPLY OF NEWS PRINT PAPER WITH-
IN CANADA

Appointed on April 16, 1917 by Order in Council P.C. 1060 under
Part I of the Inquiries Act (R.S.C., 1906, c. 104) and on the recommendation of the Minister of Finance.

Commissioner: Robert Abercrombie Pringle.

## Reports

Interim Report dated January 18, 1918. Tabled in the House of Commons on March 20, 1918. Sessional Paper no. 64-1918. Not printed in Sessional Papers Series. Copy in Sessional Paper Office, Parliament Buildings, Ottawa. 28 leaves.


205 ROYAL COMMISSION TO INVESTIGATE THE DISPUTES BETWEEN THE DOMINION COAL COMPANY, LIMITED, AND EMPLOYEES AT GLACE BAY AND SPRINGHILL, AND THE NOVA SCOTIA STEEL AND COAL COMPANY, LIMITED, AND EMPLOYEES AT SYDNEY MILLS

Appointed on April 19, 1917 by Order in Council P. C. 1102 under Part I of the Inquiries Act (R. S. C. , 1906, c. 104) and on the recommendation of the Minister of Labour. Extended by Order in Council P. C. 1278 of May 7, 1917.

Commissioners: Joseph Andrew Chisholm, Chairman, Rev. John Forrest and John T. Joy.

## Reports

Printed as:

"Reports of Royal Commission in Disputes between the Dominion Coal Company, Limited, and employees at Glace Bay and Springhill, and the Nova Scotia Steel and Coal Company, Limited, and employees at Sydney Mines," in Labour Gazette, XVII, June, 1917, pp. 452-455.

Report of Inquiry at Glace Bay: dated May 5, 1917. pp. 452-453.

Report of Inquiry at Sydney Mines: dated May 14, 1917. pp. 453-454.

Report of Inquiry at Springhill: dated May 18, 1917. pp. 454-455.

Notes: Cost: $951. 54.


206 COMMISSION TO INQUIRE INTO REPORTS OF MR. JUSTICE GALT OF MANITOBA AGAINST THE HONOURABLE ROBERT ROGERS, MINISTER OF PUBLIC WORKS

Appointed on June 6, 1917 by Order in Council P. C. 1555 under Part I of the Inquiries Act (R. S. C. , 1906, c. 104) and on the recommendation of the Secretary of State.

Commissioners: Sir Ezekiel McLeod and Louis Tellier.

Secretary: L. J. Loranger.

## Report

Dated July 26, 1917. Tabled in the House of Commons on July 27, 1917. Sessional Paper no. 230-1917. Not in Sessional Papers Series.

Printed as:

Royal Commission. Report of Commissioners re inquiry in reports of Mr. Justice Galt and Proceedings at Montreal . Ottawa,
J. de Labroquerie Taché, Printer to the King's Most Excellent Majesty,
1917. 54 p.
Notes: Hearings held June 11 - July 26, 1917. Cost: $6,648.41.


207 COMMISSION TO INVESTIGATE FISHING AND CANNING REGULATIONS
IN DISTRICT NUMBER 2, BRITISH COLUMBIA

Appointed on June 21, 1917 by Order in Council P. C. 1564 under
the Inquiries Act (R. S. C. , 1906, c. 104) and on the recommendation
of the Minister of Naval Service. Part of Inquiries Act not stated in
the Order in Council.
Commissioners: William Sandford Evans, Henry Broughton
Thompson and Frederick Thomas James.

Report

Undated. Printed as:
Report of Special Fishery Commission, 1917. Ottawa, King's
Printer, 1918. 48 p.
Notes: Cost $15,054.15.


208 COMMISSION TO INVESTIGATE THE BUSINESSES OF WILLIAM DAVIES
COMPANY, LIMITED AND MATTHEWS-BLACKWELL, LIMITED

Appointed on July 23, 1917 by Order in Council P. C. 2021 under
Part I of the Inquiries Act (R. S. C. , 1906, c. 104) and on the recom-
mendation of the Minister of Labour.
Commissioners: George F. Henderson, A. B. Brodie and
Geoffrey Teignmouth Clarkson.
Secretary: Walter L. Breckell.

Report

Dated November 1, 1917. Tabled in the House of Commons on
April 30, 1918. Sessional Paper no. 129-1918. Not in Sessional
Papers Series. Printed as:
Report of the Commissioners appointed to investigate the bus-
inesses of William Davies Company, Limited and Matthews-Blackwell,
Limited. November 1, 1917. Ottawa, J. de Labroquerie Taché,
Printer to the King's Most Excellent Majesty, 1917. 27 p.
Notes: Public hearings held at Toronto (July 30, - October 20,
1917). 14 persons gave evidence before the Commission. Cost:
$3,471.07.

209 COMMISSION TO INQUIRE INTO THE SUFFICIENCY OF THE PETITION
    FOR BRINGING INTO FORCE THE TEMPERANCE ACT IN THE CITY
    OF QUEBEC

Appointed on July 26, 1917 by Order in Council P. C. 2049 under
Part I of the Inquiries Act (R. S. C., 1906, c. 104) and on the recom-
mendation of the Secretary of State.
Commissioner: Oscar Coderre.

Report

Not located.
Notes: Cost: $223.85.

210 COMMISSION TO INQUIRE INTO THE WHOLESALE AND RETAIL COST
    OF NECESSITIES OF LIFE FOR USE BY MINERS IN DISTRICT 18,
    BRITISH COLUMBIA AND ALBERTA

Appointed on August 25, 1917 by Order in Council P. C. 2386
under Part I of the Inquiries Act (R. S. C., 1906, c. 104) and on the
recommendation of the Minister of Labour.
Commissioners: Frederick Ernest Harrison, W. F. McNeill
and Frank Wheatley.

Report

Not located.
Notes: Cost: $2,684.32.

211 COMMISSION TO INVESTIGATE AND REPORT UPON THE EXPORT OF
    HYDRO-ELECTRIC POWER TO THE UNITED STATES, IN PARTICU-
    LAR BY ONTARIO POWER COMPANY, CANADIAN NIAGARA POWER
    COMPANY AND THE ELECTRICAL DEVELOPMENT COMPANY

Appointed on September 11, 1917 by Order in Council P. C. 2531
on the recommendation of the Minister of Internal Revenue. No indication of authorizing statute given in Order in Council.
Commissioner: Sir Henry Lumley Drayton.

Report

Dated May, 1919. Tabled in the House of Commons on June 2,
1919. Sessional Paper no. 279-1919. Not printed in Sessional Papers
Series. Printed as:

Report on export of electricity from Canada, and Report of the
Power Controller. Ottawa, King's Printer, 1919. 68 p.

212 COMMISSION TO INQUIRE INTO AND REPORT UPON THE NATURE AND
    CAUSES OF THE UNREST AMONG THE EMPLOYEES OF THE CON-
    SOLIDATED MINING AND SMELTING COMPANY, OF TRAIL, IN THE
    PROVINCE OF BRITISH COLUMBIA

   Appointed on November 27, 1917 by Order in Council P. C. 3278
   under Part I of the Inquiries Act (R. S. C. , 1906, c. 104) and on the
   recommendation of the Minister of Labour.
   Commissioner: William Henry Armstrong.

                              Report
   Not located.


213 COMMISSION TO INVESTIGATE INTO AND REPORT UPON DIFFERENCES
    CONCERNING WAGES BETWEEN THE MUNICIPAL CORPORATION OF
    THE CITY OF EDMONTON AND ITS STREET CAR EMPLOYEES

   Appointed on December 8, 1917 by Order in Council P. C. 3126
   under Part I of the Inquiries Act (R. S. C. , 1906, c. 104) and on the
   recommendation of the Minister of Labour.
   Commissioner: Maitland Stewart McCarthy.

                              Report
   Not located.
   Notes: Cost: $382.75.


214 COMMISSION TO INVESTIGATE AND REPORT UPON THE CHARGES
    AGAINST DANIEL J. KEARNEY (INLAND REVENUE DEPARTMENT) -
    SPECIAL CLASS EXCISEMAN IN MONTREAL

   Appointed on December 17, 1917 by Order in Council P. C. 3406
   under Part I of the Inquiries Act (R. S. C. , 1906, c. 104) and on the
   recommendation of the Minister of Justice.
   Commissioner: Thomas J. Coonan.

                              Report
   Not located.
   Notes: Cost: $7,165.68.


215 ROYAL COMMISSION ON THE PILOTAGE DISTRICTS OF MIRAMICHI,
    SYDNEY, LOUISBOURG, HALIFAX, ST. JOHN, MONTREAL AND
    QUEBEC

Appointed on February 1, 1918 by Order in Council P. C. 264
under Part I of the Inquiries Act (R. S. C. , 1906  c. 104) and on the
recommendation of the Minister of Marine and Fisheries.  Extended
on February 28, 1918 and March 28, 1918 by Orders in Council P. C.
458 and P. C. 786 respectively.

Commissioners: Thomas Robb, Chairman, James Nunn Bales
and James W. Harrison.

Secretary: J. T. Rowan.

### Report

Dated September 10, 1918.  Tabled in the House of Commons
on March 4, 1919.  Sessional Paper no. 104-1919.  Printed as:

Report of the Royal Commission on the pilotage districts of
Miramichi, Sydney, Louisbourg, Halifax, St. John, Montreal and
Quebec.  Printed by Order of Parliament.  Ottawa, J. de Labroquerie
Taché, Printer to the King's Most Excellent Majesty, 1919.  27 p.

Also issued as a separate.

Notes: Twelve public sessions held.  96 witnesses were examined.

### 216 COMMISSION TO INVESTIGATE INTO UNREST IN THE SHIPBUILDING INDUSTRY IN BRITISH COLUMBIA

Appointed on March 2, 1918 by Order in Council P. C. 521 under
Part I of the Inquiries Act (R. S. C. , 1906, c. 104) and on the recommendation of the Minister of Labour.

Commissioners: Dennis Murphy, Chairman, J. H. Tonkin and
Gordon J. Kelly.

### Report

Not located.

Notes:  Cost: $4,556.53.

### 217 ROYAL COMMISSION ON CONDITIONS IN THE PILOTAGE DISTRICTS OF VANCOUVER, VICTORIA, NANAIMO AND NEW WESTMINSTER

Appointed on March 28, 1918 by Order in Council P. C. 787 under
Part I of the Inquiries Act (R. S. C. , 1906, c. 104) and on the recommendation of the Minister of Marine and Fisheries.

Commissioners: Thomas Robb, Chairman, James Nunn Bales
and Henry Pybus.

Secretary: J. T. Rowan.

### Report

Dated November 6, 1918.  Tabled in the House of Commons on
March 4, 1919.  Sessional Paper no. 105-1919.  Printed as:

Report of the Royal Commission on conditions in the pilotage districts of Vancouver, Victoria, Nanaimo and New Westminster. Ottawa, J. de Labroquerie Taché, Printer to the King's Most Excellent Majesty, 1919.  13 p.

Also issued as a separate.

Notes: Public hearings held in 4 towns and cities in British Columbia (May 22 - June 5, 1918).  69 witnesses were examined.  Cost: $2,567.95.

218 COMMISSION TO INVESTIGATE UNREST IN THE STEEL-MAKING, COAL-MINING AND SHIPBUILDING INDUSTRIES IN THE PROVINCE OF NOVA SCOTIA

Appointed on April 22, 1918 by Order in Council P.C. 973 under Part I of the Inquiries Act (R.S.C., 1906, c. 104) and on the recommendation of the Minister of Labour.

Commissioners: Joseph Andrew Chisholm, Chairman, Rev. John Forrest and J. B. McLachlan.

Reports

Printed as:

"Reports of Royal Commission appointed to deal with disputes in industries engaged in coal mining, steel making and shipbuilding in Nova Scotia" in Labour Gazette, XVIII, July, 1918, pp. 520-525.

Report re Nova Scotia Steel and Coal Company, Limited and employees at Sydney Mines, Nova Scotia: Dated May 18, 1918. pp. 520-521.

Report re Nova Scotia Steel and Coal Company, Limited, and employees at North Sydney, Nova Scotia, and Road Makers at the Florence Collery: Dated May 18, 1918. p. 521.

Report re Nova Scotia Steel and Coal Company, Limited and employees at Trenton, Nova Scotia: Dated May 18, 1918. pp. 522-523.

Report re Eastern Car Company, Limited, and employees at Trenton, Nova Scotia: Dated May 10, 1918. pp. 523-524.

Report re J. W. Cumming and Son, Limited, New Glasgow, Nova Scotia, and employees: Dated May 18, 1918. pp. 523-524.

Report re Dominion Iron and Steel Company, Limited, and employees at Sydney, Nova Scotia: Dated May 22, 1918. pp. 524-525.

Notes: Cost: $1,166.82.

219 COMMISSION TO INVESTIGATE AND REPORT UPON CERTAIN ALLEGED IRREGULARITIES AMONG THE MILITARY VOTERS IN THE DECEMBER 17, 1917 GENERAL ELECTION IN THE RIDING OF CHAMBLY-VERCHERES

Appointed on June 6, 1918 by Order in Council P. C. 1430 under Part I of the Inquiries Act (R. S. C., 1906, c. 104) and on the recommendation of the Minister of Justice.

Commissioner: Farquhar Stuart MacLennan.

### Report

Undated. Copy with Order in Council P. C. 2512 of October 12, 1918. (In Public Archives of Canada, R. G. 2, 1, volume 1517). 11 leaves (Includes summary of proceedings).

Notes: Public hearings held in three cities (September 12 - October 3, 1918). 36 witnesses were examined. Cost: $3,108.96.

## 220 COMMISSION TO ENQUIRE INTO AND REPORT UPON THE GRAVE FRICTION AND UNREST EXISTING BETWEEN VARIOUS EMPLOYERS IN THE CITY OF WINNIPEG AND THEIR WORKMEN

Appointed on June 26, 1918 by Order in Council P. C. 1616 under Part I of the Inquiries Act (R. S. C., 1906, c. 104) and on the recommendation of the Minister of Labour.

Commissioners: Thomas Graham Mathers, F. G. Tipping and George Fisher.

### Report

Not located.

Notes: Cost: $1,680.00.

## 221 ROYAL COMMISSION OF INQUIRY INTO THE SHIP-YARDS IN VAN-COUVER

Appointed on July 10, 1918 by Order in Council P. C. 1709 under Part I of the Inquiries Act (R. S. C., 1906, c. 104) and on the recommendation of the Minister of Labour.

Commissioners: William Edward Burns, Chairman, James H. McVety and Edward Albert James.

### Report

Interim Report: Dated September 27, 1918. Printed as:

"Interim Report of Royal Commission appointed to investigate the dispute existing on the British Columbia coast between various ship owners and their employees" in Labour Gazette, XVIII, October, 1918, pp. 810-816.

No further report located.

Notes: Hearings held during July and August in several British Columbia centres. Cost: $3,842.78.

222 ROYAL COMMISSION TO INQUIRE INTO THE ALLEGED UNREST EX-
ISTING IN THE SHIPBUILDING INDUSTRY IN THE PROVINCE OF
QUEBEC

Appointed on July 29, 1918 by Order in Council P. C. 1871 under
Part I of the Inquiries Act (R. S. C. , 1906, c. 104) and on the recommendation of the Minister of Labour.
Commissioners: Farquar Stuart MacLennan, Thomas E. Robb
and John Michael Walsh.

Report

Dated October 2, 1918. Printed as:
"Report of Royal Commission appointed to inquire into the alleged
unrest existing in the shipbuilding industry in the Province of Quebec"
in Labour Gazette, XVIII, November, 1918, pp. 954-967.
Notes: Hearings held in 3 cities (August 6 - October 2, 1918).
Cost: $4,044.78.

223 COMMISSION TO INVESTIGATE CLAIMS FROM CERTAIN ELECTION
OFFICERS IN THE WESTERN PROVINCES OF THE DOMINION,
PARTICULARLY WITHIN THE PROVINCE OF BRITISH COLUMBIA

Appointed on September 13, 1918 by Order in Council P. C. 2262
on the recommendation of the Secretary of State. No indication of
authorizing statute given in Order in Council.
Commissioner: William Francis O'Connor.

Report

Not located.

224 COMMISSION TO INVESTIGATE ALLEGED ILL-TREATMENT OF THE
MEN OF THE CANADIAN EXPEDITIONARY FORCE WHILE ON BOARD
THE TRANSPORT "NORTHLAND" ON HER VOYAGE FROM LIVERPOOL
TO HALIFAX

Appointed on January 2, 1919 by Order in Council P. C. 3210 under
Part I of the Inquiries Act (R. S. C. , 1906, c. 104) and on the recom-
mendation of the Prime Minister.
Commissioner: Frank Egerton Hodgins.

Report

Dated January 25, 1919. Tabled in the House of Commons on
February 28, 1919. Not printed. Copy in the Public Archives of
Canada (R. G. 33, no. 59). 13 leaves.

Notes: Hearings held January 2 - January 11, 1919.  86 witnesses appeared before the Commission.


225 COMMISSION TO INVESTIGATE INTO AND REPORT UPON CERTAIN REPRESENTATIONS MADE CONCERNING THE ADMINISTRATION OF THE FISHERIES IN THE BERKLEY SOUND DISTRICT, AND THE FISHERIES DISTRICT NUMBER 3, PROVINCE OF BRITISH COLUMBIA

Appointed on January 20, 1919 by Order in Council P. C. 114 under the Inquiries Act (R. S. C. , 1906, c. 104) and on the recommendation of the Minister of Naval Service.  Part of Inquiries Act not stated in the Order in Council.  Extended on March 14, 1919 by Order in Council P. C. 556.

Commissioner: David MacEwan Eberts.

Report

No report submitted as late as June 29, 1921. [1]  It seems unlikely that any Report was ever presented.  From the autumn of 1919 to mid-1921 several attempts were made to obtain a report from the Commissioner.

Notes: Hearings held at three centres in British Columbia (February 5 - October 10, 1919).  Cost: $7,867.11.


226 COMMISSION TO INVESTIGATE CHANGES IN THE COST OF LIVING IN THE COAL MINING LOCALITIES OF THE ISLAND OF VANCOUVER AFFECTING AGREEMENTS BETWEEN MINE OWNERS AND EMPLOYEES

Appointed on January 21, 1919 by Order in Council P. C. 151/53 under Part I of the Inquiries Act (R. S. C. , 1906, c. 104) and on the recommendation of the Minister of Labour.

Commissioners: D. T. Bulger, Chairman, Tully Boyce, John McAllister, [2] and Matther Gunniss. [3]

Report

Not located.

Notes: Cost: $1,873.90.

----

[1] Department of Fisheries files, W. A. Found (Assistant Deputy Minister of Fisheries to J. A. Motherwell, Chief Inspector of Fisheries, June 29, 1921.

[2] Retired.  Replaced by Gunniss.

[3] Appointed on June 15, 1921 by Order in Council P. C. 123/2045.

227 COMMISSION TO INVESTIGATE ILLEGAL LOBSTER FISHING IN THE
    SHEDIAC SUB-DIVISION OF NEW BRUNSWICK

Appointed on January 30, 1919 by Order in Council P.C. 205
under the Inquiries Act (R. S. C., 1906, c. 104) and on the recommendation of the Minister of Naval Service.   Part of Inquiries Act not stated
in the Order in Council.
    Commissioner: Ward Fisher.

Report
    Dated March 31, 1919.   Not printed.   Typewritten copy in the
Department of Fisheries files.
    Notes: Hearings held at Shediac, New Brunswick (March 11 - 12,
1919).   9 witnesses appeared before the Commission.   34 pages of
evidence taken.


228 COMMISSION TO INVESTIGATE INTO AND REPORT CONCERNING THE
    RELATIONS BETWEEN THE FIRM OF J. COUGHLAN   AND SONS,
    AND ITS EMPLOYEES

Appointed on February 6, 1919 by Order in Council P.C. 261
under Part I of the Inquiries Act (R. S. C., 1906, c. 104) and on the
recommendation of the Minister of Labour.
    Commissioners: Denis Murphy, Chairman, Harry Holgate Watson
and Frederick Wallis Welch.

Reports
    Interim Report: dated April 1, 1919.   Printed as:
    "Interim Report of Royal Commission inquiring into the differences
between the firm of J. Coughlan and Sons, Vancouver, and its employees" in Labour Gazette, XIX, April, 1919, pp. 431-432.
    Final Report: dated July 24, 1919.   Printed as:
    "The Coughlan Shipyard Dispute.   Final Report of the Royal Com-
mission appointed to enquire into the differences.   Ship Committee to
be created" in Labour Gazette, XIX, August, 1919, pp. 903-907.
    Notes: Cost: $3,883.81.


229 COMMISSION TO INQUIRE INTO AND REPORT UPON INDUSTRIAL
    RELATIONS IN CANADA

Appointed on April 4, 1919 by Order in Council P.C. 670 on the
recommendation of the Minister of Labour.   Members named on April
9, 1919 by Order in Council P.C. 784.   No indication of authorizing
statute given in Order in Council.

Commissioners: Thomas Graham Mathers, Chairman, Smeaton White, Charles Harrison, Frank Pauzé, T. Moore, J. W. Bruce and Carl Riordon.

Secretary: Thomas Bengough.

### Reports

Majority Report: dated June 29, 1919. 34 leaves.

Minority Report: (Signed by White and Pauzé): dated June 25, 1915. Tabled in the House of Commons on July 1, 1919. Sessional Paper no. 184b-1919. Not printed. Copy in Sessional Paper Office, Parliament Buildings, Ottawa.

Notes: Hearings held in 28 industrial centres (April 26 - June 13, 1919). 486 witnesses were examined. Cost: $27,973.

230 COMMISSION TO INVESTIGATE INTO AND REPORT UPON THE POTEN-TIALITIES OF THE ARCTIC AND SUB-ARCTIC REGIONS OF CANADA AS A GRAZING COUNTRY FOR THE DEVELOPMENT OF MUSK OX AND REINDEER HERDS FOR COMMERCIAL AND NATIONAL PUR-POSES

Appointed on May 20, 1919 by Order in Council P. C. 1079 under Part I of the Inquiries Act (R. S. C., 1906, c. 104) and on the recommendation of the Minister of the Interior.

Commissioners: John Gunion Rutherford, Chairman, James Stanley McLean, James Bernard Harkin and Vilhjalmur Stefansson. [1]

### Report

Dated April 1, 1921. Tabled in the House of Commons on May 4, 1921. Sessional Paper no. 162-1921. Not printed in Sessional Papers Series. Printed as:

Report of the Royal Commission appointed by Order in Council of date May 20, 1919 to investigate the possibilities of the reindeer and musk-ox industries in the Arctic and Sub-Arctic regions of Canada. John Gunion Rutherford, C. M. G., Chairman. James Stanley McLean, Commissioner. James Bernard Harkin, Commissioner. Ottawa, F. A. Acland, Printer to the King's Most Excellent Majesty, 1922. 99 p.

Notes: Hearings at Ottawa (January 24 - May 12, 1920). 35 persons gave evidence. Cost: $1,266.58.

231 COMMISSION TO INQUIRE INTO CERTAIN CHARGES BY REV. K. H.

---

[1] Resigned from the Commission on May 12, 1920.

PALMER AND SIR SAM HUGHES RELATING TO THE ADMINISTRA-
TION AT GUELPH NOVITIATE

Appointed on August 14, 1919 by Order in Council P. C. 1683
under Part I of the Inquiries Act (R. S. C., 1906, c. 104) and on the
recommendation of the Minister of the Interior.
Commissioners: William Edward Middleton and Joseph Andrew
Chisholm.

### Report

Not located.
Notes: Cost: $4,534.73.


232 COMMISSION TO INVESTIGATE INTO AND REPORT UPON THE CON-
DITIONS PERTAINING TO THE RUNNING OF RACE MEETS AND
BETTING IN CONNECTION THEREWITH IN CANADA

Appointed on August 23, 1919 by Order in Council P. C. 1646
under Part I of the Inquiries Act (R. S. C., 1906, c. 104) and on the
recommendation of the Prime Minister.
Commissioner: John Gunion Rutherford.

### Report

Dated March 9, 1920. Sessional Paper no. 67-1920. Not printed
in Sessional Papers Series. Printed as:
Royal Commission in racing inquiry. Report of J. G. Rutherford,
C. M. G., Commissioner. Printed by Order of Parliament. Ottawa,
J. de Lambroquerie Taché, Printer to the King's Most Excellent
Majesty, 1920. 96 p.
Notes: Public hearings held in 9 cities. Cost $9,332.46.


233 COMMISSION TO INVESTIGATE THE SALE OF LANDS, LIVESTOCK
AND AGRICULTURAL EQUIPMENT TO SOLDIERS IN THE EDMONTON
DISTRICT

Appointed on October 22, 1919 by Order in Council P. C. 2166
under Part I of the Inquiries Act (R. S. C., 1906, c. 104) and on the
recommendation of the Minister of the Interior.
Commissioner: John Barnett.

### Report

Not located.

234 COMMISSION TO INVESTIGATE AND REPORT UPON THE LOCKOUT
    AT GUILLET AND SONS, MARIEVILLE, QUEBEC

    Appointed on January 29, 1920 by Order in Council P. C. 203
    under Part I of the Inquiries Act (R. S. C., 1906, c. 104) and on the
    recommendation of the Minister of Labour.
    Commissioner: Joseph Perrault.

                              Report
        Not located.
        Notes: Cost: $755.64.


235 COMMISSION TO INQUIRE INTO AND REPORT CONCERNING A DISPUTE
    THAT HAS ARISEN BETWEEN THE INTERNATIONAL BROTHERHOOD
    OF TEAMSTERS, CHAUFFEURS, STABLEMEN AND HELPERS IN THE
    SAID CITY OF VANCOUVER AS TO WAGE RATES AND OTHER CON-
    DITIONS OF EMPLOYMENT AFFECTING THE ABOVE MENTIONED
    CLASSES OF LABOUR IN THE EMPLOY OF THE VARIOUS CARTAGE,
    TRANSFER, EXPRESS AND DELIVERY COMPANIES, MEMBERS OF
    THE GENERAL CARTAGE AND WAREHOUSEMAN'S ASSOCIATION OF
    THE SAID PROVINCE

    Appointed on March 5, 1920 by Order in Council P. C. 484 under
    Part I of the Inquiries Act (R. S. C., 1906, c. 104) and on the recom-
    mendation of the Minister of Labour.
    Commissioner: Rev. William H. Vance.

                              Report
        Undated.   Printed as:
        "Report of Royal Commission appointed under the Inquiries Act
    to investigate the dispute between the members of the General Cartage
    and Warehousemen's Association of British Columbia, Vancouver, B. C.,
    and certain of their employees." in Labour Gazette, XX, April, 1920,
    pp. 409-411.
        Notes: Three public sessions held.   Several days were spent in
    negotiating a basis of working conditions agreeable to both parties.
    Cost: $212.30.


236 COMMISSION TO INVESTIGATE UNIFORMITY OF LAWS RELATING TO
    INDUSTRIAL WORK IN CANADA

    Appointed on April 10, 1920 by Order in Council P. C. 721 under
    Part I of the Inquiries Act (R. S. C., 1906, c. 104) and on the recom-
    mendation of the Minister of Labour.

Commissioners: Frederick Albert Acland, Chairman, J. G. Merrick, Thomas Moore, J. Welsford Macdonald, Fulton J. Logan, John A. Gillis, C. W. Robinson, Angus McLean, G. R. Melvin, Louis O. Guyon, John Lowe, Gustave Francq, W. A. Riddell, Samuel Harris, H. J. Halford, E. McGrath, H. B. Lyall, E. Robinson, T. M. Molloy, R. K. Leckie, James Somerville, John T. Stirling, Walter F. McNeill, Robert McCreath, J. D. McNiven, John J. Coughlan and James H. McVety.

### Report

Dated May 1, 1920. Printed as:

"Uniformity of Labour laws. Report of the Dominion-Provincial Commission appointed to consider the subject" in Labour Gazette, XX, May, 1920, pp. 540-547.

Notes: The Commission opened hearings at Ottawa on April 26, 1920. Four Committees were formed within the Commission to consider various aspects of the Commission's work. Cost: $3,464.07.

237 COMMISSION TO INQUIRE INTO COAL MINING OPERATIONS IN NOVA SCOTIA AND NEW BRUNSWICK

Appointed on July 3, 1920 by Order in Council P. C. 1515 under Part I of the Inquiries Act (R. S. C., 1906, c. 104) and on the recommendation of the Minister of Labour.

Commissioners: Eugene McGrath Quirk, Sir William Stavert and William P. Hutchison.[1]

### Report

Dated September 9, 1920. Printed as:

"Report of Royal Commission to deal with disputes in connection with coal mining operations in Nova Scotia and New Brunswick" in Labour Gazette, XX, September, 1920, pp. 1169-1184.

Notes: Sittings held in 11 towns and cities in Nova Scotia and New Brunswick. Cost: $5,156.57.

238 COMMISSION TO INVESTIGATE THE TREATMENT OF SOLDIERS' DEPENDENTS ON THE S. S. SCANDINAVIAN WHO ARRIVED AT PORT OF ST. JOHN ON JANUARY 10, 1919

Appointed on July 8, 1920 by Order in Council P. C. 1558 on the recommendation of the Minister of Militia and Defence. No indication

---

[1] Appointed on July 12, 1920 by Order in Council P. C. 1592.

of authorizing statute given in Order in Council.
Commissioner: William Botsford Chandler.

Report

Not located.

239 COMMISSION TO INQUIRE INTO AND REPORT UPON PRODUCTION
COSTS OF COAL OPERATORS, DISTRICT 18, PROVINCE OF BRITISH
COLUMBIA

Appointed on November 26, 1920 by Order in Council P. C. 2876
under Part I of the Inquiries Act (R. S. C. , 1906, c. 104) and on the
recommendation of the Minister of Labour.
Commissioner: David S. Kerr.

Report

Not located.
Notes: Cost: $2,458.27.

240 COMMISSION TO INQUIRE INTO THE CIRCUMSTANCES CONNECTED
WITH THE DISPOSAL OF PRINTED MATTER IN THE DISTRIBUTION
OFFICE OF THE GOVERNMENT PRINTING AND STATIONERY OFFICE
AND AT THE SAME TIME TO INVESTIGATE THE PARTICULARS OF
ALL MATERIAL AND EQUIPMENT PURCHASED, SOLD OR OTHER-
WISE DISPOSED OF IN OR FROM THE GOVERNMENT PRINTING
BUREAU SINCE THE 1ST DAY OF JANUARY, 1919

Appointed on December 27, 1920 by Order in Council P. C. 3208
under Part I of the Inquiries Act (R. S. C. , 1906, c. 104) and on the
recommendation of the Secretary of State.
Commissioner: George Colin Snider.

Reports

Preliminary Report: dated March 10, 1921. Copy not located.
Final Report: dated June 6, 1921. Copy attached to Order in
Council P. C. 2279 of June 27, 1921. (In Public Archives of Canada,
R. G. 2, 1, volume 1636). 21 leaves.
Notes: Cost: $1,425.30.

241 COMMISSION TO INQUIRE INTO THE SUBJECT OF THE MARKETING
OF GRAIN IN CANADA

Appointed on April 12, 1921 by Order in Council P. C. 1270 under

Part I of the Inquiries Act (R. S. C., 1906, c. 104) and on the recommendation of the Minister of Trade and Commerce.

Commissioners: James Duncan Hyndman, William D. Staples, J. H. Haslam and Lincoln Goldie.

Secretary: C. Birkett.

Report

Not located.

Notes: Cost: $46,373.12.

242 COMMISSION TO INVESTIGATE INTO AND REPORT IN RESPECT TO THE "AMOUNT REQUIRED TO PAY THE PARK ST. CHARLES COMPANY, LIMITED, FOR LAND OCCUPIED BY THE QUEBEC HARBOUR COMMISSION, AS PER VERDICT OF ARBITRATOR, WHICH VERDICT WAS LATER SUSTAINED BY THE SUPERIOR COURT IN FAVOUR OF THE PLAINTIFF COMPANY, $60,000"

Appointed on June 27, 1921 by Order in Council P. C. 2170 under the Inquiries Act (R. S. C., 1906, c. 104) and on the recommendation of the Minister of Justice. Part of Inquiries Act not stated in the Order in Council.

Commissioner: Louis Edmond Panneton.

Report

Not located.

Notes: Cost: $231.90.

243 COMMISSION REGARDING STERLING FUND-REDEMPTION AT PAR TO EX-MEMBERS OF THE CANADIAN EMERGENCY FORCE

Appointed on June 27, 1921 by Order in Council P. C. 2286 under Part I of the Inquiries Act (R. S. C., 1906, c. 104) and on the recommendation of the Minister of Labour.

Commissioner: Geoffrey Teignmouth Clarkson.

Report

Dated February 28, 1922. Copy attached to Order in Council P. C. 537 of March 8, 1922. (In Public Archives of Canada, R. G. 2, 1, volume 1666). 45 leaves.

Notes: Hearings held in 5 cities. Cost: $26,203.10.

244 ROYAL COMMISSION ON REPARATION CLAIMS

Appointed on October 31, 1921 by Order in Council P. C. 4032 under Part I of the Inquiries Act (R. S. C. , 1906, c. 104) and on the recommendation of the Secretary of State.

Commissioners: Sir John Douglas Hazen, William Pugsley, [1] and James Friel. [2]

### Report

Dated December 14, 1927. Tabled in the House of Commons on May 22, 1928. Sessional Paper no. 280-1928. Printed as:

Reparations. The report of the Royal Commissioner appointed by His Excellency the Governor General in Council under the provisions of Part I of the Inquiries Act, Chapter 104 of the Revised Statutes of Canada, and Amending Act, Chapter 28, 2 George V, to investigate and report upon all claims which may be submitted to the Commissioner for the purpose of determining whether they are within the first Annex to Section I of Part VIII of the Treaty of Versailles, and the fair amount of such claims; and for the return of sequestrated property in necessitous circumstances. Dated at Ottawa this 14th day of December, 1927. Ottawa, F. A. Acland, Printer to the King's Most Excellent Majesty, 1928. 2 v. (776 p. ).

Notes: Cost: $210, 086.57.

245 COMMISSION TO INVESTIGATE FISHERIES CONDITIONS IN BRITISH COLUMBIA

Appointed on July 10, 1922 by Order in Council P. C. 1466 under Part I of the Inquiries Act (R. S. C. , 1906, c. 104) and on the recommendation of the Minister of Fisheries.

Commissioners: William Duff, Chairman, Charles Herbert Dickie, Alan Webster Neil, Alfred Stork, Lewis Herbert Martell, William Garland McQuarrie, Alexander W. Chisholm, [3] and Henry Herbert Stevens. [4]

Secretary: E. Knicle.

### Reports

Preliminary Report: dated November 18, 1922. No copy located.
Final Report: dated February 28, 1923. Printed as:

---

[1] Appointed on March 13, 1923 by Order in Council P. C. 165. Pugsley died on March 3, 1925.
[2] Appointed on June 19, 1925 by Order in Council P. C. 938.
[3] Owing to illness in his family, he was unable to take part in its deliberations.
[4] Replaced by McQuarrie (Order in Council P. C. 1544 of July 24, 1922).

British Columbia Fisheries Commission, 1922. Report and recommendations. Ottawa, F. A. Acland, Printer to the King's Most Excellent Majesty, 1923. 33 p.

Notes: Sittings held August 14 - September 14, 1922. 191 witnesses appeared before the Commission. Cost: $10,284.42.


246 ROYAL COMMISSION ON PENSIONS AND RE-ESTABLISHMENT

Appointed on July 22, 1922 by Order in Council P. C. 1525 under Part I of the Inquiries Act (R. S. C., 1906, c. 104) and on the recommendation of the Department of Soldiers' Civil Re-establishment.

Commissioners: James Layton Ralston, Chairman, Walter McKeown and Arthur Edward Dubuc.

Secretary: H. D. Dewar.

Reports

First part of investigation: dated February 1923. Tabled in the House of Commons on March 28, 1923. Sessional Paper no. 154-1923. Printed as:

Royal Commission on pensions and re-establishment. Report on first part of investigation. (Matters referred to in G. W. V. A. telegram). February, 1923. Ottawa, F. A. Acland, Printer to the King's Most Excellent Majesty, 1923. 130 p.

Also issued as a separate.

First interim report on second part of investigation: dated April, 1923. Tabled in the House of Commons on May 21, 1923. Sessional Paper no. 154a-1923. Printed as:

Royal Commission on pensions and re-establishment. First interim report on second part of investigation. April, 1923. Printed by order of Parliament. Ottawa, F. A. Acland, Printer to the King's Most Excellent Majesty, 1923. 26 p.

Also issued as a separate.

Second interim report on second part of investigation: dated May, 1924. Tabled in the House of Commons on May 12, 1924. Sessional Paper no. 203-1924. Printed as:

Royal Commission on pensions and re-establishment. Second interim report on second part of investigation. May, 1924. Printed by order of Parliament. Ottawa, F. A. Acland, Printer to the King's Most Excellent Majesty, 1924. 77 p.

Also issued as a separate.

Final report on second part of investigation: dated July 5, 1924. Tabled in the House of Commons on July 18, 1924. Sessional Paper no. 203a-1924. Printed as:

Royal Commission on pensions and re-establishment. Final report on second part of investigation. Printed by order of Parliament.

July, 1924. Ottawa, F. A. Acland, Printer to the King's Most Excellent Majesty, 1924. 191 p.

Notes: The first part of the investigation was concerned with
certain charges against the Pensions Board contained in a telegram
sent out by the Great War Veterans Association. The Commission
held public hearings on 29 days (July - November, 1922). About
3,800 typewritten pages of evidence taken.

The second part of the investigation was concerned with suggestions and complaints respecting pensions, treatment and re-establishment, particularly affecting handicapped men. Public hearings were
held at 9 different centres for 38 days. 160 witnesses gave evidence.
5,800 pages of evidence taken with 200 exhibits. Cost: $122,252.19.


247 COMMISSION TO INVESTIGATE INTO AND REPORT AS TO WHETHER
THE DISMISSAL OF ALBERT M. GOGUEN FROM THE POSITION OF
FISHERY GUARDIAN WAS JUSTIFIED ON THE GROUND OF INEFFI-
CIENCY AND WHETHER WILFRED BOURGEOIS HAS EFFICIENTLY
DISCHARGED HIS DUTIES IN A SIMILAR POSITION AND WHETHER
EITHER OF THE ABOVE NAMED FISHERY GUARDIANS WAS GUILTY
OF POLITICAL PARTIZANSHIP

Appointed on December 22, 1922 by Order in Council P.C. 2533
under the Inquiries Act (R.S.C., 1906, c. 104) and on the recommendation of the Minister of Marine and Fisheries. Part of Inquiries Act
not stated in the Order in Council.

Commissioner: Louis Robichaud.

Report

Undated. (Received in the Department of Marine and Fisheries on
January 9, 1923). Not printed. Typewritten copy in the Department
of Fisheries files. 5 leaves.

Notes: Hearings held December 5 - 6, 1922. Ten witnesses
appeared before the Commission.


248 ROYAL COMMISSION ON GREAT LAKES GRAIN RATES

Appointed on January 17, 1923 by Order in Council P.C. 118
under Part I of the Inquiries Act (R.S.C., 1906, c. 104) and on the
recommendation of His Excellency the Governor General in Council.

Commissioners: Simon James McLean, Chairman, Thomas
Lewis Tremblay and Levi Thompson.

Secretary: William Thomas Rochester Preston.

Report

Dated May 14, 1923. Tabled in the House of Commons on May 18,

1923. Sessional Paper no. 211-1923.  Printed as:
  Royal Commission.  S. J. McLean, LL. B. , Chairman, General
T. L. Tremblay, Levi Thompson.  Lake Grain Rates.  Report.  W. T. R.
Preston, Secretary.  Printed by order of Parliament.  Ottawa, F. A.
Acland, Printer to the King's Most Excellent Majesty, 1923.  53 p.
  Also issued as a separate.
  Notes: Hearings held in 4 cities.  Commissioners also visited
5 American lake ports.  Cost: $41,012.00.


249 COMMISSION TO INVESTIGATE AND REPORT UPON THE AFFAIRS OF
    THE SIX NATIONS INDIANS

  Appointed on March 20, 1923 by Order in Council P. C. 44/505
under Part I of the Inquiries Act (R. S. C. , 1906, c. 104) and on the
recommendation of the Treasury Board.
  Commissioner: Andrew Thorburn Thompson.

                          Reports
  Dated November 22, 1923.  Printed as:
  Department of Indian Affairs.  Honourable Charles Stewart,
Superintendent General.  Duncan C. Scott, F. R. S. C. , Litt. D. ,
Deputy Superintendent General.  Report by Col. Andrew T. Thompson,
B. A. , LL. B. , Commissioner to investigate and enquire into the
affairs of the Six Nations Indians.  1923.  Ottawa, F. A. Acland,
Printer to the King's Most Excellent Majesty, 1924.  26 p.
  Location: Library of Parliament, Ottawa.
  Notes: The Commissioner held personal interviews with a number
of Indians.  Several open meetings held at Ohsweken.  Cost: $5,510. 34.


250 COMMISSION TO INQUIRE INTO AND REPORT UPON PAYMENT MADE
    OR AUTHORIZED BY THE GRAND TRUNK RAILWAY COMPANY OF
    CANADA

  Appointed on April 21, 1923 by Order in Council P. C. 713 under
Part I of the Inquiries Act (R. S. C. , 1906, c. 104) and on the recom-
mendation of the Minister of Railways and Canals.
  Commissioners: Frederick Tennyson Congdon and Frederick
Henry Honeywell. [1]

                          Report
  Dated January 3, 1924.  Tabled in the House of Commons on

---

[1] Replaced Congdon.  Appointed on May 18, 1923 by Order in Council
P. C. 894.

March 17, 1924. Sessional Paper no. 99-1924. Not printed. Copy
in Sessional Paper Office, Parliament Buildings, Ottawa. 20 leaves.
     Notes: Hearings held at Montreal (July 4 - September 27, 1923).
15 witnesses appeared before the Commission. 23 exhibits placed
before the Commission. Cost: $2,450.90.


251 ROYAL GRAIN INQUIRY COMMISSION

     Appointed on May 1, 1923 by Order in Council P. C. 774 under
Part I of the Inquiries Act (R. S. C., 1906, c. 104) and on the recom-
mendation of the Minister of Trade and Commerce.
     Commissioners: Wilfred Ferdinand Alphonse Turgeon, Chairman,
James Guthrie Scott, William John Rutherford and Duncan Alexander
McGibbon.
     Secretary: Robert Dezchman.

Reports
     Interim Report: dated June 19, 1924. Tabled in the House of
Commons on July 7, 1924. Sessional Paper no. 287-1924. Not
printed in Sessional Papers Series. Printed as:
     Interim Report of the Royal Grain Inquiry Commission. Vancouver,
B. C., June 19, 1924. Printed by order of Parliament. Ottawa, F. A.
Acland, Printer to the King's Most Excellent Majesty, 1924. 32 p.
     Final Report: dated January 7, 1925. Tabled in the House of
Commons on February 9, 1925. Sessional Paper no. 35-1925. Not
printed in Sessional Papers Series. Printed as:
     Dominion of Canada. Report of the Royal Grain Inquiry Commis-
sion. Printed by order of Parliament. Ottawa, F. A. Acland, Printer
to the King's Most Excellent Majesty, 1925. 217 p.
     Notes: Public hearings opened on June 25, 1923. Cost:
$170,295.67.


252 COMMISSION TO INVESTIGATE INTO AND REPORT IN RESPECT OF
     DYNAMITE STICKS PLACED NEAR THE ROAD OUTSIDE THE HATCH-
     ERY GATE AT NORTH EAST MARGAREE, IN THE PROVINCE OF
     NOVA SCOTIA AND IN THE HATCHERY YARD; ALSO IN RESPECT
     OF THE INTERFERENCE WITH THE SCREENS IN THE SALMON
     REARING POND AND THE DAMAGE AND INJURY TO THE LANTERNS
     AT A TRAP SET FOR CATCHING PARENT TROUT FOR HATCHERY
     PURPOSES AT THAT PLACE

     Appointed on August 1, 1923 by Order in Council P. C. 1396 under
the Inquiries Act (R. S. C., 1906, c. 104) and on the recommendation
of the Minister of Marine and Fisheries. Part of Inquiries Act not
stated in the Order in Council.

Commissioner: Charles Deering La Nause.

Report

Dated October 4, 1923. Not printed. Carbon of typewritten copy in the Department of Fisheries files. 4 leaves.

Notes: Hearings held at North East Margaree, New Brunswick, (September 18 - 19, 1923). 14 witnesses appeared before the Commission.

253 ROYAL COMMISSION ON PULPWOOD

Appointed on August 14, 1923 by Order in Council P. C. 1576 under the Inquiries Act (R. S. C. , 1906, c. 104) and on the recommendation of the Minister of Finance. Part of Inquiries Act not stated in the Order in Council.

Commissioners: Joseph Picard, Chairman, William A. Anstie, Joseph G. Sutherland, Apollos Bamber Kerr and Robert W. McLennan. [1]

Secretary: E. H. Finlayson.

Report

Dated July 1924. Tabled in the House of Commons on July 18, 1924. Sessional Paper no. 310-1924. Not printed in Sessional Papers Series. Printed as:

Report of the Royal Commission on Pulpwood. Canada. Chairman: Joseph Picard. Deputy Chairman: William A. Anstie. Commissioners: Joseph G. Sutherland, R. W. McLellan, A. B. Kerr. Secretary: E. H. Finlayson, B. Sc. F. Ottawa, F. A. Acland, Printer to the King's Most Excellent Majesty, 1924. 292 p.

Notes: Hearings held in 31 towns and cities. 382 witnesses appeared before the Commission. Cost: $75,672.51.

254 COMMISSION TO INVESTIGATE AND REPORT UPON THE VALIDITY OF A CLAIM MADE BY CERTAIN INDIANS OF THE CHIPPEWA AND MISSISSAUGA TRIBES WHO HAVE CLAIMED THAT THE SAID TRIBES WERE AND ARE ENTITLED TO A CERTAIN INTEREST IN LANDS IN THE PROVINCE OF ONTARIO TO WHICH THE INDIAN TITLE HAS NEVER BEEN EXTINGUISHED BY SURRENDER AND OTHERWISE, AND SHOULD THE SAID COMMISSION DETERMINE IN FAVOUR OF THE VALIDITY OF THE SAID CLAIMS, TO NEGOTIATE WITH THE SAID INDIANS

---

[1] Did not sign the Report.

Appointed on August 31, 1923 by Order in Council P. C. 1750 under Part I of the Inquiries Act (R. S. C. , 1906, c. 104) and on the recommendation of the Superintendent General of Indian Affairs.

Commissioners: Angus Seymour Williams, Chairman, Robert Victor Sinclair and Uriah McFadden.

### Report

Not located.

Notes: Cost: $15,060.50.

## 255 ROYAL COMMISSION TO INQUIRE INTO INDUSTRIAL UNREST AMONG THE STEEL WORKERS AT SYDNEY, NOVA SCOTIA

Appointed on September 22, 1923 by Order in Council P. C. 1929 under Part I of the Inquiries Act (R. S. C. , 1906, c. 104) and on the recommendation of the Prime Minister.

Commissioners: James W. Robertson, Chairman, James J. Johnston and Fred Bancroft.

### Report

Dated February 9, 1924. Tabled in the House of Commons on March 3, 1924. Sessional Paper no. 39-1924. Not printed in Sessional Papers Series. Printed as:

Report of Commission appointed under Order in Council [ P. C. 1929] , September 22, 1923 to inquire into the industrial unrest among the steel workers at Sydney, Nova Scotia creating conditions which have occasioned the calling out of the Active Militia in aid of the Civil Power and their retention for a considerable period of time in the areas affected. Printed as a supplement to "The Labour Gazette," February, 1924. Printed at the Government Printing Bureau, Ottawa [ 1924] . 24 p.

Notes: 147 witnesses appeared before the Commission. Hearings held at Ottawa and Sydney October 31 - November 28, 1923. Cost: $14,919.93.

## 256 COMMISSION FOR THE REVISION AND CONSOLIDATION OF THE PUBLIC STATUTES OF CANADA

Appointed on December 28, 1923 by Order in Council P. C. 2520 on the recommendation of the Minister of Justice. No indication of authorizing statute given in Order in Council.

Commissioners: Sir Charles Fitzpatrick, Edward John Daly, Herbert Hartly Dewart, [1] Louis Adhemar Rivet, Finley Robert Mc-

---

[1] Replaced by McGregor.

Donald Russell, Edmund Leslie Newcombe and Alexander MacGregor.

### Report
Proclamation dated December 22, 1927.  Printed as:

The revised statutes of Canada, 1927.  Proclaimed and published under the authority of the Act;  Chapter 65 of the Statutes of Canada, 1924.  Ottawa, Printed by Frederick Albert Acland , Law Printer to the King's Most Excellent Majesty  from the roll of the said Revised Statutes deposited in the office of the Clerk of the Parliaments, as authorized by the said Act, Chapter 65 of the Statutes of Canada, 1927.  5 v. (4,913 p. )

Notes:  Cost: $138,473.53.

257 ROYAL COMMISSION TO INQUIRE INTO AND REPORT UPON AFFAIRS OF THE HOME BANK OF CANADA AND IN THE MATTER OF THE PETITION OF THE DEPOSITORS IN THE SAID HOME BANK OF CANADA

Established on February 23, 1924 by Order in Council P. C. 306 under Part I of the Inquiries Act (R. S. C. , 1906, c. 104) and on the recommendation of the Minister of Finance.  Commissioner named on February 27, 1924 by Order in Council P. C. 314.

Commissioner: Harrison Andrew McKeown.

### Report
Dated June 10, 1924.  Tabled in the House of Commons on June 11, 1924.  Sessional Paper no. 100d-1924.  Printed as:

Interim Report: Royal Commission re Home Bank.  Interim Report.  June 10, 1924.  Ottawa, F. A. Acland, Printer to the King's Most Excellent Majesty, 1924. 26 p.

Also issued as a separate.

Notes: Hearings held at Ottawa and Toronto (April 16 - May 20, 1924)  Cost: $42,630.93.

258 COMMISSION TO INVESTIGATE CHARGES THAT FRAUDS AND IRREGULARITIES HAVE OCCURED IN CONNECTION WITH CERTAIN CONTRACTS FOR THE SUPPLY OF COAL TO THE DEPARTMENT OF NATIONAL DEFENCE AT WINNIPEG

Appointed on March 26, 1924 by Order in Council P. C. 473 under Part I of the Inquiries Act (R. S. C. , 1906, c. 104) and on the recommendation of the Minister of National Defence.

Commissioner: David Campbell.

Report

Not located.

Notes: Cost: $20,738.16.


## 259 ROYAL COMMISSION ON MARITIME CLAIMS

Appointed on April 7, 1926 by Order in Council P. C. 505 under Part I of the Inquiries Act (R. S. C., 1906, c. 104) and on the recommendation of the Prime Minister.

Commissioners: Sir Andrew Rae Duncan, Chairman, William Bernard Wallace and Cyrus Macmillan.

Secretary: F. MacLure Sclanders.

Report

Dated September 23, 1926. Tabled in the House of Commons on December 10, 1926. Sessional Paper no. 9-1926/27. Printed as:

Report of the Royal Commission on Maritime Claims. Sir Andrew Rae Duncan, Kt., Chairman; Honourable W. B. Wallace, Prof., Cyrus MacMillan; F. M. Sclanders, F. R. G. S., Secretary. Ottawa, F. A. Acland, Printer to the King's Most Excellent Majesty, 1926. 45 p.

Notes: Public hearings held in 5 cities. Private sessions were held in two other cities. Over 100 witnesses were heard. Cost: $26,409.10.


## 260 COMMISSION TO EXAMINE AND INVESTIGATE THE TRANSACTIONS OF THE TORONTO HARBOUR COMMISSIONERS

Appointed on June 15, 1926 by Order in Council P. C. 927 under Part I of the Inquiries Act (R. S. C., 1906, c. 104) and on the recommendation of the Minister of Marine and Fisheries.

Commissioner: James Herbert Denton.

Report

Dated March 14, 1927. Copy attached to Order in Council P. C. 492 of March 17, 1927. (In Public Archives of Canada, R. G. 2, 1, volume 1781). 184 leaves and volume of appendices (Mostly charts and tables).

Notes: 4,207 pages of evidence taken. 114 exhibits presented to the Commission. Cost: $7,004.61.


## 261 ROYAL COMMISSION ON CUSTOMS AND EXCISE

Appointed on July 20, 1926 by Order in Council P. C. 1161 under Part I of the Inquiries Act (R. S. C. , 1906, c. 104) and on the recommendation of the Prime Minister and the Minister of Justice.

Commissioners: Sir Francois Xavier Lemieux, James Thomas Brown, Chairman, William Henry Wright and Ernest Roy.

Secretary: P. D'Auteuil Leduc.

Reports

Interim Reports Nos. 1 - 10 (December 3, 1926 - October 14, 1927) tabled in the House of Commons on February 2, 1928. Sessional Paper no. 5a-1928. Printed as:

Royal Commission on customs and excise. (Confidential). Interim Reports (Nos. 1 to 10). Ottawa: F. A. Acland, Printer to the King's Most Excellent Majesty, 1928. 119 p.

Final Report: Dated January 27, 1928. Tabled in the House of Commons on January 27, 1928. Sessional Paper no. 5-1928. Printed as:

Royal Commission on customs and excise. Final Report. Ottawa, F. A. Acland, Printer to the King's Most Excellent Majesty, 1928. 24 p.

Notes: Cost: $236,447.51.

262 ROYAL COMMISSION ON RECONVEYANCE OF LAND TO BRITISH COLUMBIA

Appointed on March 8, 1927 by Order in Council P. C. 422 under Part I of the Inquiries Act (R. S. C. , 1906, c. 104) and on the recommendation of the Minister of the Interior.

Commissioner: William Melville Martin.

Report

Letter of transmittal dated February 16, 1928. Tabled in the House of Commons on March 13, 1928. Sessional Paper no. 76a-1928. Printed as:

Report of the Royal Commission. Reconveyance of land to British Columbia. Pursuant to Order in Council of March 8, 1927. Ottawa, F. A. Acland, Printer to the King's Most Excellent Majesty, 1928. 57 p.

Notes: Sessions of the Commission held at Victoria, June, 1927. Cost: $6,976.20.

263 COMMISSION TO INVESTIGATE CHARGES OF MALADMINISTRATION, ETC. , PREFERRED AGAINST CAPTAIN JOHN D. MACKENZIE, SUPERINTENDENT OF PILOTS AT SYDNEY, NOVA SCOTIA

Appointed on March 9, 1927 by Order in Council P. C. 404 under Part I of the Inquiries Act (R. S. C., 1906, c. 104) and on the recommendation of the Minister of Marine and Fisheries.
Commissioner: Arthur McDonald.

### Report

Not located.
Notes: Cost: $423.80.

### 264 ROYAL COMMISSION TO INVESTIGATE CHARGES OF POLITICAL PARTISANSHIP IN THE DEPARTMENT OF SOLDIER'S CIVIL RE-ESTABLISHMENT

Appointed on June 30, 1927 by Order in Council P. C. 1293 under Part I of the Inquiries Act (R. S. C., 1906, c. 104) and on the recommendation of the Acting Prime Minister.
Commissioner: Alfred Taylour Hunter.

### Report

Dated January 10, 1928. Tabled in the House of Commons on February 20, 1928. Sessional Paper no. 118-1928. Printed as:
Report of the Royal Commission appointed to investigate charges of political partisanship in the Department of Soldier's Re-establishment. Ottawa, F. A. Acland, Printer to the King's Most Excellent Majesty, 1928. 31 p.
Notes: Over 100 witnesses gave evidence.

### 265 ROYAL COMMISSION TO INVESTIGATE THE FISHERIES OF THE MARITIME PROVINCES AND THE MAGDALEN ISLANDS

Appointed on October 7, 1927 by Order in Council P. C. 1949 under Part I of the Inquiries Act (R. S. C., 1906 c. 104) and on the recommendation of the Minister of Marine and Fisheries.
Commissioners: Alexander Kenneth Maclean, Chairman, Cyrus Macmillan, Henry Ryder Locke Bill, Joseph Mombourquette and John George Robichaud.
Secretary: E. S. Carter.

### Report

Dated May 4, 1928. Tabled in the House of Commons on May 8, 1928. Sessional Paper no. 256-1928. Printed as:
Report of the Royal Commission investigating the fisheries of the Maritime Provinces and the Magdalen Islands. Ottawa, F. A. Acland, Printer to the King's Most Excellent Majesty, 1928. 119 pp. and maps.

Notes: 49 hearings held.   823 witnesses appeared before the
Commission.   7,700 typewritten pages of evidence taken.   Cost:
$87,699.92.


266 COMMISSION TO INVESTIGATE AND REPORT ON CONDITIONS IN CON-
      NECTION WITH THE TOBACCO PRODUCING INDUSTRY IN THE
      PROVINCES OF ONTARIO AND QUEBEC

Appointed on February 27, 1928 by Order in Council P. C. 298
under Part I of the Inquiries Act (R. S. C., 1927, c. 99) and on the
recommendation of the Minister of Agriculture.
      Commissioners: E. S. Archibald, Chairman, E. P. Tellier
and H. B. Archibald.
      Secretary: A. J. Desfosses.

Report
Undated.   Tabled in the House of Commons on May 11, 1928.
Sessional Paper no. 266-1928.   Printed as:
Report of the Tobacco Inquiry Commission in the Provinces of
Ontario and Quebec. Ottawa, F. A. Acland, Printer to the King's
Most Excellent Majesty, 1928. 49 p.
      Notes: Held hearings in 15 towns and cities in Ontario and
Quebec.


267 COMMISSION TO INVESTIGATE AND REPORT UPON THE ILLEGAL
      REMOVAL OF ALCOHOL IN BOND BY THE SUNSET VINEGAR COM-
      PANY REORGANIZED IN 1925 UNDER THE NAME OF THE BRITISH
      COLUMBIA VINEGAR COMPANY, LIMITED, AND THE BRITISH
      COLUMBIA DISTILLERY COMPANY, LIMITED, NEW WESTMINSTER,
      AND ALSO JOSEPH KENNEDY, LIMITED

Appointed on May 30, 1928 by Order in Council P. C. 908 under
Part I of the Inquiries Act (R. S. C., 1927, c. 99) and on the recommendation of the Minister of National Revenue.
      Commissioner: Gordon Clapp Lindsay.

Report
      Not located.


268 ROYAL COMMISSION ON THE TRANSFER OF THE NATURAL RESOURCES
      OF MANITOBA

Appointed on August 1, 1928 by Order in Council P. C. 1258 under

Part I of the Inquiries Act (R. S. C. , 1927, c. 99) and on the recommendation of the Prime Minister.
    Commissioners: William Ferdinand Alphonse Turgeon, Chairman,
Thomas Alexander Crerar and Charles Martin Bowman.
    Secretary: Oliver Master.

Report

Letter of transmittal dated May 30, 1929. Tabled in the House of
Commons on June 12, 1929. Sessional Paper no. 40a-1929. Printed
as:
    Report of the Royal Commission on the transfer of the natural
resources of Manitoba. Honourable W. F. A. Turgeon, Chairman.
Honourable T. A. Crerar. Charles M. Bowman. Oliver Master, M. A. ,
Secretary. Ottawa, F. A. Acland, Printer to the King's Most Excellent
Majesty, 1929. 46 p.
    Notes: Cost: $16,294. 52.

269 COMMISSION TO INQUIRE INTO THE CLAIM OF ROBERT W. MCLELLAN,
    BARRISTER, FREDERICTON, NEW BRUNSWICK, FOR REMUNERA-
    TION FOR HIS SERVICES AS A PULPWOOD COMMISSIONER

    Appointed on August 30, 1928 by Order in Council P. C. 1589 under
Part I of the Inquiries Act (R. S. C. , 1927, c. 99) and on the recommendation of the Minister of Finance.
    Commissioners: Bennet John Roberts, Chairman, John Chisholm
and Roscoe Marritt Brown.

Report

No action taken by this Commission as late as March 27, 1933.

270 ROYAL COMMISSION ON RADIO BROADCASTING

    Appointed on December 6, 1928 by Order in Council P. C. 2108
on the recommendation of the Minister of Marine and Fisheries. No
indication of authorizing statute given in Order in Council.
    Commissioners: Sir John Aird, Chairman, Charles A. Bowman
and Augustin Frigon.
    Secretary: Donald Manson.

Report

Dated September 11, 1929. Tabled in the House of Commons on
February 24, 1930. Sessional Paper no. 74-1930. Printed as:
    Report of the Royal Commission on radio broadcasting.. Ottawa,
F. A. Acland, Printer to the King's Most Excellent Majesty, 1929.
29 p.

In English and French, the latter inverted with special title page
and separate paging.

Notes: Public hearings held in 25 Canadian cities. Commissioners
also visited 10 foreign cities. 124 written statements submitted. 164
persons submitted verbal statements at the Canadian hearings. Cost:
$41,902.99.

271 ROYAL COMMISSION ON TECHNICAL AND PROFESSIONAL SERVICES

Appointed on April 15, 1929 by Order in Council P.C. 664 under
Part I of the Inquiries Act (R.S.C., 1927, c. 99) and on the recommendation of the Minister of Finance.

Commissioners: Edward Wentworth Beatty, Chairman, Sir John
George Garneau, Walter Charles Murray and G. T. Jackson.

Secretary: W. C. Ronson.

Reports

Interim Report dated July 12, 1929. Text in Final Report, pp.
57-60.

Final Report dated February, 1930. Tabled in the House of Commons on February 25, 1930. Sessional Paper no. 101-1930. Printed
as:

Report of the Royal Commission on technical and professional
services. February, 1930. Ottawa, F. A. Acland, Printer to the
King's Most Excellent Majesty, 1930. 60 p.

Notes: 67 witnesses were examined at 8 meetings in 3 cities.
Cost: $25,095.71.

272 COMMISSION FOR THE PURPOSE OF NEGOTIATING AN EXTENSION OF
JAMES BAY TREATY NO. 9 WITH THE OJIBWAS AND OTHER INDIANS

Appointed on May 30, 1929 by Order in Council P.C. 921 on the
recommendation of the Superintendent General of Indian Affairs. No
indication of authorizing statute given in Order in Council.

Commissioners: Walter Charles Cain and Herbert Nathaniel
Awrey.

Report

Not located.

273 COMMISSION TO INVESTIGATE CERTAIN CHARGES OF ALLEGED IR-
REGULARITIES ON THE PART OF EMPLOYEES OF THE DOMINION
DISTILLERS, LIMITED, MONTREAL, AND THE OFFICER IN CHARGE
OF THE CUSTOMS BONDING WAREHOUSE

Appointed on March 29, 1930 by Order in Council P. C. 694 under Part I of the Inquiries Act (R. S. C., 1927, c. 99) and on the recommendation of the Minister of National Revenue.
Commissioner: Phillippe Brais.

Report

Not located.

274 COMMISSION TO INQUIRE INTO THE FEASIBILITY, PROBABLE COST OF CONSTRUCTION, ECONOMIC AND NATIONAL ADVANTAGES TO BE GAINED BY THE CONSTRUCTION OF A SHIP CANAL ACROSS THE ISTHMUS OF CHIGNECTO TO CONNECT THE WATERS OF THE BAY OF FUNDY WITH THE GULF OF ST. LAWRENCE

Appointed on June 11, 1930 by Order in Council P. C. 1325 under Part I of the Inquiries Act (R. S. C., 1927, c. 99) and on the recommendation of the Minister of Railways and Canals. Recinded on July 14, 1931 by Order in Council P. C. 1661. The Royal Commission was annulled.
Commissioners: Frank McKenzie Ross, Alfred Burpee Balcom, James Joseph Johnstone and Duncan Angus McArthur.

Report

Apparently no report was issued.

275 ROYAL COMMISSION ON REPARATIONS

Appointed on September 30, 1930 by Order in Council P. C. 2100 under Part I of the Inquiries Act (R. S. C., 1927, c. 99) and on the recommendation of the Secretary of State.
Commissioner: Errol Malcolm McDougall.

Reports

Special Report upon Armenian Claims: Dated May 9, 1931. Tabled in the House of Commons on April 18, 1932. Sessional Paper no. 98d-1932. Printed as:
Reparations, 1930-31. Special report upon Armenian claims. Errol M. McDougall, Commissioner. Printed by order of Parliament. Ottawa, F. A. Acland, Printer to the King's Most Excellent Majesty, 1931. 12 p.
Interim Report: Dated March 6, 1931. Tabled in the House of Commons on March 17, 1931. Sessional Paper no. 100-1931. Printed as:
Reparations, 1930-31. Interim Report. Errol M. McDougall,

Commissioner. Printed by order of Parliament. Ottawa, F. A. Acland, Printer to the King's Most Excellent Majesty, 1931. 172 p.

Supplementary Report: Dated July 21, 1931. Tabled in the House
of Commons on July 27, 1931. Sessional Paper no. 100a-1931.
Printed as:

Reparations, 1930-31. Supplementary report. Errol M. McDougall, Commissioner. Printed by order of Parliament. Ottawa, F. A.
Acland, Printer to the King's Most Excellent Majesty, 1931. 34 p.

Report on maltreatment of prisoners of war: Dated January 13,
1932. Tabled in the House of Commons on February 5, 1932. Sessional
Paper no. 98-1932. Printed as:

Reparations, 1930-1931. Report. Maltreatment of prisoners of
war. Errol M. McDougall, K. C., Commissioner. Printed by order
of Parliament. Ottawa, F. A. Acland, Printer to the King's Most
Excellent Majesty, 1932. 332 p.

Further Report: Dated November 30, 1932. Tabled in the House
of Commons on March 13, 1933. Sessional Paper no. 299-1932/33.
Printed as:

Reparations, 1932. Further report. Errol M. McDougall, K. C.,
Commissioner. Printed by order of Parliament. Ottawa, F. A.
Acland, Printer to the King's Most Excellent Majesty, 1933. 217 p.

Final Report: Dated March 4, 1933. Tabled in the House of
Commons on March 13, 1933. Sessional Paper no. 299a-1932/33.
Printed as:

Reparations, 1932-1933. Final report. March 4, 1933. Errol
M. McDougall, K. C., Commissioner. Printed by order of Parliament.
Ottawa, F. A. Acland, Printer to the King's Most Excellent Majesty,
1933. 211 p.


276 COMMISSION CONCERNING THE ADMINISTRATION OF HALIFAX HAR-
BOUR BY FORMER COMMISSIONERS

Appointed on October 24, 1930 by Order in Council P. C. 2490
under Part I of the Inquiries Act (R. S. C., 1927, c. 99) and on the
recommendation of the Minister of Marine.
Commissioner: John Fosbery Orde.

Report

Not located.
Notes: Cost: $9,400.58.


277 COMMISSION TO INQUIRE INTO AND REPORT UPON ALL MATTERS
RELATIVE TO MEANS OF COMMUNICATION FOR THE TRANSPORTA-
TION OF PERSONS, GOODS AND MERCHANDISE BETWEEN VANCOU-
VER AT THE SECOND NARROWS, BURRARD INLET, BRITISH

COLUMBIA

Appointed on December 13, 1930 by Order in Council P. C. 2908 under Part I of the Inquiries Act (R. S. C. , 1927, c. 99) and on the recommendation of the Minister of Marine.

Commissioners: Louis E. Côté, Chairman, E. E. Brydone-Jack and C. E. Cartwright.

### Report
Dated February 20, 1931. Tabled in the House of Commons on May 29, 1931. Sessional Paper no. 288-1931. Printed as:

Report on the removal of Ripple Rock. Department of Marine. Commissioners: Mr. L. E. Côté (Chairman), Dr. E. E. Brydon-Jack, Mr. C. E. Cartwright. February 20, 1931. Ottawa, F. A. Acland, Printer to the King's Most Excellent Majesty, 1931. 11 p.

Notes: Public hearings held at Vancouver and Victoria (January 28 - February 2, 1931). 44 appeared before the Commission.


278 COMMISSION TO INVESTIGATE AS TO THE CORRECTNESS OR OTHER-WISE OF CERTAIN CHARGES MADE AGAINST MR. N. CURTIS, EM-PLOYED AS STOCKYARD AGENT IN THE DOMINION DEPARTMENT OF AGRICULTURE AT EDMONTON

Appointed on December 20, 1930 by Order in Council P. C. 2971 under Part I of the Inquiries Act (R. S. C. , 1927, c. 99) and on the re-commendation of the Minister of Agriculture.

Commissioner: Percy W. Abbott.

### Report
Not located.


279 ROYAL COMMISSION TO INQUIRE INTO TRADING IN GRAIN FUTURES

Appointed on April 10, 1931 by Order in Council P. C. 853 under Part I of the Inquiries Act (R. S. C. , 1927, c. 99) and on the recom-mendation of the Prime Minister.

Commissioners: Sir Josiah Stamp, Chairman, James Thomas Brown and William Sanford Evans.

Secretary: Lester Bowles Pearson.

### Report
Letter of transmittal dated April 29, 1931. Tabled in the House of Commons on June 4, 1931. Sessional Paper no. 308-1931. Printed as:

Dominion of Canada. Report of the Commission to enquire into trading in grain futures. Ottawa, F. A. Acland, Printer to the King's Most Excellent Majesty, 1931. 90 p.

Notes: Hearings held in 3 cities (April 13 - April 22, 1931). 52 witnesses heard during the 16 sessions held. Commissioners also visited Minneapolis and Chicago. Cost: $11,817.22.

280 COMMISSION TO INQUIRE INTO THE FEASIBILITY OF CONSTRUCTING A CANAL ACROSS THE ISTHMUS OF CHIGNECTO TO CONNECT THE WATERS OF THE BAY OF FUNDY WITH THE WATERS OF THE GULF OF ST. LAWRENCE

Appointed on July 21, 1931 by Order in Council P. C. 1686 under Part I of the Inquiries Act (R. S. C. , 1927, c. 99) and on the recommendation of the Minister of Railways and Canals.

Commissioners: Arthur Surveyor, Chairman, David W. Robb, John F. Sowards, and Stephen Butler Leacock. [1]

Secretary: George W. Yates.

Report

Dated November 9 1933. Tabled in the House of Commons on May 22, 1934. Sessional Paper no. 288-1934. Printed as:

Report of Chignecto Canal Commission. Part I - The Commission's findings. Part II - Surveys and estimates. Part III - Extent and scope of Commission's investigation. Ottawa, J. O. Patenaude, Printer to the King's Most Excellent Majesty, 1933. 33 p.

Notes: Cost: $9,239.35.

281 COMMISSION TO INQUIRE INTO AND INVESTIGATE THE CIRCUMSTANCES SURROUNDING AN ACCIDENT ON MAY 19, 1928 TO GUY BENNING TO DETERMINE WHETHER THIS EMPLOYEE OF THE FOREST SERVICE WAS ENTITLED TO FURTHER COMPENSATION

Appointed on October 13, 1931 by Order in Council P. C. 2535 under Part I of the Inquiries Act (R. S. C. , 1927, c. 99) and on the recommendation of the Minister of the Interior.

Commissioner: Alexander W. Brodie.

Report

Not located.

---

[1] Leacock resigned because of his academic and literary engagements. He was replaced by Surveyor on September 21, 1931, by Order in Council P. C. 2342.

Notes: Cost: $284. 85.


282 ROYAL COMMISSION TO INQUIRE INTO RAILWAYS AND TRANSPORTA-
TION IN CANADA

Appointed on November 20, 1931 by Order in Council P. C. 2910
under Part I of the Inquiries Act (R. S. C. , 1927, c. 99) and on the
recommendation of the Minister of Finance.
Commissioners: Lyman Poore Duff, Chairman, Sir Joseph
Wesley Flavelle, Beaudry Leman, Leonon Fresel Loree, Walter
Charles Murray, John Charles Webster and Lord Ashfield.
Secretaries: Arthur Monon and George W. Yates.

Report
Dated September 13, 1932. Tabled in the House of Commons on
October 11, 1932. Sessional Paper no. 108-1932/33. Printed as:
Report of the Royal Commission to inquire into railways and trans-
portation in Canada, 1931-2. Ottawa, F. A. Acland, Printer to the
King's Most Excellent Majesty, 1932. 115 p.
Notes: 18 sittings occupying 50 days held in 9 cities. 72 written
submissions received. Cost: $92, 385. 83.


283 COMMISSION TO INQUIRE INTO AND REPORT UPON ALL MATTERS
RELATING TO THE LOSS OF THE SAILING VESSEL "GYPSUM QUEEN"
ON JULY 31, 1915

Appointed on January 27, 1932 by Order in Council P. C. 179 under
Part I of the Inquiries Act (R. S. C. , 1927, c. 99) and on the recommend-
ation of the Secretary of State.
Commissioner: Horace Harvey.

Report
Dated July 30, 1932. Copy attached to Order in Council P. C. 1737
of August 3, 1932. (In Public Archives of Canada, R. G. 2, 1, Volume
1895). 74 leaves and appendices (maps).
Notes: Hearings held in 6 cities. Cost: $23, 106. 28.


284 COMMISSION TO INVESTIGATE WHETHER OR NOT THE CANADIAN
PERFORMING RIGHT SOCIETY LIMITED IS COMPLYING WITH THE
TERMS AND CONDITIONS OF THE COPYRIGHT AMENDMENT ACT,
1931, IN RELATION TO CERTAIN RADIO BRAODCASTING STATIONS
IN ALBERTA

Appointed on January 28, 1932 by Order in Council P. C. 169 under Part I of the Inquiries Act (R. S. C. , 1927, c. 99) and on the recommendation of the Secretary of State.

Commissioner: Albert Freeman Ewing.

Report

Dated June 29, 1932. Not printed. Photocopy of typescript in the Library of Parliament, Ottawa:

Report of the Honourable Mr. Justice Ewing upon the activities of the Canadian Reforming Right Society Limited pursuant to Order in Council No. 169, dated January 28th, 1932. [Ottawa, 1932?] 16 leaves.

Notes: Sittings held in Calgary (April 18 - April 27, 1932). Evidence runs to 690 pages. 72 exhibits filed with the Commission.

285 COMMISSION TO INQUIRE INTO AND REPORT UPON THE CIRCUMSTANCES ATTENDANT UPON AN EXPLOSION WHICH OCCURRED ON JUNE 17, 1932, IN THE DRY DOCK OF THE MAISONNEUVE PLANT OF THE CANADIAN VICKERS LIMITED, WHERE A NUMBER OF EMPLOYEES OF THAT COMPANY WERE ENGAGED IN REPAIRING THE OIL TANKER S. S. CYMBELINE

Appointed on June 25, 1932 by Order in Council P. C. 1465 under Part I of the Inquiries Act (R. S. C. , 1927, c. 99) and on the recommendation of the Minister of Justice.

Commissioner: Stanislas Albert Baulne.

Report

Dated December 29, 1932. Tabled in the House of Commons on February 14, 1933. Sessional Paper no. 232-1933. Printed as:

Report of the Commissioner in the matter of the investigation into the circumstances attending the explosion in the drydock of Canadian-Vickers Limited, Montreal, June 17, 1932. S. A. Baulne, Commissioner. Printed by order of Parliament. Ottawa, J. O. Patenaude, Acting Queen's Printer, 1933. 11 p.

In English and French, the latter inverted with special title page and separate paging.

Notes: Sittings held from August 5-9, 1932. Cost: $20.00

286 ROYAL COMMISSION ON BANKING AND CURRENCY IN CANADA

Appointed on July 31, 1933 by Order in Council P. C. 1562 under Part I of the Inquiries Act (R. S. C. , 1927, c. 99) and on the recommendation of the Prime Minister.

Commissioners: Hugh Pattison Macmillan, baron, Chairman, Sir Charles Stewart Addis, Sir William Thomas White, John Edward Brownlee and Beaudry Leman.
Secretary: Bennet John Roberts.


Report
Dated September 22, 1933. Tabled in the House of Commons on January 26, 1934. Sessional Paper no. 115-1934. Printed as:
Report of the Royal Commission on banking and currency in Canada. 1933. Ottawa, J. O. Patenuade, Printer to the King's Most Excellent Majesty, 1933. 119 p.
Notes: Public hearings held in 13 cities (August 8 - September 15, 1933). 196 submissions received by the Commission. Cost: $30,953.41.


287 COMMISSION TO INVESTIGATE THE STATUS OF THE CANADIAN PER-
    FORMING RIGHT SOCIETY IN REFERENCE TO CERTAIN MUSICAL
    WORKS

Appointed on December 14, 1933 by Order in Council P. C. 2610 under Part I of the Inquiries Act (R. S. C. , 1927, c. 99) and on the recommendation of the Secretary of State.
Commissioner: Louis Arthur Audette.


Report
Not located.


288 ROYAL COMMISSION ON THE NATURAL RESOURCES OF SASKATCHE-
    WAN

Appointed on December 29, 1933 by Order in Council P. C. 2722 under Part I of the Inquiries Act (R. S. C. , 1927, c. 99) and on the recommendation of the Prime Minister.
Commissioners: Andrew Knox Dysart, Chairman, Henry Veeder Bigelow and George C. McDonald.
Secretary: Oliver Master.


Report
Dated March 12  1935. Tabled in the House of Commons on March 14, 1935. Sessional Paper no. 249-1935. Printed as:
Report of the Royal Commission on the natural resources of Saskatchewan. Honourable A. K. Dysart, Chairman. Honourable H. V. Bigelow. George C. McDonald, Esq. , C. A. Oliver Master, Secretary. Ottawa, J. O. Patenaude, Printer to the King's Most Excellent Majesty, 1935. 68 p.

Notes: Public hearings held at Ottawa and Regina (February 7 -
May 26, 1934). 276 exhibits filed. Cost: $44,549.45.


289 COMMISSION TO INQUIRE INTO CLAIMS OF ESTATE OF THE LATE
    JOHN ROSS FOR ADVANCES MADE TO CONTRACTORS, SECTIONS
    3, 6, 9 AND 15 OF THE INTERCOLONIAL RAILWAY

Appointed on July 6, 1934 by Order in Council P. C. 889 under
Part I of the Inquiries Act (R. S. C. , 1927, c. 99) and on the recom-
mendation of the Minister of Justice.
Commissioner: Louis Arthur Audette.

Report
Dated May 16, 1935. No copy located.
Notes: Cost: $727.90.


290 ROYAL COMMISSION ON PRICE SPREADS

Appointed on July 7, 1934 by Order in Council P. C. 1461 under
Part I of the Inquiries Act (R. S. C. , 1927, c. 99) and on the recom-
mendation of the Prime Minister.
Commissioners: William Walker Kennedy, Chairman,[1] Henry
Herbert Stevens,[2] Jean-Louis Baribeau, Thomas Bell, Oscar L.
Boulanger, Alexander McKay Edwards  Samuel Factor, Mark Senn,
James Ilsley, Edward James Young and Donald MacBeth Kennedy.
Secretary: Lester Bowles Pearson.

Report
Letter of transmittal dated April 9, 1935. Tabled in the House
of Commons on April 12, 1935. Sessional Paper no. 228d-1935.
Printed as:
Report of the Royal Commission on Price Spreads. Ottawa, J. O.
Patenaude, I. S. O. , Printer to the King's Most Excellent Majesty,
1935. xiii, 506 p.
Notes: The Commission was established on the recommendation
of a Select Special Committee of the House of Commons. The original
membership of the Royal Commission was unchanged from that of the
Committee. The Commission met in Ottawa from October 30, 1934 to

----

[1] Kennedy was named Chairman on October 29, 1934 by Order in
Council P. C. 2743.
[2] Stevens resigned as Chairman on October 29, 1934. However, he
remained a member of the Commission.

February 1, 1935.  270 witnesses appeared before the Committee and
Commission.  8,277 pages of evidence were taken before the Committee
and Commission.  Cost: $220,573.02.


291 COMMISSION TO INQUIRE INTO ALLEGATIONS AFFECTING THE RIGHT
    HONOURABLE ARTHUR MEIGHEN IN THE MANNER IN WHICH HE
    DISCHARGED HIS DUTIES AS COMMISSIONER OF THE HYDRO-ELEC-
    TRIC POWER COMMISSION

Appointed on July 7, 1934 by Order in Council P.C. 1462 under
Part I of the Inquiries Act (R.S.C., 1927, c. 99) and on the recom-
mendation of the Prime Minister.
Commissioner: Sir Lyman Poore Duff.

                                Report
No report issued.
Notes: Duff did not proceed with the inquiry after the appointment
of a similar Commission by the Government of Ontario.


292 ROYAL COMMISSION ON THE NATURAL RESOURCES OF ALBERTA

Appointed on July 19, 1934 by Order in Council P.C. 1588 under
Part I of the Inquiries Act (R.S.C., 1927, c. 99) and on the recom-
mendation of the Minister of Justice.
Commissioners: Andrew Knox Dysart, Chairman, Thomas
Mitchell Tweedie and George C. McDonald.
Secretary: Oliver Master.

                                Report
Dated March 12, 1935.  Tabled in the House of Commons on March
14, 1935.  Sessional Paper no. 249a-1935.  Printed as:
Report of the Royal Commission on the natural resources of
Alberta.  Honourable A. K. Dysart, Chairman, Honourable T. M.
Tweedie, George C. McDonald, Esq., C.A.  Oliver Master, Secre-
tary.  Ottawa, J. O. Patenaude, Printer to the King's Most Excellent
Majesty, 1935.  42 p.
Notes: Public hearings held at Ottawa (October 2 - December 11,
1934).  More than 250 exhibits presented to the Commission.  Cost:
$29,773.79.


293 ROYAL COMMISSION ON FINANCIAL ARRANGEMENTS BETWEEN THE
    DOMINION AND THE MARITIME PROVINCES

Appointed on September 14, 1934 by Order in Council P. C. 2231 under Part I of the Inquiries Act (R. S. C. , 1927, c. 99) and on the recommendation of the Minister of Finance.

Commissioners: Sir Thomas White, Chairman, John Alexander Mathieson and Edward Walter Nesbitt.

Secretary: C. H. Payne.

### Report

Letter of transmittal dated February 9, 1935. Tabled in the House of Commons on March 4, 1935. Sessional Paper no. 225-1935. Printed as:

Report of the Royal Commission on financial arrangements between the Dominion and the Maritime Provinces. The Right Honourable Sir Thomas White, P. C. , K. C. M. G. , Chairman. Honourable J. A. Mathieson. E. W. Nesbitt, Esquire. C. H. Payne, Secretary. Ottawa, J. O. Patenaude, Printer to the King's Most Excellent Majesty, 1935. 24 p.

Notes: Cost: $26,475.01.

294 ROYAL COMMISSION APPOINTED TO INVESTIGATE THE ACTIVITIES OF THE CANADIAN PERFORMING RIGHTS SOCIETY, LIMITED, AND SIMILAR SOCIETIES

Appointed on March 22, 1935 by Order in Council P. C. 738 under Part I of the Inquiries Act (R. S. C. , 1927, c. 99) and on the recommendation of the Secretary of State.

Commissioner: James Parker.

### Report

Dated October 29, 1935. Tabled in the House of Commons on February 27, 1936. Sessional Paper no. 113-1936. Printed as:

Report of His Honour Judge Parker, a Commissioner appointed by the Inquiries Act and the Copyright Amendment Act of 1931, pursuant to Order in Council no. 738 dated March 22nd, 1935. Ottawa, J. O. Patenaude, I. S. O. , Printer to the King's Most Excellent Majesty, 1935. 49 p.

Notes: Hearings held in 8 cities (April 9, 1935 - July 19, 1935). 33 days spent in hearing evidence. 143 witnesses appeared before the Commission and 274 exhibits were filed. Cost: $17,701.18.

295 COMMISSION TO INQUIRE INTO AND REPORT UPON CERTAIN ALLEGATIONS MADE BY THE HONOURABLE PETER VENIOT, MEMBER OF THE HOUSE OF COMMONS FOR GLOUCESTER, NEW BRUNSWICK, AS TO THE ADMINISTRATION OF THE PATROL SYSTEM UNDER

THE ROYAL CANADIAN MOUNTED POLICE, IN THE WATERS OF
BAIE DES CHALEURS IN THE PROVINCE OF NEW BRUNSWICK

Appointed on March 25, 1935 by Order in Council P. C. 708 under
Part I of the Inquiries Act (R. S. C. , 1927, c. 99) and on the recom-
mendation of the Minister of Justice.
Commissioner: John Babington Macaulay Baxter.
Secretary: W. Harold Davidson.

Report
Dated May 25, 1935. Tabled in the House of Commons on June 5,
1935. Sessional Paper no. 374-1935. Printed as:
Report of Honourable John B. M. Baxter upon certain allegations
made by Honourable P. J. Veniot, M. P. Ottawa, J. O. Patenaude,
I. S. O. , Printer to the King's Most Excellent Majesty, 1935. 17 p.
Notes: Hearings opened at Fredericton on May 2, 1935. Cost:
$3, 670. 40.

296 COMMISSION TO INVESTIGATE AND REPORT ON ALL ANY ANY COM-
PLAINTS IN REFERENCE TO THE MANAGEMENT OF THE RELIEF
CAMPS FOR SINGLE HOMELESS MEN IN THE PROVINCE OF BRITISH
COLUMBIA

Appointed on April 1, 1935 by Order in Council P. C. 861 under
Part I of the Inquiries Act (R. S. C. , 1927, c. 99) and on the recom-
mendation of the Minister of National Defence.
Commissioners: William Alexander Macdonald, Chairman,
Charles T. McHattie and E. D. Braden.

Report
Dated May 31, 1935. Tabled in the House of Commons on July 11,
1935. Sessional Paper no. 390-1935. Printed as:
Dominion of Canada. In the Matter of the Public Inquiries Act,
Chapter 99, R. S. C. , 1927 and In the matter of the Commission on
relief camps, British Columbia. Report. Commissioners: Honour-
able W. A. Macdonald, C. T. McHattie, Esquire, Rev. E. D. Braden.
Ottawa, J. O. Patenaude, I. S. O. , Printer to the King's Most Excellent
Majesty, 1935. 16 p.
Notes: Commissioners visited and inspected a majority of the
relief camps in British Columbia. Public meetings were held at the
camps. Cost: $5, 436. 29.

297 COMMISSION TO INQUIRE INTO THE QUESTION AS TO THE TRUTH OR
FALSITY OF STATEMENTS MADE BY A. C. HALL, A CONVICT OF

KINGSTON PENITENTIARY, AND MR. J. D. DAWSON, INSPECTOR
OF PENITENTIARIES IN AN INTERVIEW BETWEEN THEM IN THE
LECTURE ROOM OF THE ADMINISTRATIVE BUILDING OF THE
PENITENTIARY ON APRIL 9TH, 1934, IT BEING ALLEGED BY MISS
AGNES MACPHAIL, M. P. , THAT DURING THE COURSE OF THE
INTERVIEW INSPECTOR DAWSON USED TO HALL ABUSIVE AND
PROFANE LANGUAGE CONCERNING HER

Appointed on May 3, 1935 by Order in Council P. C. 1183 under
Part I of the Inquiries Act (R. S. C. , 1927, c. 99) and on the recom-
mendation of the Minister of Justice.
Commissioner: E. J. Daly.
Secretary: Robert Brydie.

### Report
Dated July 23, 1935. Not printed. Carbon of typewritten copy
in the Department of Justice files. 28 leaves.
Notes: Commission held hearings in Ottawa and Kingston for
11 days during the spring and early summer of 1935. 16 witnesses
examined by the Commission. 40 exhibits filed during the hearings.
Cost: $5,577.82.

298 COMMISSION TO INQUIRE INTO THE INDUSTRIAL DISPUTE INVOLVING
THE SHIPPING FEDERATION OF BRITISH COLUMBIA LIMITED AND
THE LONG-SHORE WORKERS AT VANCOUVER, BRITISH COLUMBIA

Appointed on September 10, 1935 by Order in Council P. C. 2834
under Part I of the Inquiries Act (R. S. C. , 1927, c. 99) and on the
recommendation of the Minister of Labour.
Commissioner: Henry Hague Davis.

### Report
Dated October 22, 1935. Printed as:
"Report of Royal Commission concerning industrial dispute on
Vancouver waterfront" in Labour Gazette, XXXV, November, 1935,
pp. 982-995.
Notes: Public hearings held at Vancouver (September 16 - October
9, 1935). Cost: $1,355.80.

299 ROYAL COMMISSION ON THE TEXTILE INDUSTRY

Appointed on January 27, 1936 by Order in Council P. C. 223
under Part I of the Inquiries Act (R. S. C. , 1927, c. 99) and on the
recommendation of the Minister of Finance.

Commissioner: William Ferdinand Alphonse Turgeon.
Secretary: Albert Spence Whiteley.

### Report
Letter of transmittal dated January 20, 1938. Tabled in the House of Commons on March 31, 1938. Sessional Paper no. 137b-1938. Printed as:

Report of the Royal Commission on the textile industry. Ottawa, J. O. Patenaude, I. S. O. , Printer to the King's Most Excellent Majesty, 1938. 308 p.

Notes: Public hearings held in 13 towns and cities in Quebec and Ontario. 1, 380 documentary exhibits filed with the Commission. Cost: $174, 335. 20.

### 300 ROYAL COMMISSION TO INVESTIGATE THE PENAL SYSTEM OF CANADA

Appointed on February 27, 1936 by Order in Council P. C. 483 under Part I of the Inquiries Act (R. S. C. , 1927, c. 99) and on the recommendation of the Minister of Justice.

Commissioners: Joseph Archambault, Chairman, Harry W. Anderson, [1] Richard W. Craig and James Chalmers McRuer. [2]
Secretary: Allan J. Fraser.

### Report
Dated April 4, 1938. Tabled in the House of Commons on June 14, 1938. Sessional Paper no. 190a-1938. Printed as:

Report of the Royal Commission to investigate the penal system of Canada. Ottawa, J. O. Patenaude, I. S. O. , Printer to the King's Most Excellent Majesty, 1938. vi, 418 p.

Notes: Public hearings held in Ottawa from early October to December 15, 1937. The Commissioners visited all the federal penetentiaries in Canada as well as many prison systems in Europe and the United States. A total of 113 institutions in 9 different countries were visited. 1, 840 inmates and 200 officers gave evidence.

### 301 ROYAL COMMISSION ON ANTHRACITE COAL

Appointed on June 6, 1936 by Order in Council P. C. 1356 under Part I of the Inquiries Act (R. S. C. , 1927, c. 99) and on the recom-

---

[1] Died on April 28, 1936.
[2] Appointed on September 17, 1936 to succeed Anderson by Order in Council P. C. 2424.

mendation of the Minister of Labour.

Commissioner: Henry Marshall Tory.

Secretary: A. L. Burgess.

Report

Dated February 3, 1937. Tabled in the House of Commons on February 4, 1937. Sessional Paper no. 142-1937. Printed as:

Report of the Royal Commission on anthracite coal. February 3, 1937. Ottawa, J. O. Patenaude, I. S. O., Printer to the King's Most Excellent Majesty, 1937. 120 p.

Notes: Public hearings held in 6 cities. 106 witnesses were examined by the Commission. Cost: $23,878.64.

302 ROYAL GRAIN INQUIRY COMMISSION

Appointed on June 27, 1936 by Order in Council P. C. 1577 under Part I of the Inquiries Act (R. S. C., 1927, c. 99) and on the recommendation of the Minister of Trade and Commerce.

Commissioner: William Ferdinand Alphonse Turgeon.

Secretary: T. W. Grindley.

Report

Letter of transmittal dated May 4, 1938. Tabled in the House of Commons on May 9, 1938. Sessional Paper no. 131a-1938. Printed as:

Dominion of Canada. Report of the Royal Grain Inquiry Commission, 1938. Ottawa, J. O. Patenaude, I. S. O., Printer to the King's Most Excellent Majesty, 1938. 264 p.

Notes: Sittings held in 7 Canadian cities and 8 foreign cities. 260 witnesses appeared before the Commission in its 122 days of hearings. 715 exhibits were presented. Cost: $141,413.39.

303 COMMISSION TO INQUIRE INTO ILLEGAL LOBSTER FISHING AND CANNING AND ILLEGAL SMELT FISHING IN LOBSTER FISHING DISTRICTS NUMBERS 7 AND 8 IN THE MARITIME PROVINCES IN THE YEAR 1936

Appointed on December 5, 1936 by Order in Council P. C. 3103 under Part I of the Inquiries Act (R. S. C., 1927, c. 99) and on the recommendation of the Minister of Fisheries.

Commissioner: Arthur T. LeBlanc.

Report

Dated December 4, 1937. Tabled in the House of Commons on

May 9, 1938.  Sessional Paper no. 264-1938.  Printed as:
     Report on illegal fishing and canning of lobsters and illegal fishing
of smelts in Lobster Fishing Districts Nos. 7 and 8, to Honourable
J. E. Michaud, M. P. , Minister of Fisheries, by Honourable Arthur T.
LeBlanc, Commissioner.  Ottawa, J. O. Patenaude, I. S. O. , Printer
to the King's Most Excellent Majesty, 1938.  16 p.
     Notes: Sessions held in 6 towns and cities in New Brunswick and
Prince Edward Island.  385 witnesses examined by the Commission.
Cost: $10, 304. 18.


304 ROYAL COMMISSION ON DOMINION-PROVINCIAL RELATIONS

     Appointed on August 14, 1937 by Order in Council P. C. 1908
under Part I of the Inquiries Act (R. S. C. , 1927, c. 99) and on the recommendation of the Prime Minister.
     Commissioners:  Joseph Sirois, [1] Chairman, (1937-1938), Newton
Wesley Rowell, [2] Chairman, (1938-1940), Thibaudeau Rinfret, [3] John
Wesley Dafoe, Robert Alexander MacKay, and Henry Forbes Angus.
     Secretaries:  Alex Skelton and Adjutor Savard.

                          Report
     Letter of transmittal dated May 3, 1940.  Tabled in the House of
Commons on May 16, 1940.  Sessional Paper no. 95-1940.  Printed as:
     Report of the Royal Commission on Dominion-Provincial relations.
[ Ottawa, 1940] .  3 v.  (261, 295, 219 p. )

     List of Research Studies Prepared for the Commission
                          Appendices:

Appendix 1:
     A - Dominion of Canada and Canadian National Railways compara-
          tive statistics of public finance, 1913, 1921, 1925 to 1937.
          Ottawa, 1938?  74 p.
     B - Province of Prince Edward Island comparative statistics of
          public finance, 1913, 1921, 1925 to 1937.  Ottawa, 1938?  29 p.
     C - Province of Nova Scotia comparative statistics of public finance,

---

[1] The appointment of Sirois as Chairman was approved on November 22,
1938 by Order in Council P. C. 2946.
[2] Rowell became seriously ill in May, 1938.  His resignation as chairman was not accepted until November, 1938.
[3] Resigned on November 18, 1937.  He was succeeded by Sirois whose
appointment was approved on November 18, 1937 by Order in Council
P. C. 2880.

1913, 1921, 1925 to 1937.  Ottawa, 1938?  33 p.

D - Province of New Brunswick comparative statistics of public
    finance, 1913, 1921, 1925 to 1937.  Ottawa, 1938?  38 p.

E - Province of Quebec comparative statistics of public finance,
    1913, 1921, 1925 to 1937.  Ottawa, 1938?  40 p.

F - Province of Ontario comparative statistics of public finance,
    1913, 1921, 1925 to 1937.  Ottawa, 1938?  47 p.

G - Province of Manitoba comparative statistics of public finance,
    1913, 1921, 1925 to 1937.  Ottawa, 1938?  51 p.

H - Province of Saskatchewan comparative statistics of public
    finance, 1913, 1921, 1925 to 1937.  Ottawa, 1938?  43 p.

I - Dominion of Canada and Canadian National Railways and Pro-
    vincial Governments comparative statistics of public finance,
    1913, 1921, 1925 to 1939.  Ottawa, 1939.  111 p.

J - Province of Alberta comparative statistics of public finance,
    1913, 1921, 1925 to 1937.  Ottawa, 1938?  43 p.

K - Province of British Columbia comparative statistics of public
    finance, 1913, 1921, 1925 to 1937.  Ottawa, 1938?  45 p.

Appendix 2 - Creighton, Donald Grant.  British North America at
Confederation.  Ottawa, King's Printer, 1939.  104 p.

Appendix 3 - Mackintosh, William Archibald.  The economic background
of Dominion-Provincial relations.  Ottawa, King's Printer, 1939.
102 p.

Appendix 4 - MacGregor, Donald Chalmers, John Bulmer Rutherford,
George Edwin Britnell, and John James Deutsch.  National income.
Ottawa, King's Printer, 1939.  97 p.

Appendix 5 - Minville, Esdras.  Labour legislation and social services
in the Province of Quebec.  Ottawa, King's Printer, 1939.  97 p.

Appendix 6 - Grauer, Albert Edward.  Public assistance and social
insurance.  Ottawa, King's Printer, 1939.  98 p.

Appendix 7 - Corry, James Alexander.  Difficulties of divided juris-
diction.  Ottawa, King's Printer, 1939.  44 p.

Appendix 8 - Gouin, Leon Mercier and Brooke Claxton.  Legislative
expedients and devices adopted by the Dominion and the Provinces.
Ottawa, King's Printer, 1939.  72 p.

Mimeographed studies:

Bates, Stewart.  Financial history of Canadian governments.
Ottawa, King's Printer, 1939.  iv, 309 p.

Corry, James Alexander. Growth of Government activities since
Confederation. Ottawa, 1939. ii, 174 p.

Eggleston, Wilfrid and C. T. Kraft. Dominion-Provincial subsidies and grants. Ottawa, 1939. iii, 200 p.

Goldenburg, Hyman Carl. Municipal finance in Canada. Ottawa,
1939. ii, iii, 128 p.

Grauer, Albert Edward. Housing. Ottawa, 1939. 78 p.

---. Labour legislation. Ottawa, 1939. 78 p.

---. Public Health. Ottawa, 1939. ii, 126 p.

Henry, Robert Alexander Cecil and Associates. Railway freight
rates in Canada. Ottawa, 1939. xxii, 290 p.

Knox, Frank Albert. Dominion monetary policy (1929-1934).
Ottawa, 1939. iv, 93 p.

Saunders, Stanley Alexander. Economic history of the Maritime
Provinces. Ottawa, 1939. ii, 148 p.

Waines, William John. Prairie population possibilities. Ottawa,
1939. ii, 77 p.

Notes: Public hearings held in 10 cities (November 29, 1937 -
August 8, 1938). Over 10,000 pages of typewritten evidence recorded.
427 exhibits were filed with the Commission. Cost: $533,600.

305 COMMISSION TO INQUIRE INTO THE DISPUTE AT CORNWALL, ONTARIO,
    BETWEEN CERTAIN MEMBERS OF THE CANADIAN SEAMEN'S UNION
    AND CERTAIN SHIPPING COMPANIES AND INTO ANY MATTERS OR
    CIRCUMSTANCES CONNECTED THEREWITH

Appointed on June 20, 1938 by Order in Council P. C. 1383 under
Part I of the Inquiries Act (R. S. C., 1927, c. 99) and on the recom-
mendation of the Minister of Labour.
Commissioner: Eugene McGrath Quirk.

Report
Dated November 10, 1938. Printed as:
"Report of Commissioner on certain matters relating to Great
Lakes' shipping" in Labour Gazette, XXXVIII, November 1938, p. 1318.

Notes: Meetings held from July 11 - October 13, 1938.


306 COMMISSION TO INQUIRE INTO THE DISPUTE BETWEEN THE MAN-
AGEMENT OF THE QUEBEC CENTRAL RAILWAY AND THE EMPLOY-
EES

Appointed on September 8, 1937 by Order in Council P. C. 2186
under Part I of the Inquiries Act (R. S. C., 1927, c. 99) and on the recommendation of the Minister of Labour.
Commissioner: Albert Constantineau.

Report
Dated November 30, 1937. Printed as:
"Report of Commission regarding an industrial dispute involving
the Quebec Central Railway Company and its train service employees"
in Labour Gazette, XXXVII, December, 1937, pp. 1316-1319.
Notes: The Commissioner held discussions with railway officials
in Sherbrooke and Montreal. Hearings opened in Montreal on November
3, 1937. Cost: $284.20.


307 ROYAL COMMISSION ON THE BREN MACHINE GUN CONTRACT

Appointed on September 7, 1938 by Order in Council P. C. 2251
under Part I of the Inquiries Act (R. S. C., 1927, c. 99) and on the recommendation of the Prime Minister.
Commissioner: Henry Hague Davis.

Report
Dated December 29, 1938. Tabled in the House of Commons on
January 13, 1939. Sessional Paper no. 92-1939. Printed as:
Report of the Royal Commission on the Bren Machine Gun Contract
Honourable Henry Hague Davis, Commissioner. Ottawa, J. O. Paten-
aude, I. S. O., Printer to the King's Most Excellent Majesty, 1939.
52 p.
Notes: Hearings held from September 19 - November 24, 1938.
388 exhibits placed before the Commission. 4,122 pages of evidence
taken. Cost: $29 123.62.


308 COMMISSION TO INQUIRE INTO THE ENGINEERING, ECONOMIC, FIN-
ANCIAL AND OTHER ASPECTS OF THE PROPOSAL TO CONSTRUCT
A HIGHWAY THROUGH BRITISH COLUMBIA AND THE NORTH-WEST
TERRITORIES TO ALASKA

Appointed on December 22, 1938 by Order in Council P. C. 3252
on the recommendation of the Secretary of State and the Minister of
Mines and Resources. No indication of authorizing statute given in
Order in Council.

Commissioners: Charles Stewart, Chairman, Thomas L. Tremblay Arthur Dixon, J. W. Spencer and J. M. Wardle.

### Report

Dated October 15, 1941. Tabled in the House of Commons on
November 13, 1941. Sessional Paper no. 137a-1941. Printed as:[1]

British Columbia-Yukon-Alaska Highway Commission, Canada.
Report on proposed highway through British Columbia and the Yukon
Territory to Alaska. August, 1941. Ottawa, Ontario. Ottawa, Edmond
Cloutier, Printer to the King's Most Excellent Majesty, 1942. 46 p.

309 COMMISSION TO INVESTIGATE THE CAPTURE OF SALMON BY TRAP-
NETS IN THE SOOKE AREA, BRITISH COLUMBIA AND ALSO TO
INVESTIGATE WHETHER PURSE-SEINES FOR THE CAPTURE OF
PINK SALMON AND "LATE" SOCKEYE SALMON SHOULD CONTINUE
IN A PORTION OF THE GULF OF GEORGIA, BRITISH COLUMBIA

Appointed on June 23, 1939 by Order in Council P. C. 1594 under
Part I of the Inquiries Act (R. S. C. , 1927, c. 99) and on the recommendation of the Minister of Fisheries.

Commissioner: Gordon McGregor Sloan.

### Report

Dated April 16, 1940. Tabled in the House of Commons on June 21,
1940. Sessional Paper no. 147-1940. Printed as:

Report relating to the use of (1) trap-nets at sooke Area and (2)
purse-seines in a portion of the Gulf of Georgia (Area No. 17) in salmon
fishing in British Columbia to the Honourable J. E. Michaud, M. P. ,
Minister of Fisheries, by the Honourable Gordon McG. Sloan, Commissioner. 1940. Ottawa, J. O. Patenaude, I. S. O. , Printer to the
King's Most Excellent Majesty, 1940. 28 p.

Notes: Hearings held in 3 towns and cities of British Columbia
(July 17 - October 28, 1939). 81 witnesses examined by the Commission.

310 COMMISSION TO INQUIRE INTO THE COST OF LIVING BONUS TO BE
PAID TO THE EMPLOYEES OF THE COAL MINE OPERATORS OF
ALBERTA AND BRITISH COLUMBIA

[1] The printed report includes only Part i, Volume I and Part VI, Volume.

Appointed on May 4, 1940 by Order in Council P. C. 1802 on the recommendation of the Minister of Labour. No indication of authorizing statute given in the Order in Council.

Commissioners: George Edwin Britnell, Chairman, Clement Stubbs and Garfield Graham.

## First Report
Dated August 22, 1940. Printed as:
"First Report of Commission" in Labour Gazette, XL, September, 1940, pp. 919-921, 922-925.

## Second Report
Dated August 30, 1940. Printed as:
"Second Report of Commission" in Labour Gazette, XL, September, 1940, pp. 921-922.

## Third Report
Dated January 10, 1941. Copy in Archives of Saskatchewan, University of Saskatchewan, Regina:
Government of Canada. Department of Labour. Cost of Living Commission, Coal Mining Industry, District Eighteen. Third Report. 7 leaves.

## Fourth Report
Dated May 3, 1941. Copy in Archives of Saskatchewan, University of Saskatchewan, Regina:
Government of Canada. Department of Labour. Cost of Living Commission, Coal Mining Industry, District Eighteen. Fourth Report. 7 leaves.

## Fifth Report
Dated August 29 1941. Copy in Archives of Saskatchewan, University of Saskatchewan, Regina:
Government of Canada. Department of Labour. Cost of Living Commission, Coal Mining Industry, District Eighteen. Fifth Report. 7 leaves.

No further reports located.

Notes: The Commissioners visited the mining communities of Alberta and British Columbia where they interviewed 212 of the 220 retail merchants (or their managers or bookkeepers) on its mailing list in 43 cities, towns, villages and hamlets.

311 COMMISSION TO INQUIRE INTO AND REPORT UPON THE NAVIGATION OF SMALL VESSELS IN THE ST. LAWRENCE RIVER AND UPON PILOTAGE MATTERS BETWEEN MONTREAL AND KINGSTON

Appointed on July 24, 1940 by Order in Council P. C. 214/3404
under Part I of the Inquiries Act (R. S. C. , 1927, c. 99) and on the
recommendation of the Minister of Transport.
Commissioner: Lucien Cannon.

Reports

Interim Report: Dated July 8, 1941. No copy located.
Final Report: Dated October 20, 1942. Not printed.
Canada. Department of Transport. Report Re: Inquiry into
navigation of small vessels on the St. Lawrence River. Prepared by
the Honourable Lucien Cannon, District Judge in Admiralty of the Ex-
chequer Court of Canada appointed a Royal Commissioner to inquire
and report upon navigation of small vessels on the St. Lawrence River.
[Ottawa, 1942?]  16 leaves.
Location: Library of Parliament, Ottawa; Department of Transport Library, Ottawa; Queen's University Library, Kingston (Xerox
copy).
Notes: Held sittings in four cities.

312 COMMISSION TO INQUIRE INTO THE INDUSTRIAL DISPUTE AT THE
PLANT OF COURTAULDS (CANADA) LIMITED, CORNWALL, ONTARIO

Appointed on October 18, 1940 by Order in Council P. C. 5769
under Part I of the Inquiries Act (R. S. C. , 1927, c. 99) and on the recommendation of the Minister of Labour.
Commissioner: Albert Constantineau.

Report

Not located.

313 COMMISSION TO INQUIRE INTO THE CAUSES OF THE LACK OF CAPA-
CITY PRODUCTION IN THE COAL MINES IN THE MINTO-CHIPMAN
DISTRICT OF THE PROVINCE OF NEW BRUNSWICK

Appointed on February 24, 1941 by Order in Council P. C. 1347
under Part I of the Inquiries Act (R. S. C. , 1927, c. 99) and on the recommendation of the Minister of Labour.
Commissioner: Maynard Brown Archibald.

Report

Dated July 25, 1941. Printed as:
"Report of Commissioner on Inquiry into causes of lack of capa-
city coal production in Minto-Chipman District, New Brunswick" in
Labour Gazette, XLI, September, 1941, pp. 1073-1084.

Notes: Held sittings in four centres (March 5 - April 25, 1941).
24 witnesses appeared before the Commission. The Commissioner
also held interviews with several Provincial officials in New Brunswick.


314 COMMISSION TO INQUIRE INTO THE DISPUTES OR INTO ANY MATTERS
OR CIRCUMSTANCES CONNECTED WITH THE DOMINION COAL COM-
PANY, LIMITED

Appointed on February 27, 1941 by Order in Council P. C. 1447
under Part I of the Inquiries Act (R. S. C., 1927, c. 99) and on the
recommendation of the Minister of Labour.
Commissioners: C. P. McTague, Ralph P. Bell and F. R. Scott.

Report
Dated March 7, 1941. Printed as:
"Report of Tribunal in Disputes between various Coal Mining
Companies in the Province of Nova Scotia and their employees, Mem-
bers of District 26, United Mine Workers of America" in Labour
Gazette, XLI, March, 1941, pp. 231-236.
Notes: Sittings held at Halifax (February 27 - March 1, 1941).


315 COMMISSION TO INQUIRE INTO THE LABOUR DISPUTE AT THE WINDSOR
PLANT OF THE CHRYSLER CORPORATION OF CANADA

Appointed on March 24, 1941 by Order in Council P. C. 2053 under
Part I of the Inquiries Act (R. S. C., 1927, c. 99) and on the recom-
mendation of the Minister of Labour.
Commissioner: William H. Furlong.

Report
Not located.


316 COMMISSION TO INQUIRE INTO THE STRIKE AT THE PLANT OF THE
SCHOLFIELD WOOLLEN COMPANY, LIMITED, OSHAWA, ONTARIO

Appointed on May 19, 1941 by Order in Council P. C. 3513 under
Part I of the Inquiries Act (R. S. C., 1927, c. 99) and on the recom-
mendation of the Minister of Labour.
Commissioner: John J. Robinette.

Report
Not located.

317 ROYAL COMMISSION TO INQUIRE INTO THE EVENTS WHICH OCCURRED
    AT ARVIDA, QUEBEC, IN JULY, 1941

Appointed on August 15, 1941 by Order in Council P. C. 6334 under
Part I of the Inquiries Act (R. S. C., 1927, c. 99) and on the recom-
mendation of the Prime Minister.
Commissioners: Severin Letourneau, and William Langley Bond.
Secretary: Adrien Falardeau.

Report

Dated October 4, 1941.  Tabled in the House of Commons on
November 3, 1941.  Sessional Paper no. 329-1941.  Printed as:
Royal Commission to inquire into the events which occurred at
Arvida, P. Q. in July, 1941.  Report of the Commissioners.  Ottawa,
Edmond Cloutier, Printer to the King's Most Excellent Majesty, 1941.
13 p.
Notes: Held meetings at Chicoutimi, August 25-September 9,
1941.  76 witnesses appeared before the Commission.  56 exhibits
were filed.


318 COMMISSION TO DETERMINE THE AMOUNTS, IF ANY, TO BE PAID BY
    WAY OF A COST OF LIVING BONUS TO THE EMPLOYEES OF THE
    COAL MINE OPERATORS OF THE ESTEVAN-BIENFAIT DISTRICT,
    SASKATCHEWAN

Appointed on August 29, 1941 by Order in Council P. C. 6839 under
Part I of the Inquiries Act (R. S. C., 1927, c. 99) and on the recom-
mendation of the Minister of Labour.
Commissioners: George Edwin Britnell, Chairman, Harold L.
Johnston and Vincent Clark.

First Report

Dated September 16, 1941.  Copy in Archives of Saskatchewan,
University of Saskatchewan, Regina:
Government of Canada.  Department of Labour.  Cost of Living
Commission, Coal Mining Industry, Estevan District.  First Report.
3 leaves.
No further reports located.
Notes: The Commission interviewed the proprietors, managers,
assistant managers or bookkeepers of 22 meat, grocery, clothing
and general stores serving the coal-mining communities of Estevan,
Bienfait and Roche Percee.


319 ROYAL COMMISSION ON SHIPBUILDING IN THE PROVINCES OF ONT-
    ARIO AND QUEBEC

Appointed on September 2, 1941 by Order in Council P. C. 6931 under Part I of the Inquiries Act (R. S. C., 1927, c. 99) and on the recommendation of the Minister of Labour. Extended on September 25, 1941 by Order in Council P. C. 7480 and on November 27, 1941 by Order in Council P. C. 9272. [1]

Commissioners: Leon Mercier Gouin, Chairman, Vincent C. MacDonald and F. H. Barlow.

### Report

Dated November 28, 1941. Printed as:

"Report of the Royal Commission on shipbuilding in the Provinces of Quebec and Ontario" in Labour Gazette, XLII, January, 1942, pp. 17-25.

320 ROYAL COMMISSION TO INQUIRE INTO AND REPORT UPON THE ORGANIZATION, AUTHORIZATION AND DISPATCH OF THE CANADIAN EXPEDITIONARY FORCE TO THE CROWN COLONY OF HONG KONG

Appointed on February 12, 1942 by Order in Council P. C. 1160 under Part I of the Inquiries Act (R. S. C., 1927, c. 99) and on the recommendation of the Prime Minister.

Commissioner: Sir Lyman Poore Duff.

Secretary: W. Kenneth Campbell.

### Report

Dated June 4, 1942. Tabled in the House of Commons on June 5, 1942. Sessional paper no. 302-1942. Printed as:

Dominion of Canada. Report on the Canadian Expeditionary Force to the Crown Colony of Hong Kong, by Right Honourable Sir Lyman P. Duff, G. C. M. G., Royal Commissioner pursuant to Order in Council, P. C. 1160. Ottawa, Edmond Cloutier, Printer to the King's Most Excellent Majesty, 1942. 61 p.

Notes: Hearings held from March 2, to March 31, 1941. 300 exhibits were filed. 2,288 typewritten pages of evidence taken.

321 ROYAL COMMISSION TO INQUIRE INTO THE MOST EFFECTIVE METHODS TO SECURE MAXIMUM PRODUCTION IN THE SHIPYARDS OF BRITISH COLUMBIA

Appointed on July 13, 1942 by Order in Council P. C. 5964 under

---

[1] Originally the Commission was to be concerned only with shipbuilding firms in the Province of Quebec.

Part I of the Inquiries Act (R. S. C. , 1927, c. 99) and on the recom-
mendation of the Minister of Labour.
Commissioners: Stephen Ellswood Richards, Chairman, Donald
Serviss, Hugh Lewis, Chris. Pritchard and A. A. McAuslane.

Report
Dated August 28, 1942. Copy in Department of Labour files.
28 leaves.
Notes: Public sittings held at Vancouver and Victoria (July 21 -
August 14, 1942). 46 exhibits placed before the Commission.

322 ROYAL COMMISSION TO INVESTIGATE WAGE RATES IN STEEL PLANTS
AT SAULT STE. MARIE, ONTARIO AND SYDNEY, NOVA SCOTIA

Appointed on September 14, 1942, by Order in Council P. C. 8267
under Part I of the Inquiries Act (R. S. C. , 1927, c. 99) and on the
recommendation of the Minister of Labour.
Commissioners: F. H. Barlow, Chairman, James T. Stewart
and J. King Gordon.

Report
Dated December 28, 1942. Printed as:
Report of Royal Commission appointed to report as to adjustments
(if any) of wage rates of employees in Algoma Steel Corporation Limi-
ted and Dominion Steel and Coal Corporation Limited, pursuant to
Order in Council P. C. 5963. Signed by the Honourable Mr. Justice
Barlow, Chairman and Mr. James T. Stewart, Commissioner; to-
gether with a minority report signed by Mr. J. King Gordon, Com-
missioner. [Ottawa, 1942]. 34 leaves.
Notes: Held hearings at Sault Ste. Marie, Toronto and Sydney.

323 COMMISSION TO INQUIRE INTO CHARGES CONTAINED IN ARTICLES
IN THE VANCOUVER·NEWS HERALD UNDER THE HEADING "NIPPON
BLACK DRAGON OPERATES WITHIN BRITISH COLUMBIA"

Appointed on October 24, 1942 by Order in Council P. C. 9723
under Part I of the Inquiries Act (R. S. C. , 1927, c. 99) and on the
recommendation of the Minister of Justice.
Commissioner: John Charles Alexander Cameron.

Report
Dated December 19, 1942. Not printed. Carbon of typewritten
copy in Department of Justice files. 102 leaves.

Notes: Public hearings held at Vancouver (October 30 - November 21, 1942). 45 witnesses appeared before the Commission. 34 exhibits placed before the Commission.

324 COMMISSION TO INQUIRE INTO AND REPORT UPON CERTAIN COMPLAINTS MADE AGAINST A. FORGET, LOCAL REPRESENTATIVE OF THE WARTIME PRICES AND TRADE BOARD, AT MONT LAURIER, QUEBEC

Appointed on August 17, 1943 by Order in Council P. C. 6501 under Part I of the Inquiries Act (R. S. C., 1927, c. 99) and on the recommendation of the Minister of Finance.
Commissioner: Roland Millar.

Report
Dated March 7, 1944. Copy attached to Order in Council P. C. 1615-a of March 13, 1944. (In Privy Council Office, Ottawa). 53 leaves.
Notes: 131 witnesses examined during the inquiry.

325 ROYAL COMMISSION TO INVESTIGATE THE DEMANDS OF THE COAL MINERS OF WESTERN CANADA

Appointed on October 14, 1943 by Order in Council P. C. 8020 under Part I of the Inquiries Act (R. S. C., 1927, c. 99) and on the recommendation of the Minister of Labour.
Commissioners: G. B. O'Connor, Chairman, T. W. Laidlaw,[1] and L. D. Hyndman.[2]
Secretary: F. E. Harrison.

Reports
Interim Report: Dated November 17, 1943. Printed as
First Interim Report of the Royal Commission appointed under Letters Patent of the 14th day of October, A. D. 1943, pursuant to a Minute of Meeting of the Privy Council, approved by His Excellency the Governor General, on the 14th day of October, 1943, being P. C. 8020 in Labour Gazette, XLIII, December, 1943, pp. 1632-1635.
Final Report: Dated January 24, 1944. Mimeographed copy in Public Archives of Canada, National War Labour Board files, File No. 698 (a), Box 394536. 9 leaves.

[1] Appointed on November 11, 1943 by Order in Council P. C. 8559.
[2] Appointed on November 10, 1943 by Order in Council P. C. 8620.

Notes: Sittings held at Calgary and Edmonton.

326 COMMISSION TO INQUIRE INTO THE PROVISION MADE FOR THE PERSONS OF THE JAPANESE RACE IN THE SETTLEMENTS IN BRITISH COLUMBIA

Appointed on December 14, 1943, by Order in Council P. C. 9498 under Part I of the Inquiries Act (R. S. C. , 1927, c. 99) and on the recommendation of the Minister of Labour.
Commissioners: F. W. Jackson, Chairman, G. F. Davidson, W. R. Bone and Mary Sutherland.

Report
Dated January 12, 1944. Mimeographed copy in the Department of Labour Library. 17 leaves. (Appendices missing).
Notes: Hearings held at Vancouver (December 20 - January 12, 1944).

327 COMMISSION TO INQUIRE INTO THE PECUNIARY LOSS SUFFERED AS A RESULT OF THE CRASH OF THE LIBERATOR AIRCRAFT EW148 AT MONTREAL, QUEBEC, ON APRIL 25, 1944

Appointed on May 15, 1944 by Order in Council P. C. 3654 under Part I of the Inquiries Act (R. S. C. , 1927, c. 99) and on the recommendation of the Minister of National Defence for Air.
Commissioner: O. N. Tyndale.

Report
No report was ever issued.
Notes: Commission revoked on June 7, 1946 by Order in Council P. C. 2326.

328 COMMISSION TO INQUIRE INTO THE MATTERS OF MEMBERSHIP IN THE INDIAN BANDS IN LESSER SLAVE LAKE AGENCY

Appointed on May 19, 1944 by Order in Council P. C. 3744 under Part I of the Inquiries Act (R. S. C. , 1927, c. 99) and on the recommendation of the Minister of Mines and Resources.
Commissioner: W. A. Macdonald.

Report
Report dated August 7, 1944. Printed as:
"Report by Mr. Justice W. A. Macdonald, of the Supreme Court

of Alberta" in Special Joint Committee of the Senate and the House
of Commons appointed to continue and complete the examination and
consideration of the Indian Act. Minutes of Proceedings and Evidence,
No. 12, Monday, April 21, 1947. Ottawa, Edmond Cloutier, C. M. G. ,
G. A. , L. Ph. , Printer to the King's Most Excellent Majesty, Controller
of Stationery, 1947, Appendix EK, 557-566.

Notes: Sittings held in 13 centres. (June 12 - July 18, 1944).

## 329 ROYAL COMMISSION ON COAL

Appointed on October 12, 1944 by Order in Council P. C. 7756
under Part I of the Inquiries Act (R. S. C. , 1927, c. 99) and on the
recommendation of the Minister of Munitions and Supply.

Commissioners: W. F. Carroll, Chairman, Angus J. Morrison
and Colin Campbell McLaurin.

Secretary: Robert D. Howland.

### Report

Dated December 14, 1946. Tabled in the House of Commons on
January 31, 1947. Sessional Paper no. 142-1947. Printed as:

Report of the Royal Commission on coal, 1946. Honourable Mr.
Justice W. F. Carroll, Chairman, Mr. Angus J. Morrison, Honourable Mr. Justice C. C. McLaurin. Ottawa, Edmond Cloutier, C. M. G. ,
B. A. , L. Ph. , King's Printer and Controller of Stationery, 1947. ix,
663 p.

Notes: Public hearings held from January 16, 1945 to April, 1946.
6,030 pages of evidence recorded.

## 330 ROYAL COMMISSION ON THE TAXATION OF ANNUITIES AND FAMILY CORPORATIONS

Appointed on November 13, 1944 by Order in Council P. C. 8679
under Part I of the Inquiries Act (R. S. C. , 1927, c. 99) and on the recommendation of the Minister of Finance.

Commissioners: William C. Ives, Chairman, Duncan Alexander
MacGibbon and Maxwell Weir Mackenzie.

Secretary: J. A. Michon.

### Report

Dated March 29, 1945. Made public on May 4, 1945 by the Minister of Finance, James Ilsley. Printed as:

Report of the Royal Commission on taxation of annuities and
family corporations, 1945. Ottawa, Edmond Cloutier, Printer to the
King's Most Excellent Majesty, 1945. 99 p.

Notes: 32 public sittings held. 73 witnesses examined. 305 submissions considered by the Commission.

## 331 ROYAL COMMISSION ON CO-OPERATIVES

Appointed on November 16, 1944 by Order in Council P. C. 8725 under Part I of the Inquiries Act (R. S. C., 1927, c. 99) and on the recommendation of the Minister of Finance.

Commissioners: Errol M. McDougall, Chairman, B. N. Arnason, G. A. Elliott, Jean-Marie Nadeau and J. J. Vaughan.

Executive Secretary: G. W. Ross.

### Report

Dated September 25, 1945. Tabled in the House of Commons on November 26, 1945. Sessional Paper no. 224-1945. Printed as:

Report of the Royal Commission on co-operatives. Ottawa, Edmond Cloutier, Printer to the King's Most Excellent Majesty, 1945. 245 p.

Notes: Hearings held in 11 cities. (January 15 - May 3, 1945) 175 briefs considered by the Commission.

## 332 ROYAL COMMISSION ON VETERANS' QUALIFICATIONS

Appointed on April 10, 1945 by Order in Council P. C. 2486 under Part I of the Inquiries Act (R. S. C, 1927, c. 99) and on the recommendation of the Minister of Labour. Amended on May 8, 1945 by Order in Council P. C. 3342.

Commissioners: Wilfred Bovey, Chairman, D. S. Lyons, Stewart R. Ross, [1] J. C. G. Herwig, F. S. Smelts, Hector Dupuis and F. S. Rutherford. [2]

Secretary: A. E. Fortington.

### Reports

First Interim Report: Dated June 22, 1945. Tabled in the House of Commons on October 29, 1945. Sessional Paper no. 117a-1945. Copy in Sessional Paper Office, Parliament Buildings, Ottawa. 51 p.

Second Interim Report: Dated September 14, 1945. Tabled in the House of Commons on October 29, 1945. Sessional Paper no. 117a-1945. Copy in Sessional Paper Office Parliament Buildings, Ottawa. 280 p.

Third and Final Report: Dated December 27, 1945. Tabled in the House of Commons on June 27, 1946. Sessional Paper no. 124h-1946. Copy in Sessional Paper Office, Parliament Buildings, Ottawa. 552 p.

[1] Appointed on May 8, 1945, by Order in Council P. C. 3342 to replace F. S. Rutherford.

[2] Resigned on May 8, 1945.

Notes: Hearings held in three cities (May 11 - June 25, 1945).

333 COMMISSION TO INQUIRE INTO THE PURCHASE PRICE OF CERTAIN
LAND IN THE TOWNSHIP OF SANDWICH WEST, ONTARIO, BOUGHT
UNDER THE PROVISIONS OF THE VETERANS' LAND ACT

Appointed on April 13, 1945 by Order in Council P. C. 2564 under
Part I of the Inquiries Act (R. S. C. , 1927, c. 99) and on the recommend-
ation of the Minister of Veterans Affairs.
Commissioner: D. M. Brodie.

Report
Dated February 15, 1946. Tabled in the House of Commons on
March 18, 1946. Sessional Paper no. 127b-1946. Not printed.
Typewritten copy in the Library of Parliament, Ottawa. 5 leaves.
Notes: Hearings held at Windsor, August 7, 1945.

334 ROYAL COMMISSION TO INQUIRE INTO THE DISORDERS AT HALIFAX,
NOVA SCOTIA, AND VICINITY THEREOF, DURING A CELEBRATION
OF THE DECLARATION OF VICTORY OVER GERMANY ON THE 7TH
AND 8TH MAY, 1945

Appointed on May 10, 1945 by Order in Council P. C. 3422 1/2
under the Inquiries Act (R. S. C. , 1927, c. 99) and on the recommendation of the Acting Prime Minister. Part of Inquiries Act not stated in
the Order in Council.
Commissioner: Roy Lindsay Kellock.

Report
Dated July 28, 1945. Tabled in the House of Commons on Septem-
ber 11, 1945. Sessional Paper no. 130-1945. Printed as:
Report on the Halifax disorders, May 7th - 8th, 1945, by Honour-
able Mr. Justice R. L. Kellock, Royal Commissioner. Pursurant to
Order in Council P. C. 3422 1/2 of May 10, 1945. Ottawa, Edmond
Cloutier, Printer to the King's Most Excellent Majesty, 1945. 61 p.
Notes: Sittings held at Halifax (May 17 - June 18, 1945).

335 COMMISSION TO INQUIRE INTO AN ARTICLE IN THE MONTREAL
GAZETTE ON MAY 15, 1945, REGARDING THE CAPTURE OF A
GERMAN SPY IN NOVEMBER, 1942

Appointed on May 29, 1945 by Order in Council P. C. 3858 under
the Inquiries Act (R. S. C. , 1927, c. 99) and on the recommendation

of the Minister of Justice.   Part of Inquiries Act not given in the Order
in Council.
    Commissioner:   Robert Forsyth.

Report
Copy in Department of Justice files.   Unavailable for examination.


336 ROYAL COMMISSION TO INQUIRE INTO THE ACTIVITIES AND LOYALTY
    OF THE JAPANESE IN CANADA DURING THE WAR

    Established on December 15, 1945 by Order in Council P. C. 7375
under Part I of the Inquiries Act (R. S. C. , 1927, c. 99) and on the recommendation of the Prime Minister.   Revoked on January 23, 1947
by Order in Council P. C. 269.
    Commissioners:   No indication that any members were appointed.

Report
Apparently no report was ever issued.


337 ROYAL COMMISSION TO INVESTIGATE THE FACTS RELATING TO AND
    THE CIRCUMSTANCES SURROUNDING THE COMMUNICATION, BY
    PUBLIC OFFICIALS AND OTHER PERSONS IN POSITIONS OF TRUST
    OF SECRET AND CONFIDENTIAL INFORMATION TO AGENTS OF A
    FOREIGN POWER

    Appointed on February 5, 1946 by Order in Council P. C. 411 under
Part I of the Inquiries Act (R. S. C. , 1927, c. 99) and on the recommendation of the Prime Minister.
    Commissioners:   Robert Taschereau and Roy Lindsay Kellock.
    Secretary:   W. K. Campbell.

Reports[1]
First Interim Report:   Dated March 2, 1946.   Tabled in the House
of Commons on March 14, 1946.   Sessional Paper no. 132-1946.
Printed in Final Report, pp. 693-696.
    Second Interim Report:   Dated March 14, 1946.   Tabled in the

---

[1] An Additional document was also issued:
Documents relating to the proceedings of the Royal Commission established by Order in Council P. C. 411 of February 5, 1946, including
the First and Second Interim Reports of the Royal Commission.
Ottawa, Edmond Cloutier, Printer to the King's Most Excellent Majesty, 1946.   25 p.

House of Commons on March 15, 1946.  Sessional Papers nos. 132a,
132b-1946.  Printed in Final Report, pp. 697-703.

Third Interim Report: Dated March 29, 1946.  Tabled in the
House of Commons on March 29, 1946.  Sessional Paper no. 132d-
1946.  Printed in Final Report, pp. 705-712.

Final Report: Dated on June 27, 1946.  Tabled in the House of
Commons on July 15, 1946.  Sessional Paper no. 132f-1946.  Printed
as:

The Report of the Royal Commission appointed under Order in
Council P. C. 411 of February 5, 1946 to investigate the facts relating
to and the circumstances surrounding the communication, by public
officials and other persons in positions of trust and secret and confid-
ential information to agents of a foreign power.  June 27, 1946.  Hon-
ourable Mr. Justice Robert Taschereau, Honourable Mr. Justice R. L.
Kellock, Commissioners.  E. K. Williams, K. C. , Gerald Fauteux,
K. C.  D. W. Mundell, Esq. , Counsel.  W. K. Campbell, Secretary.
J. H. Pepper, Esq. , Deputy Secretary.  Ottawa, Edmond Cloutier,
Printer to the King's Most Excellent Majesty, 1946.  733 p.

Notes: Hearings held February 13 - June 27, 1946.  116 witnesses
appeared before the Commission.  1, 000 pages of exhibits studied.
6, 000 pages of evidence taken.


338 ROYAL COMMISSION ON ADMINISTRATIVE CLASSIFICATION IN THE
PUBLIC SERVICE

Appointed on February 15, 1946 by Order in Council P. C. 563
under Part I of the Inquiries Act (R. S. C. , 1927, c. 99) and on the
recommendation of the Minister of Finance.

Commissioners: Walter Lockhart Gordon, Chairman, Edouard
de Bellefeuille Panet, Sir Horace Hamilton, [1] and Sir Thomas Gardiner. [2]
Secretary: John James Deutsch.

#### Report

Letter of transmittal dated July 4, 1946.  Tabled in the House of
Commons on July 16, 1946.  Sessional Paper no. 246-1946.  Printed
as:

Report of the Royal Commission on administrative classifications
in the public service, 1946.  Ottawa, Edmond Cloutier, B. A. , L. Ph. ,
C. M. G. , Printer to the King's Most Excellent Majesty and Controller
of Stationery, 1946.  36 p.

Notes: Public sittings held at Ottawa (March - May, 1946).  66

---

[1] Resigned due to illness.

[2] Replaced Hamilton on February 21, 1946 by Order in Council P. C.
641.

Cabinet Ministers, Deputy Ministers and other high civil servants interviewed by the Commission. 10 submissions received from organizations.

339 ROYAL COMMISSION ON THE INDIAN ACT AND INDIAN ADMINISTRATION IN GENERAL

Appointed on October 11, 1946 by Order in Council P. C. 3797 under Part I of the Inquiries Act (R. S. C., 1927, c. 99) and on the recommendation of the Minister of Mines and Resources.
Commissioners: J. Fred Johnston and Donald Ferguson Brown, Joint Chairmen, Norman McLeod Patterson, William Horace Taylor, William Bryce, William Garfield Case, Thomas Farquhar, Wilfred Gariepy, Douglas Scott Harkness and John Leon Raymond.
Secretary: Thomas L. McEvoy.

Report
Dated July 8, 1947. Tabled in the House of Commons on July 8, 1947. Sessional Paper no. 68b-1947. Mimeographed copy in Sessional Paper Office, Parliament Buildings, Ottawa. 16 leaves.
Notes: Meetings held on 19 reserves (October 20 - November 6, 1946). The Commission was originally a special Joint Parliamentary Committee.

340 ROYAL COMMISSION TO INVESTIGATE COMPLAINTS OF CANADIAN CITIZENS OF JAPANESE ORIGIN WHO RESIDED IN BRITISH COLUMBIA IN 1941, THAT THEIR REAL AND PERSONAL PROPERTY HAD BEEN DISPOSED OF BY THE CUSTODIAN OF ENEMY PROPERTY AT PRICES LESS THAN THE FAIR MARKET VALUE

Appointed on July 18, 1947 by Order in Council P. C. 1810 under Part I of the Inquiries Act (R. S. C., 1927, c. 99) and on the recommendation of the Secretary of State. Amended on September 17, 1947 by Order in Council P. C. 3737. Also extended on January 22, 1948 by Orders in Council P. C. 242 and P. C. 243.
Commissioner: Henry Irvine Bird.
Secretaries: A. Watson and V. J. White.

Report
Dated April 6, 1950. Tabled in the House of Commons on June 13, 1950. Sessional Paper no. 185a-1950. Mimeographed copy in the Sessional Paper Office, Parliament Buildings, Ottawa. 66 p.
Notes: Hearings held December 3, 1947 - March 3, 1950. 1434 claims considered.

341 COMMISSION TO INVESTIGATE COMPLAINTS MADE BY WALTER H.
KIRCHNER, M. C., D. C. M., SECRETARY, CANADIAN COMBATS
VETERANS ASSOCIATION, INC., VANCOUVER, BRITISH COLUMBIA,
REGARDING PENSION AND TREATMENT SERVICES WITH RESPECT
TO CERTAIN CASES CONCERNING WHICH MR. KIRCHNER HAS MADE
REPRESENTATIONS

Appointed on December 4, 1947 by Order in Council P. C. 4980
under Part I of the Inquiries Act (R. S. C., 1927, c. 99) and on the re-
commendation of the Minister of Veterans Affairs. Amended on Janu-
ary 8, 1948 by Order in Council P. C. 75.
Commissioners: James Joseph McCann, Chairman, Robert Henry
Winters, Chairman,[1] William Gourlay Blair, John Oliver Probe and
Moses Elijah McGarry.
Secretary: F. L. Barrow.

Report
Undated. Tabled in the House of Commons on March 9, 1948.
Sessional Paper no. 131i-1948. Copy in Sessional Paper Office,
Parliament Buildings, Ottawa. 24 p.
Notes: Commission held 35 sittings. 24 witnesses appeared
before the Commission.


342 COMMISSION ON THE FRASER VALLEY RELIEF AND REHABILITATION

Appointed on June 10, 1948 by Order in Council P. C. 2644 under
Part I of the Inquiries Act (R. S. C., 1927, c. 99) and on the recom-
mendation of the Prime Minister.
Commissioners: B. M. Hoffmeister and Eric W. Hamber.

Report
It appears that no report was issued.
Notes: Commission revoked on August 31, 1948 by Order in
Council P. C. 3839.


343 ROYAL COMMISSION ON PRICES

Appointed on July 8, 1948 by Order in Council P. C. 3109 under
Part I of the Inquiries Act (R. S. C., 1927, c. 99) and on the recommendation of the Minister of National Health and Welfare.
Commissioners: Clifford Austin Curtis, Chairman, Henri C. Bois
and Mary Sutherland.

[1] Acted in the absence of McCann.

Secretary: A. G. S. Griffin.

### Report

Letter of transmittal dated March 18, 1949. Tabled in the House of Commons on April 8, 1949. Sessional Paper no. 193-1949.

Report of the Royal Commission on prices. Ottawa, Edmond Cloutier, C. M. G. , B. A. , L. Ph. , Printer to the King's Most Excellent Majesty, Controller of Stationery, 1949. 3 v. (647 p. )

Notes: 77 public hearings held at Ottawa (August 3 - December 16, 1948). 179 witnesses examined.

### 344 ROYAL COMMISSION ON TRANSPORTATION

Appointed on December 29, 1928, by Order in Council P. C. 6033 under Part I of the Inquiries Act (R. S. C. , 1927, c. 99) and on the recommendation of the Prime Minister.

Commissioners: William Ferdinand Alphonse Turgeon, Chairman, Henry Forbes Angus and Harold Adams Innis.

Secretary: G. R. Hunter.

### Report

Letter of transmittal dated February 9, 1951. Tabled in the House of Commons on March 15, 1951. Sessional Paper no. 161-1951.

Printed as:

Report of the Royal Commission on transportation, 1951. Ottawa, Edmond Cloutier, C. M. G. , B. A. , L. Ph. , King's Printer and Controller of Stationery, 1951. 307 p.

Notes: Hearings held in 14 cities (May 2, 1949 - May 31, 1950). 214 witnesses appeared before the Commission. 143 formal submissions presented. 24,000 pages of evidence recorded. Cost: $468,853.

### 345 ROYAL COMMISSION ON THE REVISION OF CRIMINAL CODE

Appointed on February 3, 1949 by Order in Council P. C. 527 on the recommendation of the Minister of Justice. No indication of authorizing statute given in the Order in Council. Reorganized on September 26, 1950 and May 10, 1951 by Orders in Council P. C. 68/4633 and P. C. 2275 respectively.

Commissioners: William Melville Martin, Chairman, Gerald Fauteux, F. P. Varcoe, Robert Forsyth, Fernand Choquette, H. J. Wilson, Joseph Sedgwick and A. A. Moffat.

Secretary: L. J. Ryan.

### Report

Dated February 22, 1952. Tabled in the House of Commons on

April 7, 1952. Sessional Paper no. 66b-1952. Printed as:
Report of Royal Commission on the revision of Criminal Code.
Reports of Special Committee (Session 1952-53) on the Bill No. 93
(Letter O of the Senate) "An Act Respecting the Criminal Code".
House of Commons, December 16, 1953. Edmond Cloutier, C. M. G. ,
O. A. , D. S. P. , Queen's Printer and Controller of Stationery, Ottawa,
1954. pp. 1-45.
Notes: 12 meetings held. Each occupied a period of about one
week.


346 ROYAL COMMISSION ON NATIONAL DEVELOPMENT IN THE ARTS,
    LETTERS AND SCIENCES

Appointed on April 8, 1949 by Order in Council P. C. 1786 under
Part I of the Inquiries Act (R. S. C. , 1927, c. 99) and on the recom-
mendation of the Prime Minister.
Commissioners: Vincent Massey, Chairman, Arthur Surveyor,
Norman Archibald MacRae Mackenzie, Rev. Georges Henri Levesque
and Hilda Neatby.
Secretary: Archibald A. Day.

### Report

Dated May, 1951. Tabled in the House of Commons on June 1,
1951. Sessional Paper no. 189-1951. Printed as:
Report of Royal Commission on National development in the arts,
letters and sciences, 1949-1951. Ottawa: Edmond Cloutier, C. M. G. ,
O. A. , D. S. P. , Printer to the King's Most Excellent Majesty, 1951.
xxi, 517 p.

### Special Studies

A volume containing twenty-eight special studies prepared for the
Royal Commission was published in 1951:
Royal Commission studies. A selection of essays prepared for
the Royal Commission on national development in the arts, letters and
sciences. Ottawa, Edmond Cloutier, C. M. G. , O. A. , D. S. P. , Printer
to the King's Most Excellent Majesty, 1951. vii, 430 p.
Notes: Hearings held in 16 cities (August 3, 1949 - July 8, 1950).
Commissioners held 224 meetings - 114 of these were in public session.
462 briefs were presented. 1, 200 witnesses appeared before the Commission. Cost: $287,101.


347 ROYAL COMMISSION TO INQUIRE INTO THE NATURE AND EXTENT
    OF THE DAMAGE CAUSED BY THE RECENT FIRES IN THE TOWNS
    OF RIMOUSKI AND CABANO IN THE PROVINCE OF QUEBEC

Appointed on May 17, 1950 by Order in Council P. C. 2537 under the Inquiries Act (R. S. C. , 1927, c. 99) and on the recommendation of the Prime Minister. Part of Inquiries Act not stated in the Order in Council.

Commissioners: A. Theriault and Edouard Laurent.

### Reports

Preliminary Report: Dated May 27, 1950. Tabled in the House of Commons on June 16, 1950. Sessional Paper no. 180c-1950. Not printed. Copy in Sessional Paper Office, Parliament Buildings, Ottawa. 4 leaves.

Final Report on Fire at Rimouski: Dated October, 1950. Tabled in the House of Commons on January 29, 1951. Sessional Paper no. 164-1950/51. Not printed. Typewritten copy in the Sessional Paper Office, Parliament Buildings, Ottawa. 15 leaves and maps and diagrams.

Final Report on Fire at Cabano: Dated October, 1950. Tabled in the House of Commons on January 29, 1951. Sessional Paper no. 164a-1950/51. Not printed. Typewritten copy in the Sessional Paper Office, Parliament Buildings, Ottawa. 11 leaves and maps and diagrams.

Notes: Cost: $4,789.

348 ROYAL COMMISSION TO INQUIRE INTO THE NATURE AND EXTENT OF THE DAMAGE CAUSED BY THE 1950 FLOODS IN THE RED RIVER VALLEY IN MANITOBA

Appointed on May 17, 1950 by Order in Council P. C. 2536 under the Inquiries Act (R. S. C., 1927, c. 99) and on the recommendation of the Prime Minister. Part of Inquiries Act not stated in the Order in Council.

Commissioners: John Ballantyne Carswell and Donald Bruce Shaw.

### Reports

Interim Report: Dated June 6, 1950. Tabled in the House of Commons on June 9, 1950. Sessional Paper no. 182f-1950. Not printed. Copy in Sessional Paper Office, Parliament Buildings, Ottawa, 27 leaves.

Final Report: Not located.

Notes: Commission opened hearings May 17, 1950. Cost: $8,644.

349 ROYAL COMMISSION TO INQUIRE INTO, REVIEW AND REPORT ON THE RENTALS PAYABLE UNDER THE LEASES IN THE TOWNSITES AND SUBDIVISIONS OF BANFF AND JASPER NATIONAL PARKS AND THE MINIMUM VALUE OF BUILDINGS WHICH MAY BE ERECTED ON A LOT IN A TOWNSITE OR SUBDIVISION IN SAID PARKS

Appointed on December 9, 1950 by Order in Council P. C. 81/5955 under Part I of the Inquiries Act (R. S. C. , 1927, c. 99) and on the recommendation of the Treasury Board.

Commissioner: Harry O. Patriquin.

Report

Dated December 14, 1950. Typewritten copy in the Public Archives of Canada (R.G. 33, no. 29). 9 leaves.

Notes: Cost: $822.00.

350 ROYAL COMMISSION ON THE SOUTH SASKATCHEWAN RIVER PROJECT

Appointed on August 24, 1951 by Order in Council P. C. 4435 under Part I of the Inquiries Act (R. S. C. , 1927, c. 99) and on the recommendation of the Prime Minister.

Commissioners: Thomas Henry Hogg, Chairman, Geoffrey Abbott Gaherty and John A. Widtsoe. [1]

Secretary: Berton Taylor Richardson.

Report

Dated October 29, 1952. Tabled in the House of Commons on January 19, 1953. Sessional Paper no. 170-1953. Printed as:

Report of the Royal Commission on the South Saskatchewan River Project, 1952. Edmond Cloutier, C. M. G. , O. A. , D. S. P. , Queen's Printer and Controller of Stationery, Ottawa, 1952. xix, 423 p.

Notes: Public hearings held at 4 cities and towns in Alberta and Saskatchewan (May 2 - September 12, 1952). Cost: $151,165.

351 COMMISSION TO INQUIRE INTO AND REPORT UPON THE FACTS CONCERNING THE STAKING OF CERTAIN AREAS OF THE CROWN IN THE NORTH WEST TERRITORIES AND YUKON TERRITORY

Appointed on November 12, 1951 by Order in Council P. C. 6027 under Part I of the Inquiries Act and on the recommendation of the Minister of Resources and Development.

Commissioner: Kenneth J. Christie.

Report

Undated. Photocopy in the Public Archives of Canada (R.G. 33, no. 30). 24 leaves (Appendices missing).

---

[1] Dr. Widtsoe died in Salt Lake City, Utah on November 29, 1952 while the Report was being printed.

Notes: Hearings held at Hay River, North West Territories, and Calgary (November 30, 1951 - December 7, 1951). Cost: $1,358.

352 ROYAL COMMISSION ON THE LAW OF INSANITY AS A DEFENCE IN CRIMINAL CASES

Appointed on March 2, 1954 by Order in Council P.C. 1954-289 under Part I of the Inquiries Act (R.S.C., 1952, c. 154) and on the recommendation of the Minister of Justice.
Commissioners: James Chalmers McRuer, Chairman, Gustave Desrochers, Helen Kinnear, Robert Orville Jones and Joseph Harris.
Secretary: R. Noel Dickson.

Report
Dated October 25, 1956. Tabled in the House of Commons on November 15, 1957. Sessional Paper no. 194-1957. Printed as:
Report of the Royal Commission on the law of insanity as a defence in criminal cases. Hull, Edmond Cloutier, C.M.G., O.A., D.S.P., Queen's Printer and Controller of Stationery [1957] viii, 73 p.
Notes: Hearings held in 13 cities. 22 organizations made representations.

353 ROYAL COMMISSION ON THE CRIMINAL LAW RELATING TO CRIMINAL SEXUAL PSYCHOPATHS

Appointed on March 25, 1954 by Order in Council P.C. 1954-445 under Part I of the Inquiries Act (R.S.C., 1952, c. 154) and on the recommendation of the Minister of Justice.
Commissioners: James Chalmers McRuer, Chairman, Gustave Desrochers and Helen Kinnear.
Secretary: R. Noel Dickson.

Report
Dated March 21, 1958. Tabled in the House of Commons on April 16, 1959. Sessional Paper no. 218-1959. Printed as:
Report of the Royal Commission on the criminal law relating to criminal sexual psychopaths. [Ottawa, Queen's Printer 1958] x, 200 p.
Notes: Hearings held in 13 cities. 52 briefs submitted.

354 ROYAL COMMISSION TO INQUIRE INTO, REVIEW AND REPORT ON THE ADMINISTRATION OF QUARTZ MINING AND PLACER MINING IN THE YUKON TERRITORY

Appointed on April 29, 1954 by Order in Council P. C. 656 under
Part I of the Inquiries Act (R. S. C., 1952, c. 154) and on the recom-
mendation of the Minister of Northern Affairs and Natural Resources.
Commissioner: George Edwards Cole.

Report
Dated June 18, 1954. Photocopy in Public Archives of Canada
(R. G. 33, no 31). 17 leaves.
Notes: Cost: $3,625.

355 ROYAL COMMISSION ON AGREED CHARGES

Appointed on May 20, 1954 by Order in Council P. C. 1954-760
under Part I of the Inquiries Act (R. S. C., 1952, c. 154) and on the
recommendation of the Prime Minister.
Commissioner: William Ferdinand Alphonse Turgeon.
Secretary: Charles W. Rump.

Report
Letter of transmittal dated February 21, 1955. Tabled in the
House of Commons on March 24, 1955. Sessional Paper no. 137a-1955.
Printed as:
Report of Royal Commission on agreed charges. February 21,
1955. W. F. A. Turgeon, Commissioner. Ottawa, Edmond Cloutier,
C. M. G., O. A., D. S. P., Queen's Printer and Controller of Stationery,
1955. 51 p.
Notes: Public hearings held in 5 cities (September 13 - December
21, 1954). 47 briefs submitted to the Commission. Cost: $19,183.

356 ROYAL COMMISSION ON PATENTS, COPYRIGHT, TRADE MARKS AND
INDUSTRIAL DESIGN

Appointed on June 10, 1954 by Order in Council P. C. 1954-852
under Part I of the Inquiries Act (R. S. C., 1952, c. 154) and on the
recommendation of the Secretary of State.
Commissioners: James Lorimer Isley, Chairman, W. W. Buchanan
and Guy Favreau. [1]
Secretary: A. M. Laidlaw.

Reports
Report on Copyright: Dated August 1, 1957. Tabled in the House
of Commons on June 10, 1958. Sessional Paper no. 186-1958. Printed
as:

---

[1] Resigned early in 1959.

Royal Commission on Patents, Copyright, Trade Marks and Industrial Designs. Report on Copyright. Edmond Cloutier, C. M. G., O. A., D. S. P., Queen's Printer and Controller of Stationery, Ottawa, 1957. 151 p.

Report on Industrial Design: Dated June 1, 1958. Tabled in the House of Commons on August 8, 1958. Sessional Paper no. 186a-1958. Printed as:

Royal Commission on Patents, Copyright, Trade Marks and Industrial Designs. Report on Industrial Designs. Edmond Cloutier, C. M. G., O. A., D. S. P., Queen's Printer and Controller of Stationery, Ottawa, 1958. 90 p.

Report on Patents of Inventions: Dated December 31, 1959. Tabled in the House of Commons on April 4, 1960. Sessional Paper no. 244-1960. Printed as:

Royal Commission on Patents, Copyright and Industrial Designs. Report on Patents of Invention. The Queen's Printer and Controller of Stationery, Ottawa, 1960. 196 p.

Notes: Cost $42, 172.


357 COMMISSION TO INQUIRE INTO THE NATURE AND EXTENT OF THE DAMAGE CAUSED BY THE FLOOD IN AND ADJOINING THE HUMBER RIVER VALLEY IN ONTARIO

Appointed on October 20, 1954 by Order in Council P. C. 1954-1610 under the Inquiries Act (R. S. C., 1952, c. 154) and on the recommendation of the Prime Minister. Part of Inquiries Act not stated in the Order in Council.

Commissioners: John Ballantyne Carswell and Donald Bruce Shaw.

Report

Undated. Not printed. Photocopy in the Public Archives of Canada (R.G. 33, no. 33). 8 leaves.

Notes: Commission took evidence from 19 delegations representing townships and 25 delegations from cities, towns and villages in the area. Cost: $1, 000.


358 ROYAL COMMISSION ON THE COASTING TRADE

Appointed on March 1, 1955 by Order in Council P. C. 1955-308 under Part I of the Inquiries Act (R. S. C., 1952, c. 154) and on the recommendation of the Minister of Transport.

Commissioners: Wishart Flett Spence, Chairman, W. N. Wickwire and Marcel Bélanger.

Secretary: G. Gordon McLeod.

Report

Dated December 9, 1957. Tabled in the House of Commons on
May 21, 1958. Sessional Paper no. 182-1958. Printed as:

Report of the Royal Commission on coasting trade. December 9,
1957. Appointed by Order in Council P. C. 1955-308 of the 1st March
1955. Ottawa, Edmond Cloutier, C. M. G. , O. A. , D. S. P. , Queen's
Printer and Controller of Stationery, 1958. xvii, 356 p.

Notes: Public hearings held in 17 cities (July 11, 1955 - January
11, 1956). 173 briefs filed with the Commission. 6,000 pages of
evidence recorded. 257 exhibits filed. Cost: $247,461.


359 ROYAL COMMISSION ON CANADA'S ECONOMIC PROSPECTS

Appointed on June 17, 1955 by Order in Council P. C. 1955-909
under Part I of the Inquiries Act (R. S. C. , 1952, c. 154) and on the
recommendation of the Prime Minister.

Commissioners: Walter Lockhart Gordon, Chairman, Omer
Lussier, Albert Edward Grauer, Andrew Stewart and Raymond Gushue.

Secretary: Douglas V. LePan.


Reports

Preliminary Report: Dated December 3, 1956. Tabled in the
House of Commons on January 10, 1957. Sessional Paper no. 176-
1957. Printed as:

Royal Commission on Canada's economic prospects. Preliminary
report. December, 1956. [Hull, Edmond Cloutier, C. M. G. , O. A. ,
D. S. P. , Queen's Printer and Controller of Stationery, 1956].

Final Report: Dated November 28, 1957. Tabled in the House of
Commons on May 12, 1958. Sessional Paper no. 181-1958. Printed
as:

Royal Commission on Canada's economic prospects. Final report.
November, 1957. [Edmond Cloutier, C. M. G. , O. A. , D. S. P. , Queen'
Printer and Controller of Stationery, 1958] 509 p.


Special Studies:

Anderson, Roger V. The future of Canada's export trade. [Ottaw
Queen's Printer, 1957] 338 p.

Bank of Montreal. The service industries. [Hull, Queen's Print
1956] 161 p.

Barber, Clarence Lyle. The Canadian electrical manufacturing
industry. [Hull, Queen's Printer, 1956] 87 p.

Brecher, Irving and S. S. Reisman. Canada-United States economic relations. [Ottawa, Queen's Printer, 1957]   344 p.

Canada. Department of Fisheries and the Fisheries Research
Board. The Commercial fisheries of Canada. [Ottawa, Queen's Printer, 1957]   192 p.

Canada. Department of Labour. Economics and Research Branch.
Skilled and professional manpower in Canada, 1945-1965. [Hull,
Queen's Printer, 1957]   xiv, 106 p.

The Canadian Bank of Commerce. Industrial concentration: A
study of industrial patterns in the United States, the United Kingdom
and Canada. [Hull, Queen's Printer, 1956]   62 p.

Canadian Business Service Limited. The electronics industry in
Canada. [Hull, Queen's Printer, 1956]   81 p.

Canadian Congress of Labour (not the Canadian Labour Congress).
Probable effects of increasing mechanization in industry. [Hull,
Queen's Printer, 1956]   87 p.

Davis, John. The Canadian chemical industry. [Ottawa, Queen's
Printer, 1957]   182 p.

---. Canadian energy prospects. [Hull, Queen's Printer, 1957]
392 p.

---. Davis, John. Mining and mineral processing in Canada.
[Hull, Queen's Printer, 1957]   ix, 400 p.

Davis, John and others. The outlook for the Canadian forest industries. [Hull, Queen's Printer, 1957]   x, 261 p.

Drummond, William Malcolm and William Mackenzie. Progress
and prospects of Canadian agriculture. [Ottawa, Queen's Printer,
1957]   424 p.

Dubé, Yves, J. E. Howes and D. L. McQueen. Housing and social
capital. [Hull, Queen's Printer, 1957]   164 p.

Fullerton, Douglas H. and H. A. Hampson. Canadian secondary
manufacturing industry. [Hull, Queen's Printer, 1957]   264 p.

Glassco, John Grant. Certain aspects of taxation relating to investment in Canada by non-residents. [Hull, Queen's Printer, 1956]
64 p.

Hood, William Clarence.  Financing of economic activity in Canada. [ Ottawa, Queen's Printer, 1959]  xv, 700 p.

Hood, William Clarence and Anthony Scott.  Output, labour and capital in the Canadian economy.  [ Hull, Queen's Printer, 1957]  513 p.

Howland, Robert Dudley.  Some regional aspects of Canada's economic development. [ Ottawa, Queen's Printer, 1958]  302 p.

Lessard, Jean-Claude.  Transportarion in Canada.  [ Ottawa, Queen's Printer, 1957]  160 p.

Morgan, Lucy (Ingram).  The Canadian primary iron and steel industry.  [ Hull, Queen's Printer, 1956]  104 p.

National Industrial Conference Board.  (Canadian Office).  The Canadian primary textiles industry.  [ Hull, Queen's Printer, 1956] 105 p.

The Royal Bank of Canada.  The Canadian construction industry. [ Ottawa, Queen's Printer, 1957]  232 p.

Slater, David W.  Canada's imports.  [ Ottawa, Queen's Printer, 1957]  222 p.

---.  Consumption expediture in Canada.  [ Ottawa, Queen's Printer, 1957]  198 p.

Smith, John McSwam.  Canadian economic growth and development from 1939 to 1955.  [ Hull, Queen's Printer, 1957]  80 p.

The Sun Life Assurance Company of Canada.  The Canadian automotive industry.  [ Hull, Queen's Printer, 1956]  119 p.

The Trades and Labour Congress of Canada (now the Canadian Labour Congress).  Labour mobility.  [ Hull, Queen's Printer, 1956] 11 p.

Urwick, Currie Limited.  The Canadian industrial machinery industry.  [ Hull, Queen's Printer, 1956]  31 p.

---.  The Nova Scotia coal industry.  [ Ottawa, Queen's Printer, 1957]  34 p.

Woods, (J. D. ) and Gordon, Limited.  The Canadian agricultural machinery industry.  [ Hull, Queen's Printer, 1956]  47 p.

Young, John H. Canadian commercial policy. [Ottawa, Queen's Printer, 1957] 235 p.

Notes: Meetings held in 14 cities (October 18, 1955 - March 9, 1956). 330 submissions received. 750 witnesses appeared before the Commission. Cost: $1,303,819.


360 ROYAL COMMISSION ON BROADCASTING

Appointed on December 2, 1955 by Order in Council P. C. 1955-1796 under Part I of the Inquiries Act (R. S. C., 1952, c. 154) and on the recommendation of the Prime Minister.
Commissioners: Robert MacLaren Fowler, Chairman, Edmond Turcotte and James Stewart.
Secretary: Paul Pelletier.


Report
Dated March 15, 1957. Tabled in the House of Commons on March 28, 1957. Sessional Paper no. 205-1957. Printed as:
Report of Royal Commission on broadcasting. Ottawa, Edmond Cloutier, C. M. G., O. A., D. S. P., Queen's Printer and Controller of Stationery. [1957] 2 v. (755 p. )

Special Studies:

Smythe, Dallas Walker. Basic tables: Television and radio programme analysis. [Ottawa, Queen's Printer, 1957] xiv, 275, xii, 267 p.

Notes: Hearings held in 12 cities (April 30 - October 12, 1956). 274 briefs received by the Commission. Cost: $328,509.


361 ROYAL COMMISSION ON EMPLOYMENT OF FIREMEN ON DIESEL LOCOMOTIVES IN FREIGHT AND YARD SERVICE ON THE CANADIAN PACIFIC RAILWAY

Appointed on January 17, 1957 by Order in Council P. C. 1957-52 under Part I of the Inquiries Act (R. S. C., 1952, c. 154) and on the recommendation of the Prime Minister.
Commissioners: Roy Lindsay Kellock, Chairman, Campbell C. McLaurin and Jean Martineau.


Report
Dated December 18, 1957. Printed as:

Report of the Royal Commission on employment of firemen on diesel locomotives in freight and yard service on the Canadian Pacific Railway. Edmond Cloutier, C. M. G. , O. A. , D. S. P. , Queen's Printer and Controller of Stationery, Ottawa, 1958. iv, 38 p.

Notes: Hearings held in 5 cities. 119 witnesses were heard. Cost: $139,979.

362 ROYAL COMMISSION ON NEWFOUNDLAND FINANCES

Appointed on February 21, 1957 by Order in Council P. C. 1957-257 under Part I of the Inquiries Act (R. S. C. , 1952, c. 154) and on the recommendation of the Prime Minister.

Commissioners: John Babbitt McNair, Chairman, Sir Albert Joseph Walsh and John James Deutsch.

Secretary: A. Sinclair Abell.

Report

Dated May 31, 1958. Tabled in the House of Commons on July 25, 1958. Sessional Paper no. 211-1958. Printed as:

Report. Royal Commission on Newfoundland finances under the terms of Union of Newfoundland with Canada. May 31, 1958. Edmond Cloutier, C. M. G. , O. A. , D. S. P. , Queen's Printer and Controller of Stationery, Ottawa, 1958. xi, 120 p.

Notes: Public hearings held at St. John's and Ottawa (July 22 - October 9, 1957). 3 briefs submitted to the Commission. Cost: $38,148.

363 ROYAL COMMISSION ON ENERGY

Appointed on October 15, 1957 by Order in Council P. C. 1957-1386 under Part I of the Inquiries Act (R. S. C. , 1952, c. 154) and on the recommendation of the Prime Minister.

Commissioners: Henry Borden, Chairman, J. Louis Levesque, George Edwin Britnell, Gordon G. Cushing,[1] Robert Dudley Howland, Leon Johnson Ladner and Robert Macdonald Hardy.[2]

Secretary: Joseph Frederick Parkinson.

First Report

Dated October 22, 1958. Tabled in the House of Commons on

---

[1] Resigned from the Commission on April 10, 1958, pending his appointment as Assistant Deputy Minister of Labour (effective May 1, 1958.

[2] Appointed on January 13, 1958 by Order in Council P. C. 1958-58.

March 4, 1959. Sessional Paper no. 199-1959. Printed as:
Royal Commission on energy. First report. October, 1958.
[Ottawa, Queen's Printer, 1958?] xiv, 98 p.

Second Report
Dated July 20, 1959. Tabled in the House of Commons on March
30, 1960. Sessional Paper no. 240-1960. Printed as:
Royal Commission on energy. Second report. July, 1959. [Ottawa,
Queen's Printer, 1960] viii, 189 p.
Notes: Public hearings held in 6 cities (February 3, - July 22,
1958). 110 submissions received. Cost: $414,557.


364 ROYAL COMMISSION ON PRICE SPREADS OF FOOD PRODUCTS

Appointed on December 10, 1957 by Order in Council P.C. 1957-
1632 under Part I of the Inquiries Act (R.S.C., 1952, c. 154) and on
the recommendation of the Prime Minister.
Commissioners: Andrew Stewart, Chairman, Dorothy Walton,
Howard MacKichan, Romeo Martin, W. M. Drummond, Cleve Kidd
and Bernard Courvrette.
Secretary: J. A. Dawson.

Report
Volumes 1 and 2: Dated September 11, 1959. Tabled in the House
of Commons on January 15, 1960. Sessional Paper no. 186-1960.
Volume 3:[1] Dated March, 1960. Tabled in the House of Commons
on May 10, 1960. Sessional Paper no. 186a-1960. Printed as:
Report of the Royal Commission on price spreads of food products.
[Ottawa, Queen's Printer, 1959-1960] 3 v. (962 p.)
Notes: Hearings held in 13 cities (April 9 - November 21, 1958).
100 submissions received by the Commission. Cost: $290,224.


365 ROYAL COMMISSION OF INQUIRY INTO THE DISTRIBUTION OF RAIL-
WAY BOX CARS

Appointed on January 31, 1958 by Order in Council P.C. 1958-181
on the recommendation of the Minister of Trade and Commerce. No
indication of authorizing statute given in Order in Council.
Commissioner: John Bracken.
Secretary: John Rayner.

---

[1] Contains a series of studies of price spreads of particular com-
modities.

Report
Letter of transmittal dated December 10, 1958. Tabled in the
House of Commons on April 23, 1959. Sessional Paper no. 187a-1959.
Printed as:
Report of the Inquiry into the distribution of railway box cars, by
John Bracken. [Ottawa, 1959] ix, 126 p.
Notes: Hearings held at Winnipeg and 16 rural points in Western
Canada. The staff met 6,800 farmers who presented it with briefs.

366 COMMISSION TO INQUIRE INTO THE DESIRABILITY OF ESTABLISHING
A NEW BAND OF INDIANS ON SEABIRD ISLAND, BRITISH COLUMBIA

Appointed on February 18, 1958 by Order in Council P. C. 1958-
281 under Part I of the Inquiries Act (R. S. C., 1952, c. 154) and on the
recommendation of the Minister of Citizenship and Immigration.
Commissioners: George L. Cassady, Chairman, Oscar D. Peters
and Vincent Harris.

Report
Dated August 25, 1958:
August 25th, 1958. Re: Seabird Island Inquiry. Report of Chair-
man and Commissioner Harris. [Ottawa, 1958?] 3 leaves.
Locations: Department of Manpower and Immigration Library,
Ottawa; Queen's University Library, Government Documents Depart-
ment, Kingston (Xerox copy).
Notes: Commission held hearings at Seabird Island and New West-
minster (March 27 - August 18, 1958). Cost: $2,506.00.

367 ROYAL COMMISSION ON TRANSPORTATION

Appointed on May 13, 1959 by Order in Council P. C. 1959-577
under Part I of the Inquiries Act (R. S. C., 1952, c. 154) and on the
recommendation of the Prime Minister.
Commissioners: Murdoch Alexander MacPherson, Chairman,[1]
Herbert Anscomb, Archibald H. Balch, René Gobeil, Howard Mann,
Arnold Platt and Charles P. McTague.[2]
Secretary: F. W. Anderson.

Report
Volume 1: Dated March 30, 1961. Tabled in the House of Commons

---

[1] MacPherson succeeded McTague as Chairman upon the latter's resignation. (See Order in Council P. C. 1959-1628 of December 22,
1959).
[2] McTague resigned because of ill health.

on April 10, 1961.  Sessional Paper no. 197-1961.
   Volume 2:  Dated December, 1961.  Tabled in the House of Commons on January 23, 1962.  Sessional Paper no. 186-1962.
   Volume 3:[1]  Dated July, 1962.  Tabled in the House of Commons on September 28, 1962.  Sessional Paper no. 183-1962.  Printed as:
   Royal Commission on transportation.  Report. [ Ottawa, Queen's Printer]  3 v.  (1,019 p. )
   Notes:  Public hearings held in 14 cities (September 17, 1959 - January 17, 1961).  153 briefs were received by the Commission.  185 exhibits were filed with the Commission.  Cost: $574,090.

## 368 ROYAL COMMISSION ON THE GREAT SLAVE LAKE RAILWAY

   Appointed on June 4, 1959 by Order in Council P. C. 1959-705 under Part I of the Inquiries Act (R. S. C. , 1952, c. 154) and on the recommendation of the Prime Minister.
   Commissioners:  Marshall E. Manning, W. D. Gainter and John Anderson-Thompson.
   Secretary:  A. Patterson.

                                   Report
   Volume 1:  Dated June 30, 1960.  Tabled in the House of Commons on July 13, 1960.  Sessional Paper no. 274-1960. [ Ottawa, Queen's Printer, 1960]  iv, 113 p.
   Volume 2:  Dated July, 1960.  Tabled in the House of Commons on November 28, 1960.  Sessional Paper no. 182-1960/61.  Printed as:
   Report of the Royal Commission on the Great Slave Lake Railway. [ Ottawa, Queen's Printer, 1960]  2 v. (201 p. )
   Notes:  Hearings held in 4 cities (September 22, 1959 - February 18, 1960).  Cost: $46,920.

## 369 ROYAL COMMISSION TO INVESTIGATE THE UNFULFILLED PROVISIONS OF TREATIES 8 AND 11 AS THEY APPLY TO THE INDIANS OF THE MACKENZIE DISTRICT

   Appointed on June 25, 1959 by Order in Council P. C. 799 under Part I of the Inquiries Act (R. S. C. , 1952, c. 154) and on the recommendation of the Minister of Citizenship and Immigration.
   Commissioners:  Walter H. Nelson, Chairman, V. F. Valentine, Leonard L. Brown, James Koe and Baptiste Cazon.

---

[1] Contains 10 special studies prepared for the Commission.

Report

Dated December 10, 1959. Printed as:

Report of the Commission appointed to investigate the unfulfilled provisions of Treaties 8 and 11 as they apply to the Indians of the Mackenzie District, 1959. [N. p., n. d.] 9 leaves.

Notes: Commissioners held public meetings at 15 settlements in the Mackenzie District. Approximately 710 adult Indians and about 43 non-Indians attended the meetings. Cost: $8,245.

370 ROYAL COMMISSION ON COAL

Appointed on October 6, 1959 by Order in Council P. C. 1959-1293 under Part I of the Inquiries Act (R. S. C., 1952, c. 154) and on the recommendation of the Prime Minister.

Commissioner: Ivan Cleveland Rand.

Secretary: W. Keith Buck.

Report

Dated August 31, 1960. Tabled in the House of Commons on December 8, 1960. Sessional Paper no. 187-1960. Printed as:

Report of Royal Commission on coal. The Honourable I. C. Rand, Q. C., the Commissioner. August, 1960. [Ottawa, Queen's Printer, 1960] xvi, 127 p.

Notes: Public hearings held in 8 cities (February 2 - April 19, 1960). 58 submissions presented. Cost: $99,166.

371 ROYAL COMMISSION ON THE AUTOMOTIVE INDUSTRY

Appointed on August 2, 1960 by Order in Council P. C. 1960-1047 under Part I of the Inquiries Act (R. S. C., 1952, c. 154) and on the recommendation of the Prime Minister.

Commissioner: Vincent Wheeler Bladen.

Secretary: J. Elizabeth Leith.

Report

Dated April 14, 1961. Tabled in the House of Commons on June 20, 1961. Sessional Paper no. 256-1961. Printed as:

Report. Royal Commission on the automobile industry. April, 1961. Roger Duhamel, F. R. S. C., Ottawa, Queen's Printer and Controller of Stationery [1961] xiii, 110 p.

Notes: Public hearings held at Ottawa, October 24 - October 28, 1960. 26 submissions considered. The Commissioner visited automobile factories in Canada, England, France, West Germany and Sweden. Cost: $57,841.

372 ROYAL COMMISSION TO INQUIRE INTO COMPLAINTS RECEIVED CON-
CERNING CERTAIN ACTIVITIES OF STATION CHEK-TV, VICTORIA,
BRITISH COLUMBIA

Appointed on September 6, 1960 by Order in Council P. C. 1960-
1211 under Part I of the Inquiries Act (R. S. C., 1952, c. 154) and on
the recommendation of the Committee of the Privy Council.
Commissioners: Andrew Stewart, Carlyle Allison, Joseph F.
Brown, Eugene Alfred Forsey and Leslie M. Marshall.

Report
Undated.  Copy in the Library of Parliament, Ottawa, 5 p.
Notes: Public hearings held at Vancouver, September 15-16, 1960.
Cost: $4,720.


373 ROYAL COMMISSION ON GOVERNMENT ORGANIZATION

Appointed on September 16, 1960 by Order in Council P. C. 1960-
1269 under Part I of the Inquiries Act (R. S. C., 1952, c. 154) and on
the recommendation of the Prime Minister.
Commissioners: John Grant Glassco, Chairman, Robert Watson
Sellar and F. Eugene Therrier.

Reports
First report on progress: Dated April, 1961.  Tabled in the House
of Commons on May 3, 1961.  Sessional Paper no. 227-1961.  Printed
as:
Royal Commission on government organization.  First report on
progress.  April 1961.  Roger Duhamel, F. R. S. C., Queen's Printer
and Controller of Stationery, Ottawa, 1961.  v, 20 p.
Volume 1:  Dated July 18, 1962.  Tabled in the House of Commons
on July 18, 1962.  Sessional Paper no. 182-1962.
Volume 2:  Dated October 1, 1962.  Tabled in the House of Commons on October 1, 1962.  Sessional Paper no. 182a-1962.
Volume 3:  Dated December 3, 1962.  Tabled in the House of Commons on December 3, 1962.  Sessional Paper no. 182b-1962.
Volume 4:  Dated January 21, 1963.  Tabled in the House of Commons on May 23, 1963.  Sessional Paper no. 185-1963.
Volume 5:  Dated February 28, 1963.  Tabled in the House of Commons on June 12, 1963.  Sessional Paper no. 185a-1963.  Printed as:
The Royal Commission on government organization.  Published by
the Queen's Printer, Ottawa, Canada, for the Royal Commission on
government organization, 1962-1963.  5 v.  (1,998 p.)
Notes: No public hearings held.  Cost: $2,791,915.

374 ROYAL COMMISSION ON PUBLICATIONS

Appointed on September 16, 1960 by Order in Council P. C. 1960-1270 under Part I of the Inquiries Act (R. S. C. , 1952, c. 154) and on the recommendation of the Prime Minister.

Commissioners: Michael Gratton O'Leary, Chairman, John George Johnston and Claude P. Beaubien.

Secretary: P. Michael Pitfield.

Report

Dated May 25, 1961. Tabled in the House of Commons on June 15, 1961. Sessional Paper no. 197a-1961. Printed as:

Report. Royal Commission on publications. May, 1961. Published by the Queen's Printer for the Royal Commission on publications. [Ottawa, 1961] vi, 263 p.

Notes: Public hearings held in 8 cities (November 14, 1960 - January 20, 1961). 188 briefs submitted. Cost: $136,121.

375 ROYAL COMMISSION ON HEALTH SERVICES

Appointed on June 20, 1961 by Order in Council P. C. 1961-883 under Part I of the Inquiries Act (R. S. C. , 1952, c. 154) and on the recommendation of the Prime Minister.

Commissioners: Emmett Matthew Hall, Chairman, Miss Alice Girard, David M. Baltzan, O. John Firestone, Malcolm Wallace McCutcheon,[1] Cecil Leslie Strachan and Arthur F. VanWart.

Secretary: N. Lafrance.

Report

Volume 1: Dated February 26, 1964. Tabled in the House of Commons on June 19, 1964. Sessional Paper no. 274-1964/65.

Volume 2: Dated December 7, 1964. Tabled in the House of Commons on February 18, 1965. Sessional Paper no. 274d-1964/65. Printed as:

Royal Commission on health services. [Report] [Ottawa, Queen's Printer, 1964-1965] 2 v. (1,330 p.)

Special Studies:

Berry, Charles Horace. Voluntary medical insurance and prepayment. [Ottawa, Queen's Printer, 1965] xii, 255 p.

---

[1] Resigned on August 8, 1962 upon his appointment to the Senate and to the federal Cabinet as Minister without Portfolio.

Boan, J. A. Group practice. [Ottawa, Queen's Printer, 1966]
viii, 79 p.

Brown, Tillman Merritt. Canadian economic growth. [Ottawa,
Queen's Printer, 1965] ix, 316 p.

Canada. Department of National Health and Welfare. Research
and Statistics Division. Provision, distribution and cost of drugs in
Canada. [Ottawa, Queen's Printer, 1965] viii, 128 p.

Govan, Elizabeth S. L. Voluntary health organizations in Canada.
[Ottawa, Queen's Printer, 1966] vi, 202 p.

Hall, Oswald. Utilization of dentists in Canada. [Ottawa, Queen's
Printer, 1965] vii, 59 p.

Hanson, Eric J. The public finance aspects of health services in
Canada. [Ottawa, Queen's Printer, 1963?] xi, 206 p.

Hastings, John E. F. and William Mosley. Organized community
health services. [Ottawa, Queen's Printer, 1966] xix, 328 p.

Judek, Stanislaw. Medical manpower in Canada. [Ottawa, Queen's
Printer, 1964] xx, 413 p.

Kohn, Robert. Emerging patterns in health care. [Ottawa, Queen's
Printer, 1966] iv, 145 p.

---. The health of the Canadian people. [Ottawa, Queen's Printer 1967] xi, 412 p.

McFarlane, Bruce A. Dental manpower in Canada. [Ottawa,
Queen's Printer, 1965] xii, 217 p.

MacFarlane, Joseph Arthur and others. Medical education in
Canada. [Ottawa, Queen's Printer, 1965] xii, 373 p.

McKerracher, Donald G. Trends in psychiatric care. [Ottawa,
Queen's Printer, 1966] ix, 256 p.

Mills, Donald L. Study of chiropractors, osteopaths and naturo-
paths in Canada. [Ottawa, Queen's Printer, 1966] ix, 294 p.

Mussalem, Helen Kathleen. Nursing education in Canada. [Ottawa,
Queen's Printer, 1965] viii, 139 p.

Paynter, Kenneth Jack. Dental education in Canada. [ Ottawa, Queen's Printer, 1965] viii, 109 p.

Richman, Alex. Psychiatric care in Canada: Extent and results. [ Ottawa, Queen's Printer, 1966] xxviii, 459 p.

Robson, Reginald Arthur Henry. Sociological factors affecting recruitment into the nursing profession. [ Ottawa, Queen's Printer, 1967] vi, 244 p.

Wherrett, George J. Tuberculosis in Canada. [ Ottawa, Queen's Printer, 1965] vi, 76 p.

Notes: Hearings held in 14 cities (September 27, 1961 - March 11, 1963). 406 briefs submitted.

376  COMMITTEE OF INQUIRY INTO THE UNEMPLOYMENT INSURANCE
      ACT

Appointed on July 17, 1961 by Order in Council P. C. 1961-1040 under Part I of the Inquiries Act (R. S. C. , 1952, c. 154) and on the re-commendation of the Prime Minister.
Commissioners: Ernest Clark Gill, Chairman, Etienne Crevier, John James Deutsch and Joseph Richards Petrie.
Secretary: Richard Humphrys.

Report
Dated November, 1962. Tabled in the House of Commons on Dec-ember 20, 1962. Sessional Paper no. 37g-1962. Printed as:
Report of the Committee of Inquiry into the Unemployment Insur-ance Act. November, 1962. [ Roger Duhamel, F. R. S. C. , Queen's Printer and Controller of Stationery, Ottawa, Canada, 1962] ix, 207 p.

Special Studies Prepared for the Commission:

Beausoleil, Gilles and Maurice Bouchard, The role of the National Employment Service. [ Ottawa, 1962] 40 p.

Hougham, George Millard, The relationship between unemployment insurance and Canada's other income maintenance programs. [ Ottawa, 1962] 35 p.

Notes: Public hearings held at Ottawa (November 14 - December 18, 1961). 51 briefs submitted.

377  ROYAL COMMISSION ON BANKING AND FINANCE

Appointed on October 18, 1961 by Order in Council P. C. 1961-1484 under Part I of the Inquiries Act (R. S. C. , 1952, c. 154) and on the recommendation of the Minister of Finance.

Commissioners: Dana Harris Porter, Chairman, William Thomas Brown, James Douglas Gibson, Paul H. Leman, Gordon L. Harrold, John Crerar MacKeeen and William Archibald Mackintosh.

Secretaries: Harold Anthony Hampson and Gilles Mercure.

Report

Dated February 5, 1964.  Tabled in the House of Commons on April 24, 1964.  Sessional Paper no. 233-1964/65.  Printed as:

Report of the Royal Commission on banking and finance, 1964.
[Ottawa, Queen's Printer, 1964]  587 p.

Appendix Volume: Printed as:

Royal Commission on banking and finance.  Appendix volume, 1964.
[Ottawa, Queen's Printer, 1965]  435 p.

Working Papers:

Asimakopulos, A.  The reliability of selected price indexes as measures of price trends.  [Ottawa, Queen's Printer, 1964]  iv, 73 p.

Carr, D. W. & Associates.  Farm credit in Canada.  [Ottawa, Queen's Printer, 1964]  155 p.

Cork, E. K.  Finance in the mining industry.  [Ottawa, Queen's Printer, 1964]  202 p.

Johnson, Albert Wesley and J. M. Andrews.  Provincial and municipal governments and the capital market.  [Ottawa, Queen's Printer, 1964]  iii, 197 p.

Johnson, Harry Gordon and Gilles Mercure.  Lags in the effects of monetary policy in Canada.  [Ottawa, Queen's Printer, 1964]  244, x p.

Mercure, Gilles.  Credit unions and caisses populaires.  [Ottawa, Queen's Printer, 1964]  219 p.

Poapst, J. V.  The residential mortgage market.  [Ottawa, Queen's Printer, 1964]  178.

Reuber, Grant Louis.  The objectives of monetary policy.  [Ottawa, Queen's Printer, 1964]  308 p.

Shearer, Ronald Alexander. Monetary policy and the current account of the balance of international payments. [ Ottawa, Queen's Printer, 1964] ii, 189 p.

Stanley, David C. H. The financing of oil and gas exploration and production in Canada [ Toronto, Wood, Gundy & Company Limited, 1964?] 121 p.

Sutton, G. D. Corporate finance. [ Ottawa, Queen's Printer, 1964] 184 p.

Turk, Sidney. The foreign exchange market in Canada. [ Ottawa, Queen's Printer, 1964] 34 p.

Wonnacott, Gordon Paul. The height, structure and significance of interest rates. [ Ottawa, Queen's Printer, 1964] 115 p.

A note regarding the availability of other confidential studies prepared for the Commission is provided in Appendix 6 of the Report, p. 576

Notes: Held 69 days of public hearings in 11 cities (March 12, 1962 - January 22, 1963). 95 briefs were presented. Cost: $732,901.

378 ROYAL COMMISSION ON TAXATION

Appointed on September 25, 1962 by Order in Council P. C. 1962-1334 under Part I of the Inquiries Act (R. S. C., 1952, c. 154) and on the recommendation of the Prime Minister.
Commissioners: Kenneth LeM. Carter, Chairman. J. Harvey Perry, A. Emile Beauvais, Donald G. Grant, Mrs. S. M. Milne and Charles E. S. Walls.

Report
Dated December 22, 1966. Tabled in the House of Commons on February 24, 1967. Sessional Paper no. 347-1966/67. Printed as:
Report of the Royal Commission on Taxation. [ Ottawa, Roger Duhamel, F. R. S. C., Queen's Printer and Controller of Stationery, Ottawa, Canada, 1966.] 6 v. and index. (2,085 p.)

Special Studies: [1]

Number 1 - Will, Robert M. The budget as an economic document. [ Ottawa, Queen's Printer, 1966] v, 101 p.

---

[1] The studies not listed here have not been published (as of September 5, 1967).

Number 2 - Gillespie, W. Irwin.  The incidence of taxes and public expenditures in the Canadian economy.  [Ottawa, Queen's Printer, 1966] vii, 273 p.

Number 3 - Helliwell, John F.  Taxation and investment: A study of capital expenditure decisions in large corporations.  [Ottawa, Queen's Printer, 1966]  xvii, 355 p.

Number 4 - Barlow, Robin.  The effects of income taxation on work choices.  [Ottawa, Queen's Printer, 1966]  vi, 42 p.

Number 6 - Tarasofsky, Abraham.  The feasibility of a Canadian federal sales tax.  [Ottawa, Queen's Printer, 1966]  vi, 74 p.

Number 7 - Bourgeois, J. Mathias.  Sources of sales and excise tax revenues.  [Ottawa, Queen's Printer, 1966]  v, 42 p.

Number 8 - Bucovetsky, M. W.  The taxation of mineral extraction. [Ottawa, Queen's Printer, 1966]  vii, 201 p.

Number 9 - Timbrell, D. Y.  and H. Anson-Cartwright.  Taxation of the mining industry in Canada.  [Ottawa, Queen's Printer, 1967] xi, 181 p.

Number 10 - Mockler, E. J., John G. Smith and Claude Frenette, Taxation of the family.  [Ottawa, Queen's Printer, 1966]  vi, 149 p.

Number 11 - Smith, John G., D. B. Fields, and E. J. Mockler. Death duties.  [Ottawa, Queen's Printer, 1967]  viii, 110 p.

Number 12 - Burton, A. Gordon.  Comments re taxation of the oil and gas industry.  [Ottawa, Queen's Printer, 1966]  v, 30 p.

Number 13 - Mockler, E. J., and Donald B. Fields.  Gift tax. [Ottawa, Queen's Printer, 1966]  vii, 41 p.

Number 15 - Royal Commission on taxation.  Research Staff. Stripping of corporate surplus.  [Ottawa, Queen's Printer, 1967]  viii, 128 p.

Number 17 - Will, Robert M.  Canadian fiscal policy, 1945-63. [Ottawa, Queen's Printer, 1967.]  v, 101 p.

Number 22 - Bertrand, Robert J., Alice Desjardins, Rene Hurtubise and Yves Ouellette.  Legislation, administrative and interpretation processes in federal taxation.  [Ottawa, Queen's Printer, 1966] xx, 484 p.

Number 23 - Lynn, James H.   Federal-Provincial fiscal relations.
[ Ottawa, Queen's Printer, 1967]   xii, 224 p.

Notes:  Public hearings held in 12 cities.   About 700 witnesses
appeared before the Commission.   289 briefs were presented to the
Commission.


379  ROYAL COMMISSION ON PILOTAGE

Appointed on November 1, 1962 by Order in Council P. C. 1962-
1575, under Part I of the Inquiries Act and on the recommendation of
the Prime Minister.
   Commissioners:  Yves Bernier, Chairman, Harold Alexander
Renwick and Robert Knowlton Smith.
   Secretary:  G. W. Nadeau.


Report
Not yet presented.


380  ROYAL COMMISSION ON BILINGUALISM AND BICULTURALISM

Appointed on July 19, 1963 by Order in Council P. C. 1963-1106
under Part I of the Inquiries Act (R. S. C. , 1952, c. 154) and on the
recommendation of the Prime Minister.
   Commissioners:  Andre Laurendeau and Arnold Davidson Dunton,
Co-Chairmen,  Rev.  Clement Cormier, Royce Frith, Jean-Louis
Gagnon, Gertrude Laing, Jean Marchand, Jaroslav Bohdan Rudnyckyj,
Frank Reginald Scott and Paul Wyczyvski.
   Secretaries:  Paul Lacoste and Neil M. Morrison.


Reports
Preliminary Report:  Dated February 1, 1965.  Tabled in the House
of Commons on February 25, 1965.  Sessional Paper no. 354-1964/65.
Printed as:
   A preliminary report of the Royal Commission on bilingualism
and biculturalism.  [ Ottawa, Queen's Printer, 1965].  211, 217 p.
   Text in English and French.
   Further reports not yet presented.
   Notes:  Preliminary public meetings held at Ottawa, November 7 - 8,
1963.  Held meetings with the ten Provincial Premiers and Ministers of
Education (January - March, 1964).  Regional meetings held in 23 towns
and cities (March 18 - June 16, 1964).  Public meetings opened March 1,
1965.

381 COMMISSION TO INQUIRE INTO AND REPORT UPON THE CIRCUMSTAN-
CES LEADING TO THE DISMISSAL OF MR. GEORGE WALKER FROM
THE POSITION OF DISTRICT SUPERVISOR OF THE PRAIRIE FARM
ASSISTANCE ADMINISTRATION; AND IRREGULARITIES ALLEGED
TO HAVE OCCURRED IN THE PROCESSING OF CLAIMS FOR BENE-
FITS UNDER THE PROVISIONS OF THE PRAIRIE FARM ASSISTANCE
ACT AND THE PAYMENT OF SUCH CLAIMS, RELATIVE TO THE
CROP GROWN IN THE YEAR 1962 IN THE PROVINCE OF SASKATCHE-
WAN

Appointed on December 21, 1963 by Order in Council P. C. 1963-
1896 under Part I of the Inquiries Act (R. S. C. , 1952, c. 154) and on
the recommendation of the Prime Minister.
Commissioner: Harold Walpole Pope.

Report
Dated June 10, 1964. Tabled in the House of Commons on July 29,
1964. Sessional Paper no. 12A-1964/65. Printed as:
The report of the Prairie Farm Assistance Administration Com-
mission of Inquiry established under Order in Council P. C. 1963-1896
of December 21st, 1963. June 10, 1964. [Ottawa, 1964?] ii, 60, 30 p.
Notes: 103 farmers from the Swift Current PFAA Supervisory
District presented evidence before the Commission.

382 COMMISSION TO INQUIRE INTO AND REPORT UPON THE PROBLEM
RELATING TO THE FUTURE OF THE AIRCRAFT OVERHAUL BASE
MAINTAINED BY TRANS-CANADA AIR LINES AT WINNIPEG INTER-
NATIONAL AIRPORT AND INTO THE POSSIBILITY OF MAINTAINING
AND INCREASING EMPLOYMENT AT THE SAID BASE

Appointed on June 11, 1964 by Order in Council P. C. 1964-857
under Part I of the Inquiries Act (R. S. C. , 1952, c. 154) and on the
recommendation of the Prime Minister.
Commissioner: Donald Alexander Thompson.
Secretary: Robert E. Moffat.

Report
Dated March 3, 1966. Tabled in the House of Commons on May 19,
1966. Sessional Paper no. 162d-1966. Printed as:
Report of Commission of Inquiry as to the future of the Air Canada
overhaul base at Winnipeg International Airport, and related matters,
established under Order in Council P. C. 1964-857 of June 11, 1964.
March 3, 1966. [Ottawa, 1966] 175 p. and appendices (various pagings).
Notes: Hearings held at Winnipeg and Montreal (January 19 - May
13, 1965). 2,783 pages of evidence transcribed. 122 briefs were sub-

mitted to the Commission.

383 COMMISSION TO INQUIRE INTO AND REPORT UPON THE CIRCUM-
STANCES SURROUNDING THE CRASH OF A DOUGLAS DC 8F AIR-
CRAFT, REGISTRATION CF-TJN, AT STE-THERESE, QUEBEC, ON
THE 29TH DAY OF NOVEMBER, 1963

Appointed on October 8, 1964 by Order in Council P. C. 1964-1544
under Part I of the Inquiries Act (R. S. C., 1952, c. 154) and on the recommendation of the Prime Minister.
Commissioner: George Swan Challies.

Report
Dated June, 1965. Printed as:
Report of Commission of Inquiry into crash of Trans-Canada Air
Lines DC-8F Aircraft CF-TJN at Ste. Therese de Blainville, P. Q.,
on November 29th, 1963. Order in Council dated 8 October, 1964,
P. C. 1964-1544. [Ottawa, 1965] a-d, 41 p.
Notes: Public hearings held at Montreal and Ottawa (November 9,
1964 - June 9, 1965). 45 witnesses appeared before the Commission.
78 exhibits were filed with the Commission.

384 COMMISSION TO INQUIRE INTO THE PROBLEMS OF MARKETING SAL-
TED AND CURED FISH PRODUCED IN THE ATLANTIC PROVINCES

Appointed on October 29, 1964 by Order in Council P. C. 1964-
1672 on the recommendation of the Prime Minister. Part of Inquiries
Act not stated.
Commissioner: F. B. Finn.
Secretary: Roger W. Bedard.

Report
Undated. Printed as:
Report. Atlantic salt fish commission. Order in Council dated
29 October, 1964. P. C. 1964-1672 [Ottawa, n. d.] x, 170 p.
Notes: Public hearings held in 4 cities (February 1 - 14, 1965).

385 COMMISSION TO INVESTIGATE FULLY INTO ALLEGATIONS ABOUT
ANY IMPROPER INDUCEMENTS HAVING BEEN OFFERED TO OR
IMPROPER PRESSURES HAVING BEEN BROUGHT TO BEAR ON
COUNSEL ACTING UPON AN APPLICATION FOR THE EXTRADITION
OF ONE LUCIEN RIVARD AND ALL THE RELEVANT CIRCUMSTANCES
CONNECTED THEREWITH

Appointed on November 28, 1964 by Order in Council P. C. 1964-1819 under Part I of the Inquiries Act (R. S. C., 1952, c. 154) and on the recommendation of the Prime Minister.
Commissioner: Frederic Dorion
Secretary: Nicol Henry.

### Reports
Dated June, 1965. Tabled in the House of Commons on June 29, 1965. Sessional Paper no. 238-1965. Printed as:
Special Public Inquiry 1964 Report of the Commissioner the Honourable Frederic Dorion, Chief Justice of the Superior Court for the Province of Quebec. June, 1965. [Ottawa, Queen's Printer, 1965] 149 p.
Additional Report: Dated July 6, 1965. Printed as:
"An Additional report about the Special Public Inquiry 1964, which is a modification of the original that I submitted on Monday, June 28, 1965." [Ottawa, 1965] 2 leaves.
Notes: Hearings held at Ottawa, Quebec City and Montreal (December 15 1964 - April 9, 1965). 65 witnesses appeared before the Commission. More than 2,000,000 words of evidence transcribed.

386 COMMISSION TO INQUIRE INTO AND TO INVESTIGATE THE CHARGES OF IRREGULARITIES IN THE FEDERAL ELECTION OF 1963 MADE BY MR. ORMOND TURNER IN THE ISSUE OF THE VANCOUVER PROVINCE OF FEBRUARY 22, 1965, AND IN ANY OTHER ISSUES THEREOF, AND TO CONSIDER SUCH OTHER MATTERS AS MAY APPEAR TO THE COMMISSIONER TO BE RELEVANT AND TO REPORT FULLY THEREON

Appointed on March 2, 1965 by Order in Council P. C. 1965-372 under Part I of the Inquiries Act (R. S. C., 1952, c. 154) and on the recommendation of the Prime Minister.
Commissioner: Nathaniel Theodore Nemetz.
Secretary: John Noel Lyon.

### Report
Dated August 2, 1965. Printed as:
Report of the Honourable Nathaniel Theodore Nemetz, a Judge of the Supreme Court of British Columbia, appointed a Commissioner under Part I of the Inquiries Act to inquire into certain charges of election irregularities in the federal election of 1963. Counsel: C. C. Locke, Esquire, Q. C., Graham Mackenzie, Esquire, Registrar, J. N. Lyon Esquire. [Ottawa, Queen's Printer, 1965] 34 p.
Notes: Hearings held (March 16 - May 11, 1965). 15 persons appeared before the Commission.

387 COMMISSION TO INQUIRE INTO AND REPORT UPON THE MARKETING
    PROBLEMS OF THE FRESHWATER FISH INDUSTRY IN THE PROV-
    INCES OF ONTARIO, MANITOBA, SASKATCHEWAN AND ALBERTA
    AND NORTH WEST TERRITORIES

> Appointed on July 9, 1965 by Order in Council P. C. 1965-1269
> under Part I of the Inquiries Act (R. S. C., 1952, c. 154) and on the
> recommendation of the Prime Minister.
> Commissioner: George H. McIvor.
> Secretary: Roger W. Bedard.

Report

> Undated. Tabled in the House of Commons on October 17, 1966.
> Sessional Paper no. 57a-1966/67. Printed as:
> Report of Commission of Inquiry into freshwater fish marketing.
> Commissioner George H. McIvor, C. M. G. [Ottawa 1966?] xi, 130 p.
> 
> Notes: Hearings held at 16 Canadian centres (October 6 - December
> 10, 1965). The Commissioner also visited wholesalers, processors,
> and retailers in three American cities.

388 COMMISSION TO INQUIRE INTO THE INCREASES IN RATES OF PAY FOR
    CIVIL SERVANTS IN "GROUP D" ANNOUNCED BY THE GOVERNMENT
    ON JULY 16, 1965, INCLUDING EXAMINATION OF ALL CONSIDERA-
    TIONS WHICH IN THE COMMISSIONER'S VIEW APPEAR TO BE RELE-
    VANT IN DETERMINING WHETHER THE INCREASES SO GRANTED
    AND THE RATES OF PAY SO ESTABLISHED ARE FAIR AND REASON-
    ABLE, AND TO REPORT THEREON

> Appointed on July 23, 1965 by Order in Council P. C. 1965-1350
> under Part I of the Inquiries Act (R. S. C., 1952, c. 154) and on the
> recommendation of the Prime Minister.
> Commissioner: Jacob Carroll Anderson.
> Secretary: Paul Roddick.

Reports

> First Interim Report: Dated August 4, 1965. Printed as:
> [First Interim Report of Commission of Inquiry into the increases
> in rates of pay for civil servants in Group D] [Ottawa, 1965] 15 p.
> 
> Second Interim Report: Undated. Printed as:
> Second Interim Report of Commission of Inquiry into the rates of
> pay for civil servants in Group D. Order in Council dated 23 July,
> 1965, P. C. 1965-1350. [Ottawa, 1965] 63 p.
> 
> Final Report: Dated September 27, 1965. Printed as:
> Final Report of Commission of Inquiry into the rates of pay for
> civil servants in Group D. Order in Council dated 23 July, 1965,
> P. C. 1965-1350. [Ottawa, 1965] 64 leaves.

389 COMMISSION TO INQUIRE INTO THE POST OFFICE DEPARTMENT
CONCERNING GRIEVANCES RELATING TO WORK RULES, CODES
OF DISCIPLINE AND OTHER CONDITIONS OF EMPLOYMENT AP-
PLYING TO NON-SUPERVISORY OPERATING EMPLOYEES, EXCLU-
SIVE OF SALARIES; IN DOING SO, TO CONSULT WITH OFFICERS
OF THE DEPARTMENT AND OF ORGANIZATIONS REPRESENTING
EMPLOYEES; AND, KEEPING IN MIND BOTH THE WELFARE OF
EMPLOYEES AND THE EFFICIENT OPERATIONS OF THE POSTAL
SERVICE, TO REPORT THEREON AND TO RECOMMEND SUCH
CHANGES IN EXISTING PRACTICES AS MAY BE IN THE PUBLIC
INTEREST

Appointed on September 1, 1965 by Order in Council P. C. 1965-
1590 under Part I of the Inquiries Act (R. S. C. , 1952, c. 154) and on
the recommendation of the Postmaster General.
Commissioner: Andre Montpetit.
Secretary: Mrs. Helen M. Roney.

Report
Letter of transmittal dated September 14, 1966. Tabled in the
House of Commons on October 19, 1966. Sessional Paper no. 321-
1966/67. Printed as:
Report of the Royal Commission of Inquiry into working conditions
in the Post Office Department. Commissioner, The Honourable Andre
Montpetit. October-1966. [Ottawa, Queen's Printer, 1966] vii, 363 p.
Notes: No public hearings held. The Commissioner and his staff
travelled across the country and interviewed postal officials.


390 COMMISSION TO INQUIRE INTO THE DEALINGS OF THE HONOURABLE
MR. JUSTICE LEO A. LANDREVILLE WITH NORTHERN ONTARIO
NATURAL GAS LIMITED OR ANY OF ITS OFFICERS, EMPLOYEES
OR REPRESENTATIVES, OR IN THE SHARES OF THE SAID COMPANY,
AND TO ADVISE WHETHER, IN THE OPINION OF THE COMMISSIONER,
ANYTHING DONE BY MR. JUSTICE LANDREVILLE IN THE COURSE
OF SUCH DEALINGS CONSTITUTED MISBEHAVIOUR IN HIS OFFICIAL
CAPACITY AS A JUDGE OF THE SUPREME COURT OF ONTARIO,
OR WHETHER THE HONOURABLE MR. JUSTICE LANDREVILLE HAS
BY SUCH DEALINGS PROVED HIMSELF UNFIT FOR THE PROPER
EXERCISE OF HIS JUDICIAL DUTIES

Appointed on January 19, 1966 by Order in Council P. C. 1966-
128 under Part I of the Inquiries Act (R. S. C. , 1952, c. 154) and on
the recommendation of the Minister of Justice.
Commissioner: Ivan Cleveland Rand.
Secretary: Mrs. Helen M. Roney.

Report

Dated August 11, 1966.  Tabled in the House of Commons on August 29, 1966.  Sessional Paper no. 195a-1966/67.  Printed as:

Inquiry re:  The Honourable L. A. Landreville.  Commissioner, The Honourable I. C. Rand. 1966. [ Ottawa, 1966]  133 p.

Notes:  Public hearings held in four cities (March 14 - April 27, 1966).  30 witnesses appeared before the Commission.  172 exhibits entered before the Commission.  Cost: $51,314.


391 COMMISSION TO INQUIRE INTO THE CASE INVOLVING GEORGE VIC-
    TOR SPENCER

Appointed on March 7, 1966 by Order in Council P. C. 1966-395 under Part I of the Inquiries Act (R. S. C., 1952, c. 154) and on the recommendation of the Prime Minister.

Commissioner:  Dalton Courtwright Wells.

Secretary:  L. Lafrance.


Report

Letter of transmittal dated July 18, 1966.  Tabled in the House of Commons on August 30, 1966.  Sessional Paper no. 232b-1966/67. Printed as:

Commission of inquiry into complaints made by George Victor Spencer.  Report of the Commissioner, The Honourable Mr. Justice Dalton Courtwright Wells, Supreme Court of Ontario.  July, 1966. [ Ottawa, 1966]  60, 2, 2 p.

Notes:  Public hearings held at Ottawa, Vancouver and Toronto (April 13 - May 10, 1966).  32 exhibits presented to the Commission.


392 COMMISSION TO INQUIRE INTO THE CASE INVOLVING GERDA MUN-
    SINGER

Appointed on March 14, 1966 by Order in Council P. C. 1966-482 under Part I of the Inquiries Act (R. S. C., 1952, c. 154) and on the recommendation of the Prime Minister.

Commissioner:  Wishart Flett Spence.

Secretary:  J. J. Pierre Benoit.


Report

Dated September, 1966.  Tabled in the House of Commons on October 5, 1966.  Sessional Paper no. 240a-1966/67.  Printed as:

Report of the Commission of inquiry into matters relating to one Gerda Munsinger.  The Honourable Mr. Justice Wishart Flett Spence, Commissioner.  September 1966. [ Ottawa, Queen's Printer, 1966]. 93 p.

Notes: Sessions of the Commissions held April 6 - May 24, 1966.
Three in camera sessions were held. 15 witnesses appeared before
the Commission.


393 COMMISSION TO INQUIRE INTO THE COSTS OF FARM MACHINERY
    AND REPAID COSTS

Appointed on May 26, 1966 by Order in Council P. C. 1966-978
under Part I of the Inquiries Act (R. S. C. , 1952, c. 154) and on the
recommendation of the Prime Minister.
    Commissioner: Clarence Lyle Barber.
    Secretary: Mrs. Helen M. Roney.

Report

Not yet presented.
Notes: Hearings opened at Winnipeg on March 6, 1967.


394 COMMISSION TO MAKE A FULL AND CONFIDENTIAL INQUIRY INTO
    THE OPERATION OF CANADIAN SECURITY METHODS AND PRO-
    CEDURES AND, HAVING REGARD TO THE NECESSITY OF MAIN-
    TAINING (A) THE SECURITY OF CANADA AS A NATION; AND (B)
    THE RIGHTS AND RESPONSIBILITIES OF INDIVIDUAL PERSONS,
    TO ADVISE WHAT SECURITY METHODS AND PROCEDURES ARE
    MOST EFFECTIVE AND HOW THEY CAN BEST BE IMPLEMENTED,
    AND TO MAKE SUCH REPORTS FOR THIS PURPOSE AS THEY DEEM
    NECESSARY AND DESIRABLE IN THE NATIONAL INTEREST

Appointed on November 16, 1966 by Order in Council P. C. 1966-
2148 under Part I of the Inquiries Act (R. S. C. , 1952, c. 154) and on
the recommendation of the Prime Minister.
    Commissioners: Maxwell Weir Mackenzie, Chairman, Yves
Pratte and Major James William Coldwell.

Report

Not yet presented.


395 ROYAL COMMISSION ON THE STATUS OF WOMEN IN CANADA

Appointed on February 16, 1967 by Order in Council P. C. 1967-
312 under Part I of the Inquiries Act (R. S. C. , 1952, c. 154) and on
the recommendation of the Prime Minister.
    Members: Mrs. John Bird, Chairman, Mrs. Ottomar Lange,
Miss Jeanne Lapointe, Miss Elsie Gregory MacGill, Mrs. Robert

Ogilvie, Donald Gordon, Jr., and Jacques Henripin.

Report

Not yet presented.

396 COMMISSION TO INVESTIGATE AND REPORT UPON THE ADMINISTRA-
TION OF JUSTICE IN THE HAY RIVER AREA OF THE NORTH WEST
TERRITORIES AND, WITHOUT RESTRICTING THE GENERALITY
OF THE FOREGOING, TO INVESTIGATE AND REPORT UPON STATE-
MENTS IN EDITORIALS APPEARING IN ISSUES OF THE NEWSPAPER
"TAPWE" DATED MARCH 27, APRIL 3 AND APRIL 10, 1967 SUG-
GESTING THAT (A) COURT PROCEEDINGS IN HAY RIVER IN THE
NORTHWEST TERRITORIES ARE NOT OPEN TO MEMBERS OF THE
PUBLIC, (B) STEPS HAVE BEEN TAKEN TO HAMPER MEMBERS
OF THE PRESS IN EFFORTS TO INFORM THE PUBLIC ABOUT PRO-
CEEDINGS IN THE COURTS IN HAY RIVER IN THE NORTH WEST
TERRITORIES, AND (C) ALL INDIVIDUALS DO NOT RECEIVE EQUAL
TREATMENT IN THE COURTS IN HAY RIVER IN THE NORTH WEST
TERRITORIES

Appointed on July 4, 1967 by Order in Council P. C. 1967-1327
under Part I of the Inquiries Act (R. S. C., 1952, c. 154) and on the
recommendation of the Minister of Justice.
Commissioner: W. G. Morrow.

Report

Not yet presented.

# BIBLIOGRAPHY

## Books

Cole, Arthur Harrison.  A finding-list of royal commission reports in the British Dominions.  Cambridge, Massachusetts:  Harvard University Press, 1939.

## Articles

Brady, Alexander.  "Royal commissions in the Dominions:  A note on current political practice,"  University of Toronto Quarterly, VIII (1939), 284-292.

Hodgetts, John Edwin.  "The Grand Inquest on the Canadian public service," Public Administration, XXII (1963), 226-241.

---.  "The role of royal commissions in Canadian government,"  Proceedings of the third annual conference of the Institute of Public Administration of Canada (1951), 351-367.

---.  "Royal commissions of inquiry in Canada,"  Public Administration Review, IX (1949), 22-29.

---.  "Should Canada be de-commissioned?  A commoner's view of royal commissions,"  Queen's Quarterly, LXX (1964), 475-490.

Lewis, Grace S.  "Reports of Dominion and Provincial royal commissions, together with a selection of reports of British royal commissions having a bearing on Canada,"  The Canada Year Book, 1940, 1108-1110.

"Royal Commissions,"  Encyclopedia Canadiana, Vol. LX, 103-105.

Sellar, Watson.  "A century of commissions of inquiry,"  Canadian Bar Review, XXXV (1947), 1-28.

Stursburg  Peter.  "Canada and its royal commissions,"  Saturday Night, LXVI (1961), 12-13.

## Unpublished Theses

Bennett, Gordon L.  An administrator looks behind the scenes of a royal commission.  M. A. Thesis, Carleton University, 1964.

Courtney, John Childs.  Canadian royal commissions of inquiry, 1946 to 1962: An investigation of an executive instrument of inquiry.  Ph. D Thesis, Duke University, 1964.

Hodgetts, John Edwin.  Royal commissions of inquiry in Canada:  A study in investigative technique.  M. A. Thesis, University of Toronto, 1940.


## Special Studies

Callard, Keith B.  Commissions of inquiry in Canada, 1867-1949.  (A report presented to the Secretary to the Cabinet. ) [ Ottawa, 1950.]

# INDEX

Included here are entries for commissioners, secretaries, titles of special studies (underlined), authors of special studies (in capital letters), and the dominant subjects of commissions and special studies. The numbers refer to entry numbers within the Checklist.

9 781487 591618